Civilian Oversight of Police

Advancing Accountability
in Law Enforcement

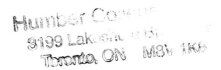

 **CRC Press**
Taylor & Francis Group
Boca Raton London New York

CRC Press is an imprint of the
Taylor & Francis Group, an **informa** business

Advances in Police Theory and Practice Series

Series Editor: Dilip K. Das

FORTHCOMING

Civilian Oversight of Police

Advancing Accountability in Law Enforcement

Edited by

Tim Prenzler
University of the Sunshine Coast
Queensland, Australia

Garth den Heyer
Police Foundation
Washington, DC, USA

CRC Press
Taylor & Francis Group
Boca Raton London New York

CRC Press is an imprint of the
Taylor & Francis Group, an **informa** business

CRC Press
Taylor & Francis Group
6000 Broken Sound Parkway NW, Suite 300
Boca Raton, FL 33487-2742

Printed on acid-free paper
Version Date: 20150803

International Standard Book Number-13: 978-1-4822-3418-3 (Hardback)

Library of Congress Cataloging-in-Publication Data

Civilian oversight of police : advancing accountability in law enforcement / editors, Tim Prenzler and Garth den Heyer.
      pages cm
Includes bibliographical references and index.
ISBN 978-1-4822-3418-3
      1. Police administration--Citizen participation. 2. Police-community relations. 3. Police misconduct. 4. Police--Complaints against. I. Prenzler, Tim, editor. II. Heyer, Garth den, editor.

HV7936.C56C547 2016
363.2068'4--dc23   2015019249

Visit the Taylor & Francis Web site at
http://www.taylorandfrancis.com

and the CRC Press Web site at
http://www.crcpress.com

Contents

Section IV

TOWARD A MODEL SYSTEM

Series Editor Preface

While the literature on police and allied subjects is growing exponentially, its impact upon day-to-day policing remains small. The two worlds of research and practice of policing remain disconnected, even though cooperation between the two is growing. A major reason is that the two groups speak in different languages. The research work is published in hard-to-access journals and presented in a manner that is difficult to comprehend for a layperson. On the other hand, the police practitioners tend not to mix with researchers and remain secretive about their work. Consequently, there is little dialogue between the two and almost no attempt to learn from one another. Dialogues across the globe, among researchers and practitioners situated in different continents, are of course even more limited.

I attempted to address this problem by starting the IPES (http://www .ipes.info), where a common platform has brought the two together. IPES is now in its twenty-sixth year. The annual meetings that constitute most major annual events of the organization have been hosted in all parts of the world. Several publications have come out of these deliberations, and a new collaborative community of scholars and police officers has been created whose membership runs into several hundreds.

Another attempt was to begin a new journal, aptly called *Police Practice and Research: An International Journal* (PPR), that has opened the gate to practitioners to share their work and experiences. The journal has attempted to focus upon issues that help bring the two on a single platform. *PPR* is completing its sixteenth year. It is certainly an evidence of growing collaboration between police research and practice that *PPR*, which began with four issues a year, expanded into five issues in its fourth year, and now it is issued six times a year.

Clearly, these attempts, despite their success, remain limited. Conferences and journal publications do help create a body of knowledge and an association of police activists but cannot address substantial issues in depth. The limitations of time and space preclude larger discussions and more authoritative expositions that can provide stronger and broader linkages between the two worlds.

It is this realization of the increasing dialogue between police research and practice that has encouraged many of us—my close colleagues and I connected closely with IPES and *PPR* across the world—to conceive and implement a new attempt in this direction. This led to the book series *Advances in Police Theory and Practice*, that seeks to attract writers from all parts of the world. Further, the attempt is to find practitioner contributors. The objective is to make the series a serious contribution to our knowledge of the police as well as to improve police practices. The focus is not only in work that describes the best and successful police practices but also one that challenges current paradigms and breaks new ground to prepare a police for the twenty-first century. The series seeks a comparative analysis that highlights achievements in distant parts of the world as well as one that encourages an in-depth examination of specific problems confronting a particular police force.

The current book reports on the advancement of police research in Israel. The studies included make important contributions to the policing literature in at least one of three ways: they replicate findings from English-speaking countries (such as in the area of hot-spots policing), and thus provide support for their validity and generalizability; they utilize the unique Israeli conditions to address questions that are difficult to test in other countries, such as in the area of counterterrorism; and they ask innovative questions in the study of policing that are yet to be addressed elsewhere. These three types of contribution are made in the context of major areas of interest in the policing literature: crime control, police–community relationships, and policing terrorism. Thus, this book not only provides the reader with a broad picture of both Israeli policing and police research carried out in Israel in the past decade, but also has important implications for policing scholars and practitioners outside of Israel and throughout the democratic world.

It is hoped that through this series, it will be possible to accelerate the process of building knowledge about policing and help bridge the gap between the two worlds—the worlds of police research and police practice. This is an invitation to police scholars and practitioners across the world to come and join in this venture.

Dilip K. Das, PhD
Founding President,
International Police Executive Symposium,
IPES, www.ipes.info

Founding Editor-in-Chief,
Police Practice and Research: An International Journal,
PPR, www.tandf.co.uk/journals

The Prologue

This book explores the complex and controversial topic of civilian oversight of police. More specifically, this multiauthored work analyzes the issues and debates entailed in oversight by providing worldwide perspectives, in-depth case studies, and a wealth of survey data. Key topics include jurisdictional differences in oversight, civilian oversight and democratization, stakeholder preferences and experiences in relation to the management of complaints against police, and innovative means by which oversight agencies can work with police departments to improve police conduct.

At the time of finalizing the book, international news reports featured stories of heated debates, public demonstrations, and riots in the United States over fatal shootings by police and alleged racism in street policing practices. Critics of police tactics repeatedly called for greater citizen oversight to stop rogue officers escaping accountability and to increase pressure on police leaders to improve tactics through better analysis of conduct issues and better management of complaints.

At the same time, conduct problems in policing go well beyond the recent high-profile media exposés in the United States. Excessive force in law enforcement is a worldwide problem and comes in many forms, including assaults on suspects, deaths in custody, dangerous high speed vehicle pursuits, and misuse of Tasers and pepper spray. Bribery and other forms of financial corruption are commonplace in many jurisdictions, as is neglect of victims of crime. Furthermore, in many less developed democracies, and in all autocracies, police remain instruments of state repression, often serving as little more than the "muscle" of governments that bear all the features of organized crime gangs—systematically and violently repressing and exploiting their citizens. Civilian oversight of police is now included as an essential element of democratic reform as advocated by major international bodies including the United Nations and Transparency International.

What is more, ethical and responsible police officers suffer from the stigma of the tarnished image that comes from inadequate integrity management, and police "whistleblowers" are often the targets of ostracism and threats. Responsible police are also frequently the victims of poor management practices that place them unnecessarily in the line of fire and at risk from a wide range of physical and psychological forms of workplace injury. Improved civilian oversight is also touted as a way of ensuring better scrutiny of police management practices, with a large potential for win–win outcomes for both citizens and officers from enhanced accountability. The right kind of democratic oversight should generate significant improvements in the working environment of police.

Since the 1960s, the oversight of police by civilian bodies has been a key emerging feature of modern policing, and it is timely to reflect on the many issues associated with this trend. The book presents these issues by organizing the chapters under four major themes. This structure provides the opportunity to illustrate local jurisdictional issues, debates, and contrasts and the common underlying factors in the development of oversight agencies.

Section I of the book sets the context by reviewing key historical and theoretical developments in police oversight. Chapter 1 examines policing conduct scandals, inquiries, and reform programs that have driven major shifts in responsibility for complaints investigation and police integrity from internal to external processes. The chapter presents three models of complaints and discipline systems: "internal affairs," "civilian review," and "civilian control," and then tracks how reliance on these models has moved across the spectrum in major exemplar countries: the United States, England and Wales, Northern Ireland, and Australia. Generally speaking, repeated processes of scandal, inquiry, and partial reform have demonstrated the need for strong civilian oversight measures to break the constant tendency for police to slip back into patterns of misconduct and self-protection. The complexities involved in implementing the idea of greater independent input into police complaints and discipline are untangled in Chapter 2. The author shows the importance of avoiding simple binary oppositions that assume that all involvement by police or former police in complaints and discipline is bad and all external nonpolice involvement is good. Operationalizing the primary principle of independence needs to be a carefully managed process and should, where appropriate, utilize the knowledge, expertise, and commitment of police in various capacities.

Section II explores stakeholder perspectives on police complaints systems. Chapter 3 summarizes available quantitative surveys and focus group studies of public opinion on the topic. The findings show overwhelming support for the principle of external independent processing, but with some scope for police handling of minor matters. Chapter 4 shows how inadequate independence generates high levels of dissatisfaction in surveys of people who have made complaints against police. Satisfaction appears to be correlated not only with independence but also with process aspects of communication, timeliness, and perceived fairness. These surveys also show that complainants, in general, are neither vindictive nor punitive but want to communicate their concerns and improve police behavior in the future. They are also keen to engage in face-to-face mediation with the police officer concerned and are much more satisfied with this process than with more perfunctory informal dispute resolution options. The following chapter on police views shows clearly that police are not consistently wedded to in-house processes. They can also be dissatisfied with apparent bias in police investigations and discipline and can acknowledge the benefits to all stakeholders from a well-managed civilian controlled system. Police also report very high rates of satisfaction with mediation.

Section III provides regional, national, and jurisdictional accounts of external oversight in Chapters 6 to 10. Chapter 6 reports on the situation in Africa, whereas Chapter 7 provides an account of developments in the Asian region. Chapter 8 provides a more legally oriented review of developments in Europe, including the United Kingdom. Chapter 9 navigates the complexities of the situation in Canada and the United States, with their myriad policing agencies. Chapter 10 completes this section with a summary of the situation in Australia and New Zealand. These chapters include descriptions and critiques of current systems, as well as historical accounts of the factors behind contemporary arrangements. The section reveals wide variation in the internal/external mix and in the powers, resources, and methods of different oversight agencies. The critiques usefully show the ongoing large gap between stakeholder aspirations and contemporary practice in many places and the urgent need to improve police accountability through more substantive and sophisticated forms of oversight.

The fourth and final section of the book brings together the key issues from the preceding sections in proposing more democratic and effective means of addressing police accountability deficits with enhanced citizen oversight. In Chapter 11, the author examines successful cases of collaboration between police departments and oversight agencies in addressing police conduct problems, focusing on the application of the classic Problem-Oriented Policing model to this specific area of police performance management. Chapter 12, the final chapter, marshals evidence from all the preceding chapters to propose core elements of a model system for responding to complaints against police, addressing police–citizen alienation and conflict, minimizing misconduct, and optimizing police accountability. The model allows some flexibility for local conditions and public sector resources but should be applicable in most situations. The three main guiding principles involve (1) independence in investigations and adjudication of complaints, (2) the availability of alternative dispute resolution mechanisms, especially an independently managed mediation program, and (3) the importance of the internal and external elements of a police integrity system working together to advance ethical policing, including through the deployment of a proactive complainant profiling and early intervention system.

The book summarizes and integrates a great deal of research from many locations over many decades. There are some very clear and consistent findings that emerge from this mass of work. Nonetheless, we hope the book will stimulate further research, including collaborative work between researchers and practitioners, to enlarge the stock of knowledge about what works in police integrity management and democratic accountability.

We thank all the chapter authors for their willingness to contribute to the book and agreement to fit in with the schedule and parameters of the project. We also owe a very special debt of gratitude to series editor Professor Dilip Das and CRC Press Forensics, Criminal Justice, and Homeland Security Editor Carolyn Spence for proposing and supporting the project.

Tim Prenzler
Garth den Heyer

About the Editors

Tim Prenzler is a professor at the University of the Sunshine Coast, Australia, where he is program convenor of the Bachelor in Criminology and Justice. He was a chief investigator in the Australian Research Council Centre of Excellence in Policing and Security based at Griffith University, Brisbane, Australia, from 2008 to 2014, where he managed the Integrity Systems Research Program. He was also a member of the School of Criminology and Criminal Justice at Griffith University from 1991 to 2014. He is the author of *Police Corruption: Preventing Misconduct and Maintaining Integrity* (CRC Press–Taylor & Francis, 2009); coauthor, with Adam Graycar, of *Understanding and Preventing Corruption* (Palgrave Macmillan, 2013); editor of *Policing and Security in Practice: Challenges and Achievements* (Palgrave Macmillan, 2012); and editor of *Professional Practice in Crime Prevention and Security Management* (Australian Academic Press, 2014).

Garth den Heyer is a qualitative researcher whose interests include police organizational reform and performance and police service delivery effectiveness. He is a New Zealand police officer with more than 30 years of service, currently serving as principal advisor for strategic development and planning. Garth is also a senior research fellow with the Police Foundation in Washington, DC. He has a doctorate in public policy from Charles Sturt University and has recently completed a research project funded by the Community-Oriented Policing Services that included an international assessment of cost-reducing strategies adopted by police agencies to maintain the effective and efficient delivery of services. Dr. den Heyer is also working with the Scottish Institute of Policing Research on a project examining the establishment of Police Scotland.

Contributors

Geoffrey P. Alpert
School of Criminology and Criminal Justice
Griffith University
Brisbane, Australia

Alan Beckley
Office of Widening Participation
University of Western Sydney
Penrith, Australia

Julie Berg
Centre of Criminology
Department of Public Law
University of Cape Town
Cape Town, South Africa

Tyler Cawthray
School of Criminology and Criminal Justice
and
Australian Research Council Centre for
    Excellence in Policing and Security
Griffith University
Brisbane, Australia

Garth den Heyer
Police Foundation
Washington, DC

Frank Ferdik
Department of Criminology and Criminal
    Justice
University of West Florida
Pensacola, Florida

Simon Howell
Centre of Criminology
Department of Public Law
University of Cape Town
Cape Town, South Africa

Mahesh K. Nalla
School of Criminal Justice
Michigan State University
East Lansing, Michigan

Louise Porter
School of Criminology and Criminal Justice
Griffith University
Brisbane, Australia

Tim Prenzler
University of the Sunshine Coast
Queensland, Australia

Jeff Rojek
University of Texas, El Paso
El Paso, Texas

Stephen P. Savage
Institute of Criminal Justice Studies
University of Portsmouth
Portsmouth, United Kingdom

Graham Smith
School of Law
University of Manchester
Manchester, United Kingdom

Setting the Context

I

Historical and Theoretical Perspectives on Police Oversight

Scandal, Inquiry, and Reform

The Evolving Locus of Responsibility for Police Integrity

1

TIM PRENZLER

Contents

This chapter analyzes the evolution of police complaints and discipline systems in selected locations where government reviews and judicial inquiries have supported interventionist forms of civilian oversight. The first section presents three models of complaints and discipline systems: "internal affairs," "civilian review," and "civilian control," as a basis for critique. The second section examines developments in the United States, England and Wales, Northern Ireland, and Australia. The analysis provides some historical background to the more contemporary critiques in other chapters of the book. The present chapter highlights common processes of scandal, inquiry, and incomplete reform, followed by repetition of the cycle. In general, inquiries condemn police for failing to manage complaints in a fair and effective manner, and they also identify a problem of significant distrust of internal processes. Consequently, reports make strong in-principle statements about the need for independence in the response to complaints. At the same time, concerns about police abandoning responsibility for integrity, and practical concerns about external control, inform a compromise package of recommendations that stymie reform, triggering new scandals. By bringing these findings together, the chapter makes a strong case for a substantive role for independent agencies as part of a comprehensive set of misconduct prevention strategies.

Models of Police Complaints and Disciplinary Systems

Police complaints systems have been conceptualized and categorized in different ways. For example, Kerstetter (1985) adopted a typology of civilian "review," "input," and "monitor." Goldsmith (1988) employed a six-part model, covering more complex types of civilian involvement in the investigation and adjudication of complaints (see also Finn, 2001). The three-part model of Prenzler and Ronken (2001) used here—consisting of "internal affairs," "civilian review," and "civilian control"—includes in-house systems as a starting point and then extends the model to include a fully developed concept of independence.

Internal Affairs

Internal affairs is a traditional American term for integrity units within police departments—what have also been called "internal investigation divisions" or "units" and are now normally referred to as "professional standards units" or similar (Prenzler & Ronken, 2001). For much of the history of policing, complaints and discipline were managed in-house. Cases were assigned to supervising officers of different ranks, depending on seriousness. Corruption scandals and a high volume of complaints prompted larger police departments to create specialist units to investigate and adjudicate allegations and, to a lesser extent, initiate prevention programs. The system was meant to ensure department-wide consistency and some independence from local affiliations. Usually, there were direct lines of reporting from the internal affairs unit to the police chief or commissioner.

In-house systems were not usually devoid of external scrutiny. Elected officials, including mayors or police ministers, provided one line of accountability to the electorate, although politicians tended to have a vested interest in hiding scandals and protecting police. In response to a citizen's suit, a civil court could require evidence from police. Some oversight was also provided by criminal courts in scrutinizing police evidence and excluding material illegally obtained (Sarre, 1989). One obvious problem here was that a great deal of police work never reached the courts. In addition, police were often adept at lying, and juries generally wanted to believe authority figures. Inquests and ad hoc inquiries provided other forms of judicial oversight.

However, criminal courts could not normally make use of incriminating testimony provided by police in the inquisitorial setting of an inquest. Judicial inquiries were often constrained by limited terms of reference designed to minimize political damage and were often blocked by the notorious "blue wall of silence" (Lewis, 1999).

Since the 1970s, better equipped inquiries, armed with covert investigative capabilities and powers to indemnify witnesses, have almost always condemned the record of internal affairs units in deflecting complainants and favoring police (Prenzler & Ronken, 2001). Inquiries also found that internal affairs systems not only failed to bring individual officers to justice but also patterns of misconduct were ignored and primary prevention strategies were underdeveloped (Wood, 1997). Furthermore, complainants were almost universally dissatisfied with police treatment of their complaint, often because of the inevitable conflict of interest entailed in the process of police investigating police (Landau, 1996). Scandals and inquiries in other domains have highlighted the natural tendency of all organizations toward self-protection (Wood, 2007). Police are not unique in their capacity to evade outside scrutiny and to intimidate and malign complainants and whistleblowers. However, the nature of police work and police organizations—including a hostile working environment and history of narrow recruitment—intensified this tendency (Skolnick, 1966).

Civilian Review

In response to recurring misconduct scandals, cover-ups, and inaction, a number of governments reluctantly introduced civilian review agencies. Civilian review takes diverse forms, but the principle idea is to provide an independent check on possible bias without excessive interference in police management (Goldsmith, 1988). A review agency usually consists of a government-appointed citizen board, reflecting community interests and professional skills, with an executive arm, including a director, usually with legal qualifications, and civilian staff. Typically, police will carry out investigations and apportion discipline, with the external agency taking a monitoring role. This normally involves paper-based audits of complaint investigation files and responses to appeals by complainants, with a capacity to criticize police work and recommend alternative findings and outcomes. This is a minimalist model, with scope for some enlargement of authority, such as the capacity to conduct independent investigations of serious matters and appeal disciplinary decisions to a mayor or a tribunal, police commission, or board (Finn, 2001).

Civilian review involves a mixed model and a clear political compromise between supporters and opponents of fully independent systems. It appears to have wide appeal and constitutes the dominant model internationally.

Available performance indicators—such as public confidence, complainant satisfaction, complaint substantiation rates, and police conduct indicators—suggest some achievements (Prenzler, 2009b, Chapter 10). A capacity to hold open inquisitorial hearings and refer matters to a public prosecutor or administrative tribunal significantly enhances the democratic accountability process, as is the ability to publish reports. Nonetheless, most review systems allow too much scope for police to control or subvert the process. One major problem is that civilian review holds out a false promise. Agencies look like they will investigate and adjudicate allegations against police. It is hardly surprising, then, that complainants' anger and disillusionment with authorities are compounded when the oversight agency refers the complaint to the police (Landau, 1996).

Civilian Control

Although *civilian control* is used to describe a type of agency within a police "oversight" system, it implies much more than is suggested by the term *oversight*. Civilian control takes the problems of real and perceived internal bias and takes them to their logical conclusion: Police should not investigate nor adjudicate complaints against their own. The assumption of natural justice entailed in this view is summed up in the following critique of review systems:

> When a person reports a crime, it would never be expected that police would allow colleagues of the alleged offender to conduct the investigation, even under police superintendence. Nor would it be considered appropriate for police to merely recommend an outcome, with the colleagues of the accused left free to choose the disciplinary response. Yet this is essentially what happens with complaints against police under the weak civilian oversight systems that operate in many jurisdictions. Reactive review processes frequently fail the most basic test of independence… "Independence should be demonstrated by the person or body concerned having control of the process." (Hayes, 1997, p. vi). (Prenzler, 2004, p. 106)

This basic principle is increasingly being applied to organizations outside police—whether it be churches, charities, defense forces, trade unions, or corporations—where victims of abuse and other stakeholders call for fully independent and transparent investigations. Independent regulatory agencies are now de rigueur for a wide range of occupations, including the health sector, construction, consumer and financial services, and the security industry (Ransley & Prenzler, 2012). Remarkably, legal services commissions, which investigate and adjudicate complaints against lawyers, have come on the scene in recent years, with little controversy regarding the demise of a long tradition of self-regulation (Graycar & Prenzler, 2013, p. 98).

In policing, the trend internationally appears to be in the direction of the civilian control model, but in very limited forms (see Chapters 6–10 of this book). Hong Kong provides a good example of a mixed profile. The Independent Commission Against Corruption (ICAC), established in 1974, appears to embody the civilian control model (Graycar & Prenzler, 2013). Its many successes include shutting down highly organized police graft. At the same time, police misconduct issues outside corruption, such as assaults, are dealt with by a limited review agency, the Independent Police Complaints Council. In other examples, police oversight agencies independently investigate a range of serious misconduct allegations, but the large bulk of cases remain in police hands, subject perhaps to some form of audit. Some agencies independently investigate all complaints, but their disciplinary recommendations can be rejected by the police department, which retains control over final outcomes. Others again are institutionally separate from police but so dependent on former or seconded police that they can hardly be said to be genuinely independent. In Northern Ireland, the Police Ombudsman, established in 2000, appears as the one agency that has gone the furthest in putting independence into practice across all aspects of the complaints and discipline process (Savage, 2013).

A variety of arguments have been put forward for rejecting civilian control. Putting the model into practice involves a significant cost, including through proper regionalization. Oversight agencies need to be accessible to the public outside capital city centers, and investigators need to access police stations and critical incidents—such as police shootings—on a timely basis. One obvious answer to this concern about the financial cost is that the work needs to be done anyway, so it is simply a matter of shifting resources. In addition, it has been argued that integration of police oversight within a larger integrity agency provides considerable efficiencies (Prenzler & Faulkner, 2010). The public sector-wide model also means that police should be treated the same as other public servants and politicians. This addresses a common police concern about equality (Oppal, 1994).

An additional argument against civilian control concerns the supposed unique investigative expertise of police. This is an argument that ignores the wide range of investigative functions carried out in the public and private domains and the long-term capacity of oversight agencies to train nonpolice investigators. There is also an argument that police will close ranks against outside investigators. However, this view is belied by the successes obtained by properly equipped inquiries in supporting police whistleblowers.

Finally, it is argued that external regulation will undermine police internal authority and strip police managers of the responsibility to keep their house in order (McDonald, 1981). The simple rejoinder is that, under the civilian control model, police retain responsibility for the primary prevention of misconduct—through recruitment, training, supervision, and other standard integrity management techniques. The outside agency assesses the effectiveness of these methods and provides a safety net when the internal system fails or underperforms (Bayley, 1995). Nor does the system exclude all in-house investigations and discipline. In theory, civilian control can operate effectively with various degrees of lower-level police authority, depending on circumstances. The Police Federation in the United Kingdom argued for a division of labor along these lines as far back as 1981. Part of the motivation was a concern that officers were subject to excessively harsh discipline. The Federation suggested that everything above administrative matters should be externalized, while police would have responsibility for dealing with:

> Lateness for duty, impertinence or insubordination, failure to carry out administrative orders and so forth … the chief officer would continue to be responsible for the good government of the force in much the same way as a Regimental Commander in the army and with the same ability to refer any more serious misconduct upwards to a court martial. (Working Party, 1981, p. 4)

There is also a potentially large role for police in informal resolution of complaints.

Reviews and Inquiries

The following subsections summarize the findings of major reviews and inquiries into police integrity matters on the question of internal and external responsibility for complaints and discipline.

The United States

The situation in the United States is marked by significant complexity, given that there are approximately 18,000 police departments organized primarily at the local level (Reaves, 2011). The fortunes of civilian review bodies have waxed and waned as political support and opposition shifted ground and policing scandals broke and subsided. Debate and protests have often been protracted and "bitter" (Finn, 2001, p. vii; see Chapter 9 of the present book).

The first embodiment of the idea of civilian oversight of police in the United States has been attributed to a nongovernment Committee on Constitutional Rights, with no official powers, established by the Los Angeles Bar Association in 1928 to "receive complaints about police misconduct" (Walker, 2006, p. 3). The National Commission on Law Observance and Enforcement—the Wickersham Commission—was instigated in 1929 over concerns about police involvement in the illegal liquor industry. The commission found widespread police complicity in serious and organized crime and that torture and intimidation to coerce confessions were widespread. One report, *Lawlessness in Law Enforcement*, recommended that "every locality" should have a "disinterested agency...to which a citizen, especially one who is poor and uninfluential, may report abuses with the knowledge that they will be protected against retaliation and that his complaint will be searchingly investigated" (National Commission on Law Observance and Enforcement, 1931, p. 192), but with no apparent affect. In New York City, a 1935 Mayor's Task Force on racial conflict supported the creation of a mixed-race committee to receive complaints of mistreatment by police. However, the mayor rejected the idea as "too radical" (Walker, 2006, p. 3). According to Walker (2006), the first genuine civilian review board was set up in Washington, DC, in 1948.

The 1960s civil rights movement included calls for citizen oversight to address police abuses. Concerns about police racism were a key driver. Review boards were set up in Minneapolis and York (Pennsylvania) in 1960 (U.S. Commission on Civil Rights, 1981, p. 125). In 1966, in New York City, the Civilian Complaint Review Board, first established in 1953, was given a 4–3 civilian majority (Walker, 2006). The federal Kerner Commission, which reviewed the race riots of 1967, found that minority groups' perceptions of police discrimination were aggravated by "the lack of effective mechanisms for handling complaints against the police" (Kerner, 1968, p. 14). However, it did not explicitly recommend independent processing.

The 1972 report of the Knapp Commission of Inquiry into the New York City Police Department was a watershed in demonstrating the vulnerability of policing to corruption and the need for complex sustained prevention measures (Newburn, 1999). The commission revealed extensive, almost universal, corrupt practices, which involved the systematic exploitation of police tasks and powers. The Knapp report emphasized how previous corruption inquiries were part of recurring cycles of weak reform, followed by a return to corruption. A significant part of the problem was that allegations and disclosures were not properly investigated and misconduct was not addressed. The system failed to deter corrupt officers, and police whistleblowers were persecuted and shut down. Consequently, the report emphasized the need for an external mechanism (Knapp, 1972, p. 14):

At the present time a citizen wishing to make a complaint about a policeman knows that his complaint will ultimately be investigated by other policemen. This discourages complaints, because many New Yorkers just don't trust policemen to investigate each other ...

This distrust is not confined to members of the public. Many policemen came to us with valuable information which they consented to give us only upon our assurance that we would not disclose their identity to the Department or to any District Attorney.

Any proposal for dealing with corruption must therefore provide a place where policemen as well as the public can come with confidence and without fear of retaliation. Any office designed to achieve this must be staffed by persons wholly unconnected with the Police Department.

Despite these strong statements, the Knapp recommendations were focused on in-house integrity management (Henry, 1994). There was only a limited attempt to remedy the systemic internal problems through the relatively weak Special Prosecutor's Office, established in the wake of the Inquiry. The 1992–1994 Mollen Commission report found that serious corruption reappeared because "the vigilance of the [post-Knapp] generation failed to survive the department's natural desire to protect itself from scandal" (Mollen, 1994, p. 148). Mollen (1994) castigated police accountability processes (p. 4):

Even corruption investigators understood that avoiding scandal was often more important than uncovering corruption. As one Internal Affairs detective testified… "They [IAD's commanders] didn't want us to be effective… They didn't want us to uncover…any kind of misconduct that would bring bad press to the Department."

Reformed police departments would inevitably slide back into corruption, "unless some countervailing pressure compels the Department to do what it naturally strays from doing" (Mollen, 1994, p. 148). The findings obliged the commission to recommend a powerful independent agency to perform continuing audits of police disciplinary processes, with the capacity to:

Conduct its own intelligence gathering operations, self-initiated investigations, and integrity tests…[with] unrestricted access to the Department's records and personnel … powers to subpoena witnesses…take testimony in private and public hearings; and the power to grant immunity. (Mollen, 1994, pp. 153–154)

Again, however, the logic of this view was denied by the belief that it was the police department's "responsibility to investigate itself" (Mollen, 1994, p. 152), and by the assumption that police possess a unique skill set: "It is the Department that best understands the corruption hazards facing cops, the culture that protects it, and the methods that can most effectively uncover it" (Mollen, 1994, p. 152).

The compromise to emerge from this involved two external agencies: the Civilian Complaint Review Board, established in 1993 as an all-civilian board, and the Commission to Combat Police Corruption, established in 1995, both of which continue to be restricted by limited powers. In 2013, the controversy over racially biased stop-and-frisk practices by New York police led to the creation of a third oversight agency, the Office of the Inspector General (Taylor & Goodman, 2014).

The Christopher Commission in Los Angeles provided another landmark report on police accountability. The Los Angeles Police Department (LAPD) is rarely far from controversy. Perhaps the most notorious case concerned the systematic beating of Rodney King in 1991, revealed to the world on a home video. The subsequent acquittal of four accused officers by an all-white jury sparked 6 days of rioting in Los Angeles, in which 55 people were killed and over 800 buildings destroyed by fire (Prenzler, 2009b). The case led to the Independent Commission on the Los Angeles Police Department—the Christopher Commission—which identified routine police brutality and cover-ups. It concluded that,

> No area of police operations received more adverse comment during the Commission's public hearings than the Department's handling of the citizen complaints against LAPD officers... Many community groups and members of the general public firmly believe that the Department is incapable of disciplining its own officers. (Christopher, 1991, p. 153)

This included the failure to address chronic misbehavior by individual officers with large numbers of complaints. However, the commission failed to tackle the problem head on, bizarrely supporting the police view that an external complaints agency would deter police whistleblowers, would be politicized, and would be unable to attract "professional" staff (Christopher, 1991, p. 172).

The potential of civilian oversight in the United States continues to be undermined by attachment to the review model. The situation has not changed significantly since a 1981 report, *Who Is Guarding the Guardians? A Report on Police Practices*, by the U.S. Commission on Civil Rights (1981), which found that, "while encountering some successes, (review) boards largely failed. Their basic flaw was that they were advisory only, having no power to decide cases or impose punishment" (p. 125). The fallout from this failed reform process is high levels of ongoing violence and corruption in U.S. policing and a particular problem with toxic police departments that continually resist accountability agendas (e.g., see U.S. Department of Justice investigation reports at http://www.justice.gov/crt/about/spl/). It should be no surprise, therefore, that a 2014 United Nations report on police violence and racism in the United States found that officers were largely immune from accountability. It concluded that:

> All instances of police brutality and excessive use of force by law enforcement officers (should be) investigated promptly, effectively and impartially by an independent mechanism with no institutional or hierarchical connection between the investigators and the alleged perpetrators. (Committee Against Torture, 2014, p. 13)

England and Wales

In England and Wales, the development of external input into police complaints management has been traced back to the Royal Commission on the Police, established in 1960 (Russell, 1976). The inquiry, chaired by Henry Willink, did not introduce civilian oversight but identified classic problems with internal control. It was triggered by a number of instances of corruption and assaults and by allegations that complaint management processes were inadequate. The report was unusual in being generally positive about police conduct, the quality of police investigations of complaints—including timeliness and communication with complainants—and the appropriateness of disciplinary outcomes. An examination of complaint files led the commission to conclude that "many of the records testify to the patience of the police under great provocation from unreasonable members of the public" (Royal Commission on the Police, 1962, p. 124).

At the time, complaint investigations and discipline were almost entirely under the control of chief constables. While the inquiry established that only 5% of complaints resulted in formal disciplinary action, it also found that up to 25% were found to have some substance. "Informal advice" to officers, amounting to "effective rebuke" in many cases, was fairly common (Royal Commission on the Police, 1962, p. 124). Available evidence suggested that complainants were evenly divided in regard to satisfaction with the process. The report indicated that satisfaction could be linked to an intrinsic problem with potential bias in police processes and perceptions of bias:

> A system in which the investigation of complaints is the concern of the police alone may not have the appearance of justice being done... A chief constable might well be inclined either to partiality or to over-severity in trying one of his own men; in any case it cannot be easy for him, with a natural sympathy towards his own officers, to adopt the attitude of mind which is necessary if justice is to be done—and, almost as important, if justice is seen to be done. It was with this in mind, rather than on the ground of specific allegations of miscarriages of justice, that some witnesses contended that the investigation of complaints against the police should be handed over to a person or body outside the force. (Royal Commission on the Police, 1962, p. 125)

The report considered this "a persuasive line of argument" (Royal Commission on the Police, 1962, p. 125) but went on to argue that civilian control would undermine the authority of police managers and undermine police confidence in the capacity of their superiors to protect them from false allegations.

The key compromise recommendation was that complaints should be investigated by an officer "from a division of the force other than that in which the alleged offender is serving" (Royal Commission on the Police, 1962, p. 131) and that all decisions about complaint outcomes be taken by the chief constable. A number of other recommendations were made to improve procedures, including the recording and reporting of complaints and complaint dispositions, a capacity for police to appeal disciplinary decisions, and an option for complainants to attend disciplinary hearings and put questions to the accused officer. The inquiry also recommended that the public prosecutor in England and Wales have sole responsibility for the course of action "wherever an allegation discloses that a criminal offence may have been committed by a police officer against a member of the public" (Royal Commission on the Police, 1962, p. 149). The majority of inquiry members supported these recommendations, believing they "will always provide for the proper and impartial investigation of complaints against the police" (Royal Commission on the Police, 1962, p. 150).

In hindsight, 50 years later, we can see that the report was naïve at best in its view of the capacity of police to effectively manage complaints. The recommendation regarding police investigators from outside divisions failed to address the general perceptions of police occupational solidarity (Russell, 1976). The glaring problem with assignment of all criminal cases to the public prosecutor was that police control of complaints reception and investigation meant the prosecutor received only matters already screened by police. In light of these problems, three inquiry members supported the appointment of a Commissioner of Rights to independently review complaint processes (Russell, 1976, p. 150).

The Royal Commission recommendations were embodied in the Police Act of 1964. However, a study in the mid-1970s (Russell, 1976) identified highly questionable low substantiation rates and a lack of confidence in the system. A series of scandals in the 1970s, focused on detectives in the Metropolitan Police, and continuing criticism of a lack of substantive independence in complaints management prompted the establishment of the Police Complaints Board (PCB) in 1977 (Waters & Brown, 2000). The Board was a weak review type agency. Although it had a power to "direct a chief officer to commence disciplinary proceedings, which would be heard by a disciplinary tribunal consisting of two PCB members unconnected with the case" (Smith, 2009, p. 124), it was widely considered to be "virtually toothless," engaged in little more than "'rubber stamping' police reports" (Maguire & Corbett, 1991, p. 8).

The inadequacies of the PCB were highlighted by ongoing misconduct cases. The 1981 Scarman Report into the Brixton race riots, with findings of police provocation, led directly to the establishment of the Police Complaints Authority (PCA) in 1985 (Maguire and Corbett, 1991). In a key statement, Scarman declared that ([1981] 1986, pp. 182–183):

> Many will continue to criticise [the complaint system] so long as the investigation of complaints remains in police hands… Only the establishment of an independent service for the investigation of all complaints against the police will silence their criticisms.

Scarman failed to apply this principle, recommending ongoing reliance on the review-based process, with some scope for civilian control of only the most serious cases. Subsequently, however, in his preface to the book edition of the report, he argued that operationalization of the principle was now possible, especially in light of Police Federation support (Scarman, 1986).

The PCA was established by the Police and Criminal Evidence Act 1984. It was tasked with supervising investigations of serious matters and reviewing the outcomes of police investigations. A review of the system by Maguire and Corbett (1991), begun in 1987 and instigated by the Home Office and the PCA, found that the work of the PCA had no apparent effect on how police operated. A survey showed that more than half of complainants were "very dissatisfied" with the process of police-based investigations. The report commended the quality of work done by full-time staff working in the system and supported the recent introduction of informal resolution. At the same time, it comprehensively critiqued the system in the following summary:

> Against these positive features have to be weighed the very low levels of satisfaction among complainants; a sense of alienation—felt by complainants and police officers alike—from a complex, long-winded and secretive investigation process; failures in communication of the reasons for, and implications of, decisions; little external understanding of the role and input of the PCA; the difficulty for PCA members, given their present location and resources, in undertaking active and direct supervision of more than a few investigations; and despite the undoubted improvements made by the Police and Criminal Evidence Act 1984, a continuing belief in many quarters that a system in which police "investigate themselves" is both wrong in principle and biased in practice. (Maguire & Corbett, 1991, p. xiv)

Little happened in response, despite these glaring problems and the exposure of corruption by senior police in major terrorist-related wrongful conviction cases. The Police Federation acknowledged that police and the public had a mutual interest in an independent system:

> The system needs to be changed so that it becomes, and is seen by the public to be, wholly independent of the police service. Although we believe that all investigations are conducted in a thoroughly scrupulous fashion, the fact that police officers undertake the investigations, albeit under direct supervision of PCA members, lays the system open to allegations of partiality and even cover-up. For this reason, we also want to see a system of independent adjudication of disciplinary charges brought against police officers following an independent investigation. (in Prenzler & Ronken, 2001, p. 169; see also http://www.polfed.org/aboutus/179.aspx)

A breaking point was created by the high-profile 1999 Stephen Lawrence Inquiry into the failed investigation of the apparently racially motivated murder of teenager Stephen Lawrence in 1993. The inquiry, headed by William MacPherson, criticized the PCA's reliance on police investigators and its limited input into police discipline. The weaknesses in the process were found to exacerbate the problems of ethnic minority dissatisfaction with police. MacPherson (1999) concluded that "investigation of police officers by their own or another Police Service is widely regarded as unjust, and does not inspire confidence" (p. 33).

The Stephen Lawrence Inquiry led to the replacement of the PCA with the Independent Police Complaints Commission (IPCC), which became operational in 2004. The IPCC was given enlarged powers to independently investigate serious matters involving police and to handle appeals. Other matters were subject to varying degrees of IPCC "management" or more detached "supervision," depending on their seriousness (Prenzler, 2011). The Commission has appeared to be fairly well resourced. At the same time, it directly investigated only a very small number of complaints—for example, just under 4% of all complaints made by the public in 2009/2010 (Prenzler, 2011).

Ongoing dissatisfaction with this limited input prompted the IPCC to enlarge its scope of operations. It acknowledged that what may appear to police to be a minor complaint, treatable in-house, "may be a serious, unique and often frightening event for a citizen" (IPCC, 2009, p. 7). Further impetus for change was generated by the U.K. "Phone Hacking Scandal" of 2011–2012. The Leveson (2012) Inquiry and Filkin (2012) Review revealed major problems with inappropriate relationships between senior police and the media, facilitated by gifts and benefits to police. Confidence in the police was also rocked by a number of other scandals in the mid-2000s/early 2010s. These included the shooting death of Jean Charles Menezes (a man wrongfully suspected of being a terrorist), the bashing death of Ian Tomlinson (an innocent passerby at a demonstration), and revelations by the Hillsborough Independent Panel (2012) that police had systematically covered up their contributing role in the 1989 "Hillsborough disaster," in which 96 persons were crushed to death at a soccer stadium.

In 2012, with these scandals squarely in the background, the Home Affairs Committee of the House of Commons commenced an inquiry into the IPCC, drawing on a range of evidence from complainants, police, the IPCC, and legal groups. The Committee pulled few punches in its conclusions:

Police officers are warranted with powers that can strip people of their liberty, their money and even their lives and it is vital that the public have confidence that those powers are not abused. In this report, we conclude that the Independent Police Complaints Commission is not yet capable of delivering the kind of powerful, objective scrutiny that is needed to inspire that confidence.

Compared with the might of the 43 police forces in England and Wales, the IPCC is woefully underequipped and hamstrung in achieving its original objectives. It has neither the powers nor the resources that it needs to get to the truth when the integrity of the police is in doubt. Smaller even than the Professional Standards Department of the Metropolitan Police, the Commission is not even first among equals, yet it is meant to be the back-stop of the system. It lacks the investigative resources necessary to get to the truth; police forces are too often left to investigate themselves; and the voice of the IPCC does not have binding authority. The Commission must bring the police complaints system up to scratch and the Government must give it the powers that it needs to do so. (House of Commons Home Affairs Committee, 2013, p. 4)

In a section titled "The Basis of Mistrust," the report noted that there was a widespread perception that police were "getting away with misconduct and criminality" (House of Commons Home Affairs Committee, 2013, p. 6). A clear double standard was identified in the treatment of police officers subject to allegations of wrongdoing, compared with police treatment of members of the public subject to similar allegations. The whole approach, including actions by the IPCC, was marked by a lack of rigor. The absence of substantive independence lay at the heart of the problem, in large part driven by the fact that (House of Commons Home Affairs Committee, 2013, pp. 6–7):

1. Complaints are often investigated by the force about which a complaint or referral has been made; [and]
2. The IPCC continues to employ a significant number of former police officers, some who held senior posts in the force, who may naturally favor their former colleagues.

Despite these damning findings, and the example of a successful independent agency across the water in Northern Ireland, the Committee held back in its recommendations. It suggested greater resources for the IPCC, but without specifying an appropriate budget; a vague widening of the number of cases it investigated and greater control of investigations; reduction in the number of ex-police investigators to 20%; and a complicated process for producing binding findings in appeal cases.

Northern Ireland

Northern Ireland has been the site of the most complete evolution of oversight in the direction of civilian control (Savage, 2013). The Police Ombudsman for Northern Ireland became operational in 2000 in the wake of the 1998 Good Friday Agreement and decisive moves to end the bitter civil war in which the Royal Ulster Constabulary was deeply complicit on the side of English rule. The establishment of the Ombudsman occurred as part of a major reform of policing, including the creation of a new Police Service of Northern Ireland.

In 1995, the Secretary of State appointed Maurice Hayes to review the police complaints system. Hayes audited the existing system—which was based on the English model—consulted widely with diverse stakeholders, and examined academic reports and overseas complaints systems. The Independent Commission for Police Complaints, established in 1988, was characterized by Hayes as exemplifying all the standard problems of the review model in failing to properly expose, discipline, or prevent police misconduct and in losing stakeholder confidence. The primary problem lay in the fact that all complaints were investigated by police and disciplinary decisions were dominated by police, and this undermined the impartiality and effectiveness of the system (Hayes, 1997, pp. 38–40). Hayes (1997) did not equivocate on the central problem (p. v):

> The overwhelming message I got from nearly all sides and from all political parties was the need for the investigation to be independent and to be seen to be independent. While there were systemic failings in the present arrangements they lacked credibility because of a lack of independence, because it was the Chief Constable who decided what was a complaint, because there was no power of initiative, and because the complaints were investigated by police officers... The main value which was impressed upon me was independence, independence, independence.

The Independent Commission for Police Complaints itself expressed frustration with the limits on its authority. To fix the problem, Hayes (1997) recommended that "the Complaints Body should have complete control of the process" (p. 47).

This core position on independence was not, however, as categorical as it appeared when translated into specific recommendations. Hayes (1997) recommended the adoption of a "mixed model" (p. 55). Within a three-part hierarchy of complaints matters, varying degrees of input and control by the Ombudsman and police were envisioned (Hayes, 1997, p. 55):

> Under this arrangement complaints would be categorized under three headings: serious complaints possibly involving criminal action (such as death in custody, serious injury etc.), which the Complaints Body has a statutory duty to investigate; less serious but still substantial complaints which might, at the discretion of the Complaints Body, be remitted to the police for investigation and report, either supervised or unsupervised; and quality of service type complaints which would be remitted to the police for informal resolution.

Hayes (1997) also recommended that the Complaints Body include a balance of nonpolice and ex-police investigators, at the discretion of the Ombudsman (p. 84). Some scope was allowed for seconding officers on a short-term basis (Hayes, 1997, p. 58). This position on the division of labor in complaints processing was, however, qualified by the view that confidence in the system in Northern Ireland was so low that in the early stages, the Ombudsman should "take control of all complaints" and "progressively delegate some of the investigation to the police as public confidence was established" (Hayes, 1997, p. 55).

Hayes' recommendations on discipline were also consistent with a mixed model. In keeping with normal practice, criminal matters would be referred to the public prosecutor. For disciplinary matters, the Ombudsman would make a recommendation to the chief constable for action. If the chief constable and Ombudsman disagreed, the matter would then go to an "independent tribunal" (Hayes, 1997, p. 60). Ultimately, however, "the question of discipline once the facts had been established would be a matter for the Chief Constable…or Police Authority for senior officers" (Hayes, 1997, p. 60).

The Hayes Report was subsequently endorsed by the Independent Commission on Policing for Northern Ireland (1999). The Commission was a product of the Good Friday Agreement and was charged with making recommendations for optimizing democratic and accountable policing. It supported a "fully independent Ombudsman" within the terms set out by Hayes and also recommended a capacity to investigate matters without receiving a complaint and for the Ombudsman to analyze complaint patterns and address problems in cooperation with the Police Service (Independent Commission on Policing for Northern Ireland, 1999, pp. 37 and 111).

The Police Ombudsman for Northern Ireland was established by the Police (Northern Ireland) Act 1998. Section 51(4) makes the Ombudsman responsible for the police complaints and discipline system:

> The Ombudsman shall exercise his powers under this Part in such manner and to such extent as appears to him to be best calculated to secure—
>
> (a) The efficiency, effectiveness and independence of the police complaints system; and
> (b) The confidence of the public and of members of the police force in that system.

Despite discretion for the Ombudsman to introduce devolved responsibilities, as set out in the previous discussion, successive Ombudsmen have maintained direct control. It appears that all, or almost all, investigations are conducted by the Office. In addition, while the Ombudsman makes disciplinary recommendations to the Chief Constable, section 59 of the Act gives the Ombudsman authority to direct disciplinary proceedings if required. As a result, scholars have accepted that the Office fits the civilian control model and is possibly the only oversight agency in the world that ticks enough boxes to be categorized that way (Criminal Justice Inspection Northern Ireland, 2011; Savage, 2013; Seneviratne, 2004).

Australia

Police accountability in Australia has been characterized by a strong trend toward inclusion of police matters within the jurisdiction of public sector-wide anticorruption commissions (see Chapter 10). Police became subject to weak review with the establishment of ombudsmen from the 1970s. Ombudsman reports were marked by repeated criticisms of the failure of police to conduct proper investigations or act on recommendations (Prenzler, 2011). A key turning point occurred in 1989, when New South Wales police became subject to scrutiny by the new ICAC. The Wood (1997) Royal Commission into the New South Wales Police Service noted that both the ICAC and the New South Wales Ombudsman (which dealt with lower level complaints) had remedied some cases of individual and organized misconduct. However, they failed to penetrate the deeply entrenched police corruption in the State. The Ombudsman was considered to have been underresourced and overdependent on police investigations. The ICAC was said to have educative and investigation functions across the public sector that distracted it from the need for intensive investigations of police. Wood identified "an inherent bias in investigations as the result of which the Service failed to carry out impartial investigations or pursue allegations with the same rigour or approach seen in ordinary criminal inquiries" (p. 201).

A major outcome of the inquiry was the creation of a new body, the New South Wales Police Integrity Commission (PIC), with responsibility for the independent investigation of serious misconduct and monitoring of police internal investigations. The PIC was also given extensive covert and coercive powers. At the same time, the Wood Commission argued that the Police Service needed to retain primary responsibility for controlling corruption, "otherwise there was a risk that it might abandon all responsibility and interest in maintaining high standards of integrity" (Wood, 1997, p. 524). As a result, the PIC's authority was severely curtailed by the fact that it could only recommend "consideration" of action against an officer, either by the Police Service or the public prosecutor (Wood, 1997, p. 525). In addition, the majority of complaints were left in police hands. Stakeholders acknowledge that serious and organized corruption has been suppressed. However, complaints remain at high levels and misconduct remains a major feature of policing in New South Wales, particularly in the area of excessive force (Prenzler, 2011).

Policing in Queensland was characterized by decades of scandal, inquiry, and failed reform. The Fitzgerald Inquiry (1987–1989) identified widespread process corruption and graft associated with vice operations. It was highly critical of police handling of complaints:

> The Internal Investigations Section has been woefully ineffective, hampered by a lack of staff and resources and crude techniques. It has lacked commitment and will and demonstrated no initiative to detect serious crime... The

Section has provided warm comfort to corrupt police. It has been a friendly, sympathetic, protective and inept overseer. It must be abolished. (Fitzgerald, 1989, p. 289)

The Fitzgerald Inquiry recommended the creation of a cross-sector integrity agency, with extensive coercive powers and a special mission for monitoring and directing police reform. The report prescribed independent investigations of intermediate and criminal matters, with a large role for an independent tribunal in adjudicating cases. However, the Criminal Justice Commission, created out of the inquiry, and its later replacement, the Crime and Misconduct Commission, confined their investigations to very small numbers of cases. Audits revealed ongoing problems with police handling of the bulk of complaints (Prenzler, 2009a). The functioning of the tribunals appears to have been undermined by an overly adversarial approach. The independence of the two commissions was also subverted by reliance on seconded police as investigators, and they were distracted by the unusual inclusion of major and organized crime in their portfolios. The system failed to satisfy complainants and stakeholders in the media, law, and academia and failed to prevent recurring scandals. In 2009, a former supreme court judge and leading corruption investigator called for an end to "cops investigating cops" (in Koch and McKenna, 2009, p. 1). The Queensland Council for Civil Liberties (2010) called for a judicial inquiry into the management of complaints against police, claiming (p. 1):

We are back to the bad old pre Fitzgerald days where police investigate police and run dead on too many complaints against police... The CMC (Crime and Misconduct Commission) is enamoured of its crime fighting/super police force role and has seriously neglected over the last ten years its police oversight role.

Victoria Police also had a long history of diverse and serious misconduct. A series of inquiries identified inherent problems with internal investigations. The 1978 Beach Inquiry found that:

There was no satisfactory avenue through which a citizen could lodge a complaint against Police misbehaviour in the expectation it would be thoroughly and impartially pursued. Regrettably, this is apparently due in no small measure to an attitude of the Police mind, which is affronted by the impertinence of the civilian in making a complaint at all, and which then in a defensive reflex, classifies him as a troublemaker, or as being anti-Police, or motivated by malice or ill-will. (Beach, 1978, pp. 106–107)

The 1983 Grieve Inquiry found that attempts to introduce citizen representation into a Police Inquiry Committee and a Police Appeal Board resulted only in tokenism: "In both cases, a significant police presence on the bodies erodes a sense of independence" (Grieve, 1983, pp. 11–12). The 1987 Richardson inquiry found that:

> Many lawyers and members of the public had so little confidence in the present system of investigations by the Internal Investigations Department that many serious complaints about the police were not being lodged. (Richardson, 1987, p. 17)

In 1986, the PCA took over the police review functions of the Ombudsman, established in 1973. However, in 1988, opposition from police and the Police Association led to the disestablishment of the PCA (Freckelton, 1991). Police subversion of the recommendations of the Ombudsman and a series of major scandals then led to the creation of a new Office of Police Integrity (OPI) in 2004, with commission-style powers. However, like its counterparts in other states, the OPI was unable to take disciplinary action against police. Despite some successes in shutting down corrupt activities, it failed to engender fundamental reform and referred most complaints back to the police—generating extensive stakeholder dissatisfaction (Prenzler, 2011). A wider movement supporting a public sector anticorruption agency led to the OPI being subsumed within a new Independent Broad-based Anti-corruption Commission, established in 2012, but still with no real prospect for adequate police accountability (Ferguson, 2014).

The Royal Commission into Aboriginal Deaths in Custody covered all areas of policing in Australia and concluded that in-house investigations of allegations against police were so poor that the report recommended:

> At least as far as they involve complaints by Aboriginal people, investigations of alleged police misconduct should be carried out as much as possible by persons other than police officers. It may be that a civilian investigator might be a team leader of a group including police officers, as there are some investigatory skills and processes, such as physical evidence collection and analysis, which are best done by police, but it is vital that there be a "hands on" investigation leader who is not currently or formerly a police officer. (Johnston, 1991, s. 29.5.23.)

The recommendation was generally ignored.

At the federal level, the contradictory nature of many police reviews and inquiries was manifested in a set of Australian Law Reform Commission reports on police complaints systems, beginning in the 1970s. In a typical finding, the 1995 report stated boldly that:

> The record of internal units is generally inadequate in terms of the effective conduct of investigations and there are excessive delays. A siege like mentality

of police officers and their own police culture means that there are strong
risks that they will not be able to conduct thorough and fair investigations.
(Australian Law Reform Commission, 1995, pp. 149–150)

The Commission went even further in positing an intrinsic inability for
police to impartially investigate police:

> To ask the police to investigate complaints against their own places them in
> a "hopeless conflict of interest position." Police investigators, whether con-
> sciously or otherwise, will tend to be sceptical of complainants and will be
> "softer" on the police concerned. (Australian Law Reform Commission, 1995,
> pp. 149–150)

The report concluded that "the model most likely to engender confidence
must be one which gives as much power and responsibility as possible to
an external agency" (Australian Law Reform Commission, 1995, p. 149).
However, in a typical back down, the report went on to conclude that:

> Only the police force or former members have the necessary investigatory skill
> and expertise to investigate serious misconduct… There would be tremendous
> difficulties in finding suitably experienced and qualified staff if an external
> investigation unit was to avoid police and ex staff… A wholly external body
> would reduce police morale service wide. Lines of management responsibility
> would be interrupted by investigations conducted by outsiders whose priori-
> ties would interfere with the operational priorities of the police. (Australian
> Law Reform Commission, 1995, pp. 151–152)

These equivocations entailed numerous delays, until the Australian Commission for Law Enforcement Integrity was introduced in 2006, necessi-
tated by intermediate-level misconduct issues. Nonetheless, the Australian
Federal Police and other federal law enforcement agencies retain a major role
in complaints investigations and adjudication (Prenzler, 2011).

Implications and Issues

Who should investigate and adjudicate complaints against police? This
chapter canvassed evidence from numerous inquiries and reviews in different jurisdictions, which suggests strongly that even the best investigations
of police by police are undermined by perceptions or suspicions of bias. It
would also seem that in most cases, these suspicions are well founded—
although this is not invariably the case. In sum, it appears that the only way to
effectively deal with these real and perceived deficiencies is to adopt civilian
control for the whole process. However, behind this simple proposition lie a

number of challenging complexities. The question of what constitutes "independence" is taken up in the next chapter. Can ex-police work in oversight agencies? What about seconded police? Can lower-level matters be effectively dealt with by police, including through informal dispute resolution, subject to external review where there is a capacity to intervene and redirect findings? Can oversight agencies work in collaboration with police or does this compromise their position?

There are other important questions, which are addressed in subsequent chapters. What can be done to ensure that an ineffective internal process is not simply replaced by an ineffective external process? What kind of standards should apply to oversight agencies in terms of the rigor of investigations and prosecutions? Is it a good idea to prioritize an efficient administrative process—utilizing a lower civil standard of proof—and then pursue criminal cases where appropriate on top of administrative outcomes, or is this unfair "double jeopardy?" Furthermore, it is well known that a proportion of police misconduct, especially graft, is unlikely to be revealed by complaints, especially public complaints. How far, then, should oversight agencies go in pursuing corruption outside the realm of complaints investigations—including through the use of covert tactics, including controversial techniques such as integrity testing?

Given the strength of the arguments in favor of the civilian control model, its general absence around the world testifies to the poverty of public policy and the antidemocratic tendencies of many government decision makers. The Police Ombudsman for Northern Ireland does, at least, provide one example of an established oversight agency consistent with the civilian control model. Subsequent chapters of this book review the performance of the Ombudsman's office across a range of criteria. On these measures, the office appears to have been successful and it remains the standout agency internationally. The unlikely fact that this has occurred in one of the world's worst trouble spots gives hope for the democratic control of police everywhere.

Conclusion

In 2009, British academic Graham Smith made the following observation in relation to the treatment of complaints against the police in England and Wales:

> A consequence of unequal representation of stakeholders' interests is that, regardless of the intentions of policy makers and practitioners, the impact of reform has been limited in practice which, in turn, ensures that public demand for meaningful change continues undiminished, and the inevitability of further controversy leads to another reform cycle. (Smith, 2009, p. 127)

This chapter has provided evidence from major investigative forums to support this view. The failure to respond to stakeholders' expectations of an independent hearing of their grievance not only creates a disaffected constituency, it also means that police misconduct is not addressed and remedied for the future. "Independence" is a core principle of justice that traditionally has not been extended to "complainants"—both members of the public and police—who make an allegation or report of wrongdoing by police. The failure to deliver on this most basic requirement means that systems remain broken and calls for reform continue. What is needed are politicians and policy makers with the intelligence and courage to make civilian control a reality in their jurisdiction. Perhaps, their prevarications are motivated by the precedent that substantive oversight of police sets for control of their own conduct.

References

Australian Law Reform Commission. (1995). *Under the spotlight: Complaints against the AFP and NCA*. Canberra: Australian Law Reform Commission.

Bayley, D. (1995). Getting serious about police brutality. In P. Stenning (Ed.), *Accountability for criminal justice: Selected essays* (pp. 93–109). Toronto: University of Toronto Press.

Beach, B. (1978). *Report of the Board of Inquiry into Allegations against Members of the Victorian Police Force*. Melbourne: Government Printer.

Christopher, W. (1991). *Report of the Independent Commission on the Los Angeles Police Department*. Los Angeles: Independent Commission on the LAPD.

Committee Against Torture. (2014). *Concluding observations on the third to fifth periodic reports of United States of America*. Geneva: United Nations.

Criminal Justice Inspection Northern Ireland. (2011). *An inspection into the independence of the Office of the Police Ombudsman for Northern Ireland*. Belfast: Criminal Justice Inspection Northern Ireland.

Ferguson, M. (2014, April 1). Labor promises an overhaul of anti-corruption body. *The Australian*, p. 6.

Filkin, E. (2012). *Ethical issues arising from the relationship between police and the media*. London: Metropolitan Police Service.

Finn, P. (2001). *Citizen review of police: Approaches and implementation*. Washington, DC: National Institute of Justice.

Fitzgerald, G. (1989). *Report of a commission of inquiry pursuant to orders in council*. Brisbane: Government Printer.

Freckelton, I. (1991). Shooting the messenger: The trial and execution of the Victorian Police Complaints Authority. In A. Goldsmith (Ed.), *Complaints against the police: The trend to external review* (pp. 63–114). Oxford: Clarendon.

Goldsmith, A. (1988). New directions in police complaints procedures: Some conceptual and comparative departures. *Police Studies, 11*(2), 60–71.

Graycar, A., & Prenzler, T. (2013). *Understanding and preventing corruption*. Houndmills: Palgrave-Macmillan.

Grieve, I. (1983). *Report of the Committee on Complaints against the police*. Adelaide: The Committee.

Hayes, M. (1997). *A police ombudsman for Northern Ireland?* Belfast: Home Office Stationery Office.

Henry, V. (1994). Police corruption: Tradition and evolution. In K. Bryett & C. Lewis (Eds.), *Un-peeling tradition: Contemporary policing* (pp. 160–176). Melbourne: Macmillan.

Hillsborough Independent Panel. (2012). *The report of the Hillsborough Independent Panel*. London: The Stationery Office.

House of Commons Home Affairs Committee. (2013). *Independent Police Complaints Commission*. London: House of Commons.

Independent Commission on Policing for Northern Ireland. (1999). *A new beginning: Policing in Northern Ireland*. Belfast: Independent Commission on Policing for Northern Ireland.

Independent Police Complaints Commission. (2009). *Annual report 2008/09*. London: Independent Police Complaints Commission.

Johnston, E. (1991). *Royal Commission into Aboriginal Deaths in Custody: National Report* (Vol. 4). Canberra: Australian Government Publishing Service.

Kerner. (1968). *Report of the National Advisory Commission on Civil Disorders: Summary of report*. Retrieved from http://www.eisenhowerfoundation.org /docs/kerner.pdf.

Kerstetter, W. (1985). Who disciplines the police? Who should? In W. Geller (Ed.), *Police leadership in America: Crisis and opportunity* (pp. 149–183). New York: Praeger.

Knapp, W. (1972). *The Knapp Commission report on police corruption*. New York: George Braziller.

Koch, T., & McKenna, M. (2009, July 24). Judge calls for ban on cops investigating cops. *The Australian*, pp. 1, 4.

Landau, T. (1996). When police investigate police: A view from complainants. *Canadian Journal of Criminology, 38*(3), 291–315.

Leveson, B. (2012). *An inquiry into the culture, practices and ethics of the press* (Vol. II). London: The Stationery Office.

Lewis, C. (1999). *Complaints against the police. The politics of reform*. Sydney: Hawkins Press.

MacPherson, W. (1999). *The Stephen Lawrence inquiry: Report of an inquiry by Sir William MacPherson of Cluny*. London: HMSO.

Maguire, M., & Corbett, C. (1991). *A study of the police complaints system*. London: HMSO.

McDonald, D. (1981). *Commission of inquiry concerning certain activities of the Royal Canadian Mounted Police, second report—Volume 1*. Ottawa: Canadian Government Publishing Centre.

Mollen, M. (1994). *Commission to investigate allegations of police corruption and the anti-corruption procedures of the Police Department: Commission report*. New York: City of New York.

National Commission on Law Observance and Enforcement. (1931). *Report on lawlessness in law enforcement*. Washington, DC: United States Government Printing Office.

Newburn, T. (1999). *Understanding and preventing police corruption*. London: Home Office.

Oppal, W. (1994). *Closing the gap: Policing and the community*. Victoria: Policing in British Columbia Commission of Inquiry.

Prenzler, T. (2004). Stakeholder perspectives on police complaints and discipline: Towards a civilian control model. *Australian and New Zealand Journal of Criminology, 37*(1), 85–113.

Prenzler, T. (2009a). An assessment of reform in politics, criminal justice and the police in post-Fitzgerald Queensland. *Griffith Law Review, 18*(3), 576–595.

Prenzler, T. (2009b). *Police corruption: Preventing misconduct and maintaining integrity*. Boca Raton, FL: CRC Press.

Prenzler, T. (2011). The evolution of police oversight in Australia. *Policing and Society, 21*(3), 284–303.

Prenzler, T., & Faulkner, N. (2010). Towards a model public sector integrity commission. *Australian Journal of Public Administration, 69*(3), 251–262.

Prenzler, T., & Ronken, C. (2001). Models of police oversight: A critique. *Policing and Society, 11*(2), 151–180.

Queensland Council for Civil Liberties. (2010). Call for judicial inquiry into police complaints process. *QCCL Media Release*. Retrieved from http://www.qccl.org.au/documents/Media_TOG_17June10_Call_JudicialInquiry _PoliceComplaints.pdf.

Ransley, J., & Prenzler, T. (2012). White collar crime. In H. Hayes & T. Prenzler (Eds.), *An Introduction to Crime and Criminology* (pp. 125–140). Sydney: Pearson.

Reaves, B. A. (2011). *Census of local and state law enforcement agencies, 2008*. Washington, DC: Bureau of Justice Statistics.

Richardson, J. (1987). *Review of the investigation of complaints by the Internal Investigation Department of the Victoria Police*. Melbourne: Victorian Government.

Royal Commission on the Police. (1962). *Final report*. London: HMSO.

Russell, K. (1976). *Complaints against the police: A sociological view*. Leicester: Milltak.

Sarre, R. (1989). Towards the notion of policing 'by consent' and its implications for accountability. In D. Chappell & P. Wilson (Eds.), *Australian policing: Contemporary issues* (pp. 102–119). Sydney: Butterworths.

Savage, S. P. (2013). Thinking independence: Calling the police to account through the independent investigation of police complaints. *British Journal of Criminology, 43*, 94–112.

Scarman, L. G. (1986). *Scarman report*. London: Penguin.

Seneviratne, M. (2004). Policing the police in the United Kingdom. *Policing & Society, 14*(4), 329–347.

Skolnick, J. (1966). *Justice without trial: Law enforcement in democratic society*. New York: Wiley.

Smith, G. (2009). A most enduring problem: Police complaints reform in England and Wales. *Journal of Social Policy, 35*, 121–141.

Taylor, K., & Goodman, D. J. (2014, March 28). Inspector General for New York Police Department is named. *New York Times*. Retrieved from http://www .nytimes.com/2014/03/29/nyregion/inspector-general-for-new-york-police -department-is-named.html?hpw&rref=nyregion&_r=0.

U.S. Commission on Civil Rights. (1981). *Who is guarding the guardians? A report on police practices*. Washington, DC: U.S. Commission on Civil Rights.

Walker, S. (2006). The history of citizen oversight. In J. C. Perino (Ed.), *Citizen oversight of law enforcement* (pp. 1–10). Chicago: ABA Publishing.

Waters, I., & Brown, K. (2000). Police complaints and the complainants' experience. *British Journal of Criminology, 40*(2), 617–638.

Wood, J. (1997). *Royal Commission into the New South Wales Police Service: Final report.* Sydney: Government of the State of NSW.

Working Party. (1981). *The establishment of an independent element in the investigation of complaints against the police, Report of a Working Party appointed by the Home Secretary.* London: HMSO.

Independent Minded
The Role and Status of "Independence" in the Investigation of Police Complaints

2

STEPHEN P. SAVAGE

Contents

In discourses surrounding police complaint machineries, few notions carry more weight and evoke more passion than the principle of *independence*. The extent of the independent dimension within police complaints processes, particularly the independence of the investigative process, is widely used by policy analysts and politicians alike as a sort of litmus test of the robustness and effectiveness of a complaints system. Alongside other parallel notions such as "civilian" or "citizen" oversight, independence appears to offer solutions to the fundamental challenges of dealing with complaints against the police that police-led systems cannot. Furthermore, the trajectory of complaints agencies seems to be one of a relentless, if sometimes stuttering, march toward a greater role for independent mechanisms within police complaints arrangements (Filstad & Gottschalk, 2011). A lot rests, therefore, on how independent elements and processes within machineries for the oversight of policing operate in practice and are interpreted and made to function by actors responsible for them.

This chapter examines *independence* as a working principle of police oversight by focusing less on constitutional frameworks for independent oversight, important as they are, and more on the social and cultural dynamics of independent (civilian, citizen) oversight. Although much of the literature on independent oversight focuses on the *extent* or *reach* of the independent element in police oversight, the concern here is with the simple question:

What does independence look like, or feel like, when you have it? Within that question, the focus will be on what many consider to be the "end game" of the pursuit of fully effective oversight of the police: the independent *investigation* of complaints against the police—a core element of what has been referred to as the "civilian control" model of police complaints systems (Prenzler, 2004; Prenzler & Ronken, 2001). In examining the role and nature of independence within police oversight, there is no better starting place than with the framework that most commentators agree is "where we want to be": a framework that allows for complaints against the police, or at least the most serious allegations against the police, to be investigated by a body and group of people not "of" the police. In this respect, the chapter will draw heavily from empirical research undertaken by the author (Savage, 2013a,b) on what might be called "independence workers," primarily complaints investigators themselves, operating within three police oversight bodies in the British and Irish islands: the Garda Siochana Ombudsman's Commission (GSOC) in the Republic of Ireland, the Independent Police Complaints Commission (IPCC) for England and Wales, and the Office of the Police Ombudsman for Northern Ireland (OPONI).

The chapter is presented in three main sections. First, it begins by considering the principle of independence as a solution to a problem: how the invocation of independence has played a key role in state responses to identified system failures within policing. Second, drawing from research undertaken by the author, it examines the "social profile" of central players in the independent oversight business: complaints investigators. Finally, also drawing from that research, it discusses "independence at work," how those charged with the delivery of independent oversight articulate independence as a working philosophy and perceive any constraints on the attainment of independence as an organizational outcome.

Independence: A Nonpolice Solution to a Policing Problem

System failures—or "things going wrong"—are a major force for change and reform in policing (Punch, 2009; Savage, 2007; Sherman, 1978). As in other areas of public policy (Dunleavy, 1995), when major system failures in policing occur, or are at least recognized by the state as having occurred, a clarion call for independent scrutiny and/or oversight is often soon to follow. This might take the form of an independent inquiry, perhaps chaired by that potent symbol of independence, a judge, which may in turn recommend new independent elements and machineries within the oversight and accountability framework. In the policing context, such responses are not hard to find. In Britain, the state response to the Brixton Riots of 1981, which were widespread disorders involving mainly Black youth directed largely at the police, was to hold an independent inquiry under the senior judge Lord Scarman. In turn, Scarman was to call, among other things, for a range of independent (i.e., nonpolice) mechanisms to be introduced to enhance police accountability, including lay visitors to police stations and, with some considerable foresight (not to be realized for more than 30 years later in the shape of the IPCC), a fully independent system for the investigation of police complaints (Scarman, 1981). In the Republic of Ireland, the state response to serious allegations of police misconduct in the county of Donegal, including malpractices in the policing of terrorist activity, was to establish a tribunal of inquiry under Justice Frederick Morris. The Morris Tribunal was to recommend a number of major institutional reforms (Conway & Walsh, 2011), one of which was the formation of an independent inspectorate, another, again, the creation of a body to independently investigate complaints against the police—this was to become the GSOC.

The history of police oversight is littered with such examples of the principle of independence being invoked to solve or help solve problems of system failure within policing. In Queensland, Australia, the Fitzgerald Inquiry into police corruption and corruption in the wider public sector called for the establishment of an independent tier in the handling of police complaints, which led, in part, to the Queensland Criminal Justice Commission, whatever its subsequent shortcomings (Hopkins, 2009; Prenzler, 2000). In Jamaica, in direct response to the growing problem of widespread civilian fatalities resulting from police shootings, the Government, in 2010, set up the Independent Commission for Investigations (INDECOM) with powers to conduct independent investigations, through a cadre of nonpolice investigators, into the more serious allegations of police misconduct (and in this case also misconduct among military personnel). INDECOM doubly embodies the independence principle through the requirement in law that its most senior role holder, the Commissioner, must be qualified to be a judge.

In the United Kingdom, both the OPONI and the IPCC had their roots in attempts to employ the principle of independence as a solution to systemic policing problems. In the case of the OPONI, often referred to as the "gold standard" in the world of independent oversight of policing (Hopkins, 2009, p. 45; Seneviratne, 2004), much was owed to its potential role in assisting and supporting the peace process in Northern Ireland. The Hayes Report, published in 1997, a review of the controversies surrounding the role of the then Royal Ulster Constabulary in exacerbating community conflicts in Northern Ireland, recommended what was then the quite radical step of establishing a machinery for the fully independent investigation of *all* complaints against the police (Hayes, 1997). This model, to become the "Ombudsman" model, was subsequently endorsed by the hugely significant Patten Commission, charged with devising a blueprint for the future of Northern Ireland policing

(Patten, 1999; Savage, 2007, pp. 70–73); the OPONI went live in 2000. The IPCC, on the other hand, came into existence in part due to the fallout of the flawed police investigation into the murder of Black teenager Stephen Lawrence in 1993. The subsequent Stephen Lawrence Inquiry, under senior judge Lord Macpherson, among many other recommendations for policing and public sector reforms, proposed the establishment of a body providing for the fully independent investigation of complaints against the police (Macpherson, 1999, p. 333; Savage, 2007, pp. 38–40). The IPCC was duly launched in 2004 following the Police Reform Act 2002.

In these ways, the independence principle has been invoked as a (part at least) solution to identified systemic policing problems. In that sense, it carries with it enormous significance as a state response to system failures in policing. However, of course, that principle goes beyond the nation state. As Chapter 8 in this book testifies, independence lies at the core of internationally binding principles of human rights law. This has been particularly evident through the European Court of Human Rights in implementing the European Convention on Human Rights (Smith, 2010). After a series of cases involving police complaints and alleged human rights breaches had defined various aspects of the law relating to the "effective investigation" of police complaints, the European Commissioner for Human Rights brought the rulings together in a codified single "opinion" document and found there to be five principles of an effective investigation: independence, adequacy, promptness, public scrutiny, and victim involvement. Independence was defined in these terms: "there should not be institutional or hierarchical connections between the investigators and the officer complained against and there should be practical independence" (CHR, 2009, p. 8). In this sense, independence is written into international law as a fundamental principle protecting human rights.

If the independence principle and, in particular, the principle that police complaints should be investigated independently carry such weight, both as a national solution to a policing problem and as an internationally binding concept, this begs the question of how that principle translates into a *working philosophy*—how independence works in practice (what the European Commissioner referred to as "practical independence") and how independence translates into an operational tool. I have attempted to broach these questions and others related to them through empirical research on the three bodies in the British and Irish islands that have established machineries for the independent investigation of police complaints, albeit with differing degrees of "reach": the GSOC, the IPCC, and the OPONI. Police complaints arrangements in Scotland were not part of this research because at the time of the study, Scotland had not moved toward independent investigation; it now has done so in the form of the Police Investigations and Review Commissioner. Over a period of less than 10 years, first Northern Ireland, then England and

Wales, and subsequently the Republic of Ireland all moved to adopt machineries for the independent investigation of police complaints. Such developments were ripe for research; my research involved over 100 semi-structured interviews with representative samples from each of the three bodies. The sample included investigators and senior investigators (sampled in terms of prior background, role, and gender; $n = 83$), caseworkers/complaints officers (frontline "gatekeepers" of the complaints bodies, sampled on the basis of role and gender; $n = 20$), and senior role holders (sampled in terms of role; $n = 18$). The research also involved observations of training events, briefings, and a small number of consultations with complainants. Research questions sought to examine two related themes: on the one hand, what might be called the "social profile" of complaints investigation and, on the other hand, how independence operates as a working principle. Although the findings relate to three specific organizations, all in close proximity, I would argue that they might apply to independent oversight across the board internationally, although this would need to be subject to further exploration.

The Social Profile of Independent Oversight

Clearly, a central platform of the "civilian control" model of police oversight (Prenzler & Ronken, 2001) is that a body of people who are not "of" the police carry out functions independently of the police to service the needs and concerns of complainants, make the police accountable for their actions, and in the longer term, contribute to the improvement of policing itself. In the case of the three bodies in question, and it would seem in other jurisdictions as well, this involves three levels of actors. First are the frontline operatives—caseworkers or complaints officers in these cases—who receive the initial complaints from the public or via the police and who then determine next steps, such as whether the complaint comes within the "remit" of the organization, where it should be routed next if it is determined to be within remit, and so on. This is, in many ways, a "gatekeeping" role that can be very significant to the handling of a complaint and does involve a degree of investigation and judgment in its own right. Second are the investigators themselves—investigating officers, deputy, and senior investigators—who carry out the actual investigations or who oversee those who do. Complaints investigations involve pretty much the same activities as police investigations (and indeed they may run in "tandem" with a live police investigation, e.g., where police have discharged firearms at an armed robbery and where, therefore, both the police actions and those of the armed robbers are under investigation). Complaints investigations involve interviews (complainants, police officers, and witnesses), CCTV footage, document analysis, forensic evidence, and so on. Third are the senior role holders, who variously include directors of investigations, communications/press and media officers, legal officers, human resource managers, chief executives, and, centrally, as the guardians of independence itself, the "commissioners"—the Ombudsman in the OPONI, the Commissioners in the IPCC (now nine in total), and the GSOC (three in total). There are, as in the case of the IPCC and the GSOC (and as we have seen in a different way with INDECOM in Jamaica), sometimes stipulations in law that the commissioners must not have been former police officers. No such stipulations apply to the investigator element in these three bodies.

Given that a central focus of the research was with the nature of independence within an independent investigatory framework, a main concern from a social and cultural perspective was with the body of investigators themselves—their backgrounds, their motivations, and their perceptions of how the cadre of investigators worked together. The question of how investigators work together was driven not least by an issue that was difficult to avoid: that a feature of all three bodies, and clearly in some others internationally (Hopkins, 2009; Prenzler, 2000), is that a proportion of complaints investigators are former police officers; in these three bodies, between a quarter and a third of their investigators had previous backgrounds in policing. Of course, this need not necessarily be problematic or unexpected, but it does raise some interesting questions about the cultural dynamics within such agencies, given that they were each created under an independence banner defined by its very *nonpolice* (independent, civilian) status. In that regard, I found that it was useful and informative to (cautiously) socially classify complaints investigators according to their backgrounds prior to joining their organizations and in terms of the "distance" between those backgrounds and the world of policing. In doing this, I reworked a classificatory framework used by Brown (1996) to reflect upon police research along a continuum between "insider" and "outsider" researchers.

Insider investigators were those who had a police background and had worked in the same force as that being overseen by the agency in question. They were relatively few in number and seemingly were becoming rarer over time, but they had been appointed in most cases directly on retirement from the force whose complaints they then went on to investigate; in other words, they could end up investigating former police colleagues. Their appointment could be justified on the grounds that not only did they have the requisite investigative skills but they also knew from personal experience all about the internal procedures, both formal and informal, of the force under investigation. They were, truly in that sense, insiders.

Insider outsiders are far greater in number (just under a third of all investigators interviewed as part of the research) and are investigators who were former police officers—or, as in the case with some staff in the OPONI, serving officers on secondment—but from police forces other than the force being investigated. Such investigators might have worked elsewhere in the United Kingdom or be former officers from countries further afield (Australasia featured on a number of occasions). What they can potentially bring to their role is awareness of the "realities" of policing—of the challenges the police face but also how they can cover their tracks when they have broken or bent rules—yet coupled with an awareness that there are other ways to police than those of the force under investigation. Arguably, they are less likely to accept police narratives in question in terms of "this is the way things are done around here" and be more challenging as a result. Furthermore, they are not as tainted by the charge of being "one of them" as are insiders.

Outsider insiders are investigators who have never been part of the police but who have previously experienced forms of law enforcement and investigative processes. They include former welfare benefits investigators, health and safety investigators, inland revenue investigators, and so on. They may also have worked under similar legislation, such as the Police and Criminal Evidence Act, as police officers themselves. They may, in their line of work, have also come into close contact with the police. They have practical previous experience of investigations and, indirectly at least, the way policing works, which gives them a degree of insider knowledge, but they do not (it could be claimed) have the "police mindset" and so may be less susceptible to being seduced into acceptance of police narratives. Around a quarter of those interviewed (representing broadly their numbers across the three agencies) came under this category, the most common background being welfare benefits investigators.

Outsiders, constituting just over a third of investigators interviewed, have a profile probably closest to the image of the "independent investigator" that most advocates have in mind when they state the case for the independent investigation of police complaints. They come to their role with neither policing nor previous investigative experience and, as such, are what some senior role holders interviewed referred to as "homegrown" investigators, in the sense that they acquire their investigative skills "in the job" through in-service training and mentoring, rather than bring those skills with them on entry to the complaints organization. In many cases, they have joined the organization soon after completing study at university or as a career change, and they tend to be, on average, younger than colleagues in the other categories. Female investigators are also more likely to be found in this grouping than in the others. The major benefit that outsiders are seen to bring to the organization, and this was a view taken by many former police officers themselves, is what was frequently referred to as a "fresh pair of eyes": They can bring an "untainted" perspective to the investigative process, which can be more challenging and less accepting of police narratives than perhaps at least some of their colleagues. Their worldview is typically one some distance from the police mindset, and as such, they may be closest to a model of independence as being not "of" the police.

The proportions of investigators in each grouping have changed over time in the three organizations in question in this research and will continue to do so, in some cases as a deliberate strategy to shift the balance of the profile of investigators to one more in favor of those without police backgrounds. For example, the incoming new chair of the IPCC, Dame Ann Owers, announced on taking office in 2012 that there would be an explicit policy of targeting future investigator recruitment at nonpolice investigators (Owers, 2012); this was a timely move given that shortly after, the IPCC was criticized in the British Parliament by the Home Affairs Select Committee as a "second home for police officers" (HAC, 2013; see also Smith, 2013). However, and this may be of relevance to all attempts internationally to establish machineries for the independent investigation of police complaints, the on-entry profile of the investigator cadre of such organizations may be affected by less strategic concerns. Particularly in early stages of development of oversight bodies, senior staff may take the view that they have little alternative but to recruit experienced former police investigators because they can bring with them an immediate capacity to launch investigations, whereas homegrown investigators will need time to acquire the necessary skills to conduct an investigation and will need to be mentored by those with more extensive experience. Furthermore, public sector financial pressures may mean that the recruitment of inexperienced investigators, who would then need training funded out of the oversight body's budget, cannot be easily afforded and that the recruitment of experienced police investigators is then seen as the sensible alternative. For these reasons, oversight bodies may have to live with this sort of mix of investigator backgrounds for some considerable time; indeed, they may even take the view that such a "hybrid" model for the investigator cadre, with a combination of insider and outsider backgrounds, is a desirable balance to strike in any case.

There is no doubt that the recruitment of former police officers into the ranks of oversight investigators is a source of controversy for the three bodies that were the subject of this research and, it could be argued, will be for all such bodies as they emerge internationally with the expansion of independent investigatory bodies worldwide. In this regard, the question is whether the presence of former police officers as investigators within oversight bodies is primarily a matter of the *appearance* of independence rather than independence per se. In other words, is it a question of the *legitimacy* of such oversight bodies, of the perception rather than the reality of independence, which is most at issue in this respect? Most certainly, oversight bodies face a challenge to their legitimacy in the eyes of many, including complainants, when it is revealed that some of those conducting independent investigations, at times leading those investigations, are themselves former police officers. The British Home Affairs Select Committee referred to this as one "basis of mistrust" in the IPCC (HAC, 2013, paragraph 13). Of course, legitimacy is central to the whole edifice of independent oversight of policing; if the body in question is not seen as independent, then independence is severely compromised, to say the least. However, could it be that the presence of former police officers in the investigative resource of police oversight bodies has substantive and not just presentational consequences for the delivery of independent oversight?

For a number of reasons, the research underpinning this chapter indicates that the issue of former police officers operating within police oversight bodies goes further than the presentational dimensions of independent oversight and penetrates deeper into the culture of independent oversight itself. There is evidence that the on-entry profile of oversight investigators plays some role in shaping the attitudinal profile of those investigators and, more significantly, may in part shape their practices and occupational philosophies.

One indicator of the significance of on-entry profile in shaping the attitudinal profile of oversight investigators was revealed in responses to one line of questions posed by the research: What attracted oversight investigators to that line of work? The creation of new, independent police oversight bodies is typically associated with intensive levels of publicity and expansive expectations. Their work is high profile, imbued with explicitly value-based ambitions and often, in their decisions and outcomes, deeply contentious. In that context, the motivational drivers behind the decision to seek that line of work are of interest: What was the appeal of working in the police oversight world? Three types of "job appeal" emerged, some aspects of which seemed to fall along the fault lines of previous experience.

First, around a quarter of those interviewed expressed the attraction of oversight in terms of what might be termed *value-based* motivations: the appeal of oversight work lay in its association with values and principles which those concerned could identify with. These included such principles as the pursuit of justice, enhancing the accountability of the police, protecting human rights, representing the "public" in the complaints process, and more simply, improving policing itself. This sentiment was nicely captured by one investigator as "getting involved with something that would make a difference" (cited in Savage, 2013b, p. 891).

Second, and overlapping to some extent with value-based motivations, around one third of interviewees expressed the appeal of oversight work in terms of it looking like "challenging" or highly "interesting" work. This was related variously to oversight being seen as a "novel" line of work (reflecting the newness of oversight agencies themselves), as involving potentially exciting work, dealing with such matters as miscarriages of justice, and as "affecting people's lives" and therefore "tangible" as a line of work (Savage, 2013b, p. 893).

The third type of job appeal was very different from the other two. Rather than focus on values, principles, or what is novel about oversight work, this motivation was concerned with the similarity between such work and the work that respondents had experienced in their previous careers. Some 40% of interviewees expressed the appeal of oversight work in terms of its continuity with work they had done in the past: police oversight working appealed in short because it was seen as a similar line of work. As one investigator put it: "I saw it as something that was…very similar to work I had done before as a Sergeant" (cited in Savage, 2013b, p. 893). This latter statement also identifies what type of work police oversight work is typically seen as "similar" to: police work. Although investigators who were formerly police officers were among those who saw the appeal of police oversight work in terms of values, principles, and new challenges, and some spoke with passion about that motivation, over two thirds of investigators with police backgrounds took the view that police oversight work was "similar type of work" to their previous career in the police.

One must expect that a variety of motivations will be at play in any organization when it comes to what it was that attracted personnel to that line of work, and so in that sense, there is little at issue here. However, two considerations present themselves with the scenario just painted. On the one hand, it can and has been argued that it is essential that police oversight bodies, to do their job effectively, need to develop a distinctive organizational or occupational culture of their own (KPMG, 2000). One facet of the independence of police oversight could, even should, be their distinctive organizational ethos and mission, one clearly separate and different from the bodies they have oversight of. However, this is challenged to an extent by what seems to be a perception for many investigators that oversight work is not that different from, or is even similar to, work within the police organization. On the other hand, it does seem that the motivational drivers underpinning working within police oversight varies by on-entry profile; in other words, that to an extent, those with no police backgrounds are, in general, attracted to police oversight work for reasons different from those with police backgrounds. This points to possible attitudinal variations over what it means to work within police oversight, which may be of cultural significance to the police oversight body in question and, if present as my research implies, may be something that police oversight bodies should seek to address, if not challenge. To use the rather crude terms referred to earlier by the British Home Affairs Select Committee (HAC, 2013), this would be one dimension of avoiding police oversight bodies becoming a "second home for police officers."

However, motivations for joining an organization are less important than the attitudes and behaviors which are evident once those recruited are actually fulfilling their roles. Is the on-entry profile of oversight staff, and particularly the investigator cadre, relevant to the way oversight is carried out? Another central research question was how oversight personnel read the way in which the mix of oversight investigators, and in particular the mix of insiders and outsiders as referred to earlier, plays out in practice. This embraces both attitudinal and behavioral dimensions of oversight work. There seemed clear evidence that the social profile of oversight investigators—with a mix of those with and those without police backgrounds— is significant to the way investigators approach their work and operate in practice; what is less clear is whether this works in a positive or less positive way.

To begin with, there was almost unanimous agreement among all of those interviewed that former police officers play a significant, if not crucial, role in contributing to providing for the investigative capacity of independent police oversight. They can bring to the table a range of skills, both formal and informal, which are valued by senior staff and fellow investigators alike. First, they can bring in specialist technical skills, which can give critical support to a complaints investigation: specialist interviewing skills, skills in managing complex investigations, scene management, and so on. Although these skills can of course be acquired in time by all investigators, oversight bodies can "buy in" those skills through the recruitment of certain types of former police officers and run investigations from the outset on that basis. Second, they bring with them a practically based awareness of police laws and procedures, the alleged breach of which is often the basis of a complaints investigation. This can assist in the investigative process, which often involves determining the levels of compliance of officers with established rules, and in assessing whether officers had behaved in a "proportionate" manner in particular cases. Third, they can bring with them an awareness of police culture and the informal practices employed in police work, their knowledge of which can assist in reading "behind" police narratives or, putting it more crudely, they know where the bodies are buried!

Interestingly, there was almost total agreement that those without police experience also bring critical characteristics to the table of complaints investigation. Both those with and those without previous police experience were generally of the view that not having a police background adds a number of important dimensions to the investigative process. First, such outsiders can bring an "open-mindedness" to complaints investigation, being less weighed down by preconceptions about "acceptable" ways of doing policing— expressed earlier as bringing a "fresh pair of eyes" to investigations—and can be more critical and less accepting of police traditions as a result. Second, outsiders can bring a "public perspective" into the investigative process, perhaps with a more empathetic understanding of complainants' motives and reasoning than one with a police background may provide. Third, again as indicated earlier with reference to the question of legitimacy, those without police backgrounds can be more accepted by complainants and victims precisely because they cannot be accused of being "one of them" in an investigation of alleged police misconduct. They, more than any other group, can directly support the narrative of the oversight body as being an independent agency with no connection to the police.

In these senses the mix of on-entry profiles of oversight investigators may be seen to work effectively and positively; indeed, this is how many senior role-holders interviewed held the mixed social profile of investigators to operate in practice. However, there were less positive views in some quarters about either how some of those with police backgrounds functioned or, more extensively, whether the balance between the on-entry backgrounds of investigators was all it could be. In terms of the less positive views on the behavioral concerns about former police officers, claims were made by a number of respondents (almost exclusively outsiders) that former police officers, in some cases, tend to "box off" investigations prematurely—in other words make early decisions on investigatory outcomes and not shift that position in due course—and not pursue alternative lines of inquiry sufficiently. The issue of "premature closure" has been identified as a central problem with police investigative culture in the past (McConville, Sanders, & Leng, 1993; Savage & Milne, 2007; Shepherd & Milne, 1999); may that tendency be reemerging within the police oversight context? The flipside of bringing in valuable police experience to oversight investigations is that former police investigators may also be inhibiting the investigative process to an extent because they are operating within a police investigative mindset not necessarily conducive to complaints investigations. As one senior role holder expressed it, "when we have produced very weak investigations…it has nearly always come from ex-police officers who were unable to detach themselves from being police detectives" (cited in Savage, 2013b, p. 899).

It should be made clear that such sentiments are expressed in relation to some, but certainly not all, former police officers and that, to reiterate, the general consensus is that former officers do bring with them valuable skills and experiences. Nevertheless, there is evidence of concern that some former officers cannot break from the very police culture oversight agencies are seeking to penetrate—in the words of one interviewee, some former officers cannot "de-policify." This must present a challenge at least for police oversight agencies wedded to the notion of the independent investigation of police misconduct. At this point, we can move to examine the notion of independence itself as an organizing principle of the civilian control model of police oversight.

Independence at Work

Reference was made earlier to the European Commissioner's conception of independence as involving a twofold requirement, that on the one hand there should not be an institutional or hierarchical connection between the police under investigation and the investigatory body, and on the other hand, that there shall be practical independence (European Commissioner for Human Rights, 2009, p. 8). This begs the question of what *practical independence* means. In my research, the central line of questioning was precisely what independence in investigating police misconduct means in practice to those who operate under its banner and, linked to that, what obstacles and limitations exist in the eyes of those who practice it to inhibit the realization of independence in practice.

There is a sense in which the attempts by nation states to establish an independent machinery for the investigation of police complaints and misconduct focus almost exclusively on institutional and constitutional forms; independence is to be delivered by institutional and functional separation between the police organization and the police oversight body. However, it could be argued that institutional formation is only the beginning, not the end, of the process of securing independence in police oversight. The baton is then passed to practitioners—commissioners, senior staff, investigators, and front-end staff—to deliver independence in practice. In this respect, two questions may be posed: first, how do practitioners articulate independence as a "working philosophy?" Second, how do practitioners assess the level of realization of independence in the practical context?

Interpreting Independence

Independence is written into the constitution of many police oversight bodies and may even be written into the title of those organizations—such as the IPCC (England and Wales) or the INDECOM (Jamaica). In which case it was interesting to pursue in the research the question of how practitioners charged with delivering independence translate the principle into a "working philosophy," what it means to them, and how they see that as a guiding principle of their activities, particularly those involved in oversight investigations. In these respects, three primary interpretations of independence emerged, which, although overlapping, are actually quite different.

The most prominent conception of independence, cited by nearly half of all interviewees, was of it being essentially concerned with *impartiality* or *neutrality*. That is, independence is defined as being impartial or neutral in relation to the two typical parties of a complaint—the complainant and the police. Police complaints investigations normally involve "contested narratives": on the one hand, the allegations made by the complainant or victim, and on the other hand, the police case as to what happened. From this perspective, an independent investigation is one that steers a path between the two narratives favoring neither one nor the other until the investigation is complete—expressed by one investigator as not "taking sides" and by being "in the middle" (cited in Savage, 2013a, p. 101). Impartiality is a powerful message to portray to the parties to the complaint and to stakeholders more generally: it can be used to reassure the police that the complaints body is not acting on behalf of the complainant (which is how police oversight might be perceived by the police); conversely, it can be used to reassure the complainant or victim that the complaints body is not part of the police—and the research did reveal that many complainants found it difficult to grasp that the complaints body was not itself part of the police.

The second most cited conception of independence, expressed by just under a quarter of all interviewees, was that of *distance*. More specifically, independence was defined primarily in this case as being about distance from the police. So rather than independence being about neutrality between two parties, this interpretation focuses on the "nonrelationship" with one of them: the police. This was expressed variously in terms of "separateness" from the police, not being "answerable to" the police and "not feeling any sort of attachment to the police" (cited in Savage, 2013b, p. 102). Not only was this seen as a working philosophy of independent oversight, it was also used as a presentational tool when dealing with complainants and victims. It was evident that to reassure complainants where it was felt necessary, some investigators made statements along the lines "we've nothing to do with the police"; in this sense, the distance and separateness of oversight investigators were notions employed tactically to facilitate the investigation.

The third most cited interpretation of independence, involving just under one-fifth of those interviewed, was that independence was fundamentally about *objectivity*, being "evidence based" or being, more dramatically, a matter of the "search for the truth." In this case, independence is defined not by a relationship between the parties involved in the complaints process (neutral between, separate from) but by a relationship with "facts." The rooting of independent investigation in the facts and in evidence, so the argument runs, ensures objectivity and militates against any sort of prioritization of one party over the other. Again, this working philosophy can also be used tactically and presentationally in an attempt to reassure the parties to the complaint along the lines of, as one investigator expressed it: "we are solely and strictly driven by the evidence" (cited in Savage, 2013a, p. 103).

These various interpretations of independence are unlikely to be unique to the three oversight bodies that were the subject of my research. There is every reason to assume, but it remains to be examined, that they would be part of the working philosophies and underlying principles of police oversight work in other contexts internationally, although not necessarily with this pattern of distribution. In that respect, there are at least two sorts of considerations regarding the practice of independence in terms of interpretations of the very meaning of independence itself. First, that the apparent lack of consensus within oversight agencies as to what independence means in practice, as evidenced by the variations in responses by practitioners outlined in this section, presents challenges for consistency of practice and the coherence of organizational ethos and mission. In other words, oversight bodies might need to have a more definitive conception of what they are about in terms of independence and take more steps to ensure that this is embedded across their own internal organizational culture. Second, there is then the question of which interpretation of independence is most appropriate. This is more contentious: it could be argued that it is for each oversight agency, or its government, to form judgment as to how that organization will interpret and operationalize the principle of independence—whether that be as impartiality, as separateness, or as evidence based or indeed other conceptions of what independence means.

However, there is a case for saying that in reaching such a judgment, some notice or guidance might be taken of two "steers" in this direction, which have emerged in the European context, largely under case law, and which could be of global significance. On the one hand, the European framework for independent oversight as spelled out by the European Partners Against Corruption (EPAC), a body representing oversight bodies across Europe, includes a number of key principles, one of which is that "The police oversight body shall be sufficiently *separated* from the hierarchy of the police or other law enforcement agencies that are the subject of its remit" (EPAC, 2011, p. 7, emphasis added). Does this mean that separateness from the police should be prioritized over impartiality or neutrality as a core principle of independent police oversight practice? On the other hand, as already noted earlier, the European Commissioner for Human Rights (2009) has, as part of the five stated principles of an effective investigation of police complaints, included both independence and victim involvement (p. 8) as two of those five principles.

One might argue on that basis that impartiality or neutrality as interpretations of independence pays insufficient homage to the case for mainstreaming complainant and victim concerns; rather than steering a path between those concerns and those of the police, there is a case for anchoring the ethos of police oversight bodies very firmly with complainants and victims. At the very least, questions of this kind need to inform the debate about the organizational ethos and practices of independent police oversight bodies as they expand internationally and come to terms with the realities and practicalities of independent or civilian oversight.

These issues come into sharper light when the second set of questions regarding the practice of independent oversight is pursued: what do independence workers perceive to be the inhibitors or constraints on delivering independence, if they are present at all?

Delivering Independence—Constraints and Limitations

The question of what, if any, are the inhibitors in delivering independence addresses issues that the international debate over appropriate machineries for police oversight can at times overlook: that although institutional forms may create a formal framework for independence, substantive independence may be shaped by many of the factors that constitute the lived realities of police oversight. My research sought to address these issues by examining the extent to which independence workers saw obstacles in the way of delivering the independent oversight they aspired to.

To begin with, nearly one-fifth of those interviewed were of the view that there were no real constraints on independence within their own organization, and this rose to over one-third of interviewees from the Police Ombudsman for Northern Ireland (PONI); this latter point may reflect the proportionately higher level of resources directed at the OPONI in comparison with the IPCC and the GSOC and also perhaps the wider remit of the OPONI in terms of its being charged with investigating all complaints against the police (Prenzler, 2011, p. 285; Savage, 2013a, p. 98; Seneviratne, 2004, p. 340). Nevertheless, a large majority of interviewees were of the view that factors did inhibit or constrain the delivery of independence in their own organization. Three main factors were cited.

First—and interesting given that one of the main interpretations of independence is, as has been seen, distance from the police—over one-third of independence workers cited forms of what may be termed *proximity* to the police as a major source of constraint on their independence. Put crudely, being "too close to the police" was seen as a root cause of inhibiting the realization of independence in practice. This was explained in a number of ways, but two stood out. On the one hand, proximity to the police was identified with a tendency to be "overcautious" in dealings with the police—one investigator expressed it as "pulling punches" (Savage, 2013a, p. 104)—largely because it seems efforts are made to maintain good working relations with the police. This may be reflected in allowing the police to determine the pace and even the form of a complaints investigation, in terms of making officers available or making evidence, such as officers' notebooks, available. On the other hand, proximity is identified with a cultural tendency of some investigators, including those without previous police experience, to have an overly empathetic attitude to the police and even to adopt elements of the police mindset in the way they operate; one senior investigator, himself a former police officer, expressed it as "going native" (cited in Savage, 2013a, p. 104).

Second, just over one-fifth of those interviewed cited *resources* as a major source of constraint on delivering independence (although this was less evident among the OPONI interviewees for reasons stated previously). It is of course a common refrain to cite lack of resources as a factor inhibiting organizational performance; however, in this context, it is primarily a question of the comparative lack of resources available to oversight bodies as compared with those available to the police body under investigation. This is most evident in what are termed *tandem investigations*, where the police are investigating a crime at the same scene or in similar circumstances to an oversight investigation. The prime example of this was a set of incidents surrounding an armed robbery in one of the jurisdictions included in the research, which involved both the use of arms by an armed gang and the fatal use of arms by police officers at the scene of the robbery. It was made clear that in such circumstances, the police had five or six times the number of investigators at the scene (and who were at the scene somewhat earlier) than oversight investigators. Such an inequality of available resources places the oversight investigation in challenging circumstances relative to the police organization under investigation. This includes, as has been indicated, difficulties in maintaining "scene preservation": oversight bodies typically have very wide geographic areas to cover with small numbers of investigators, so that maintaining the forensic integrity of a possible crime scene, for example, a police cell after a death in custody, is often very difficult to achieve.

This relates to the third cited source of constraints on delivering independence, cited by around one-fifth of interviewees: *reliance on police support*. Police oversight bodies have to have forms of engagement and cooperation with the police organization to undertake their role effectively; however, many independence workers were of the view that oversight investigations are often overreliant on that "cooperation." Again, this took two primary forms. On the one hand, linked to a point made in the previous paragraph, most complaints investigations are routed through an identified single point of contact (e.g., an officer working in Professional Standards) and work within agreed sets of protocols—such as all requests for documentation such as officers' notebooks should go to that single point of contact. These arrangements clearly cause some frustration among oversight investigators, as they may be the cause of delay, lack of appropriate access (for example to interview officers), and other factors inhibiting the realization of prompt investigations, as required by European guidelines (EPAC, 2011, p. 13) and, as noted previously, mean that the police can exert control over the pace of the oversight investigation. On the other hand, reliance on police support included the need to use police-based technical and forensic support services or to share with the police specialists such as forensic pathologists, in the absence of such services within the oversight agency itself. This reliance is seen by many to compromise the independence of oversight investigations, not least because it limits the degree of separation between the oversight body and the police organization under investigation.

Taken together, these identified constraints on independence in police oversight give us some possible insight into the classic problem of regulatory capture in police complaints (Prenzler, 2000) and expose the mechanisms by which capture actually works. Furthermore, there is every reason to assume that these identified constraints on the delivery of independence in oversight investigations would apply equally, if not more than equally, to other oversight agencies in the international context. In which case it is evident that, whatever the institutional and constitutional forms independent police oversight might take, what has been termed *practical independence* might look very different and, on that basis, we can draw an overall conclusion.

Conclusion

As has been made clear, much of the debate around the civilian control model of police oversight and the independent oversight of police complaints and misconduct has focused on institutional forms, constitutional frameworks and legal frameworks. For example, there has been much discussion of the "reach" of police oversight agencies in terms of their remit for independent investigations (Filstad & Gottschalk, 2011; Porter & Prenzler, 2012; Seneviratne, 2004). Critical though these debates are to the future of police oversight, this chapter and my research have sought to cast light on what might be termed the *lived realities* of independent oversight and in particular focus on the social, cultural, and practical dimensions to the pursuit of independence in investigating police misconduct.

In this regard, an overall conclusion is that independence in police oversight—and perhaps in other contexts in which the principle of "independence" is invoked—is in a process of constant interaction. Rather than viewing independence as a "thing" or a "status" attached to particular institutional forms, independence operates within a constant interaction between the aspirations and goals of those who seek independence and civilian oversight and the social, cultural, political, and financial environments within which it is forced to operate, including the internal environments and cultural dynamics of oversight agencies themselves. I have termed this a *relational* conception of independence: independence, rather than something you are or are not, you have or do not have, exists within sets of relationships, internal and external, which make independence conditional, negotiable, and contingent. In that sense, the critical creation of appropriate institutional and constitutional forms to enable the independent, civilian, or citizen oversight of police misconduct is only the beginning, not the end, of the road to independence.

References

Brown, J. (1996). Police research: Some critical issues. In F. Leishman, B. Loveday & S. Savage (Eds.). *Core issues in policing*. Harlow: Longman.

CHR. (2009). *Opinion Concerning Independent and Effective Determination of Complaints Against the Police*. Council of Europe, CommDH.

Conway, V., & Walsh, D. (2011). Current developments in police governance and accountability in Ireland. *Crime, Law and Social Change, 55*, 241–257.

Dunleavy, P. (1995). Policy disasters: Explaining the UK's record. *Public Policy and Administration, 10*(2), 52–70.

EPAC. (2011). *European police oversight principles*. Laxenburg: Author.

Filstad, C., & Gottschalk, P. (2011). Performance evaluation of police oversight agencies. *Policing and Society, 21*(1), 96–109.

HAC. (2013). *Home Affairs Committee Eleventh Report: The Independent Police Complaints Commission*. London: House of Commons.

Hayes, M. (1997). *A police ombudsman for Northern Ireland?* Belfast: HMSO.

Hopkins, A. (2009). *An effective system for investigating complaints against the police*. Melbourne: Victoria Law Foundation.

KPMG. (2000). *Feasibility of an independent system for investigating complaints against the police*. London: Home Office.

Macpherson, W. (1999). *The Stephen Lawrence inquiry*. London: Home Office.

McConville, M., Sanders, A., & Leng, R. (1993). *The case for the prosecution: Police suspects and the construction of criminality*. London: Routledge.

Owers, A. (2012). *Independent oversight of police complaints: The IPCC eight years on*. John Harris Memorial Lecture. London: The Police Foundation.

Patten, C. (1999). *A new beginning: Policing in Northern Ireland, report of the Independent Commission on Policing for Northern Ireland*. London: HMSO.

Porter, L., & Prenzler, T. (2012). Police oversight in the United Kingdom: The balance of independence and collaboration. *International Journal of Law, Crime and Justice, 40*(3), 152–171.

Prenzler, T. (2000). Civilian oversight of police: A test of capture theory. *British Journal of Criminology, 40*, 659–674.

Prenzler, T. (2004). Stakeholder perspectives on police complaints and discipline: Towards a civilian control model. *Australian and New Zealand Journal of Criminology, 37*(1), 85–113.

Prenzler, T. (2011). The evolution of police oversight in Australia. *Policing and Society, 21*(3), 284–303.

Prenzler, T., & Ronken, C. (2001). Models of police oversight: A critique. *Policing and Society, 11*(3), 155–180.

Punch, M. (2009). *Police corruption*. Cullompton: Willan.

Savage, S. (2007). *Police reform: Forces for change*. Oxford: Oxford University Press.

Savage, S. (2013a). Thinking independence: Calling the police to account through the independent investigation of police complaints. *British Journal of Criminology, 53*(1), 94–112.

Savage, S. (2013b). Seeking "civilianness": Police complaints and the civilian control model of oversight. *British Journal of Criminology, 53*(4), 886–904.

Savage, S., & Milne, B. (2007). Miscarriages of justice. In T. Newburn, T. Williamson & A. Wright (Eds.), *The handbook of criminal investigation*. Cullompton: Willan.

Scarman, Lord. (1981). *The Scarman report: The Brixton disorders*. London: HMSO.

Seneviratne, M. (2004). Policing the police in the United Kingdom. *Policing and Society, 14*(4), 329–347.

Shepherd, E., & Milne, B. (1999). Full and faithful: Ensuring quality practice and integrity of outcome in witness interviews. In A. Heaton-Strong, E. Shepherd & D. Wolchover (Eds.), *Analysing witness statements: A guide for legal practitioners and other professionals*. London: Blackstone Press.

Sherman, L. (1978). *Scandal and reform: Controlling police corruption*. Berkeley: University of California Press.

Smith, G. (2010). Every complaint matters: Human Rights Commissioner's opinion concerning independent and effective determination of complaints against the police. *International Journal of Law, Crime and Justice, 38*, 59–74.

Smith, G. (2013). Oversight of the police and residual dilemmas: Independence, effectiveness and accountability deficits in the United Kingdom. *Police Practice & Research: An International Journal, 14*(2), 92–103.

Stakeholder Perspectives on Complaints against Police

II

Democratic Policing, Public Opinion, and External Oversight

3

TIM PRENZLER

Contents

This chapter reviews surveys of a major stakeholder group in the police complaints and discipline process: the public. Twenty-eight surveys and two focus group studies from three countries are discussed. This includes two sets of repeated surveys. In general, public opinion is strongly supportive of independent processing of complaints, and some surveys show extremely high levels of support—over 90%. Several surveys have included a set of breakdown questions about different types of complaints. In these cases, responses show that support for independent investigations is focused more on serious matters, with some allowance for police retention of lower-level matters. As far as can be ascertained, while distrust of police has some bearing on opinions, the main reason relates to the principle of institutional independence to ensure impartiality in investigations. What these surveys also highlight is the enormous gap between public standards and current practice in most locations. Public opinion surveys also show high levels of support for existing oversight agencies, although it appears that respondents often assume these agencies are much more engaged in investigations than they are. The chapter concludes by emphasizing the need for external investigations of serious and intermediate matters. In addition, the data show that there is value to be obtained from consulting with complainants about how their allegations should be addressed, even for "minor" matters, as well as focusing on restorative justice options, especially in the areas of apology and mediation.

Background

The introduction of police oversight agencies has been driven largely by major scandals and associated judicial inquiries and government reviews, which have highlighted poor internal investigation and disciplinary processes (Chapter 1). Findings show that weak internal mechanisms protect officers engaged in misconduct and foster an environment where corrupt police feel safe (Goldsmith, 1991; Hopkins, 2009). Complainant dissatisfaction has fed into inquiries and reviews at times, and police views have also been taken into account on occasions. Another key factor influencing inquiry and review recommendations favoring external oversight has been the fact that testimony from police whistleblowers has frequently been buried by internal processes, and police whistleblowers have been harassed and threatened (e.g., Fitzgerald, 1989; Knapp, 1972). Inquiries and reviews have also considered general arguments in relation to due process principles, natural justice, and fairness. However, the process of scandal, inquiry, and reform has generally ignored public opinion on the issue.

This neglect of public views is perhaps surprising given that "democratic policing" is considered the most legitimate form of policing, and major policing improvement methods, including community policing and problem-oriented policing, have emphasized the essential requirement of public consultation and input for success (Stone & Ward, 2000). Public satisfaction with police, measured through surveys, is also an essential element of modern accountability processes, including survey questions about police integrity.

The issue of who should investigate complaints against police has, however, been of sufficient salience to find a place at times in some public opinion surveys. One of the earliest involved canvassing responses to a simple statement—"Serious complaints against police should be investigated by an independent body, not by the police themselves"—included in the 1990 British Social Attitudes Survey (Tarling & Dowds, 1997, p. 206). In a journal article, "Reconciling Stakeholder Interests in Police Complaints and Discipline Systems," Prenzler, Mihinjac, and Porter (2013) briefly summarized a limited set of public opinion surveys up to 2011. The present chapter updates and enlarges on this study, and the following two chapters in this book update and enlarge findings from the other two stakeholder groups covered in the paper: complainants and police. The present chapter also provides more background information on the surveys where available.

The Prenzler et al. (2013) paper expressed the following view in relation to the rationale for canvassing stakeholder opinions and experiences (p. 156):

> Improved public confidence is a major goal of complaints handling bodies. Therefore, the general public, together with complainants and police, are viewed as key stakeholders in these systems. While agencies are not expected to serve a particular client base, participant satisfaction—particularly in relation to perceived impartiality and fairness—is one indicator of the effectiveness and legitimacy of a system... While individual views may be biased by personal perspectives or agendas, triangulation between sources minimises these effects. Thus, if stakeholders with potentially different agendas can be satisfied by the same system, this goes some way to validating its effectiveness.

The inclusion of public attitude surveys in this mix has the advantage of assessing opinion across a wide range of persons, including many of those who do not have a direct and personal stake in the complaints process—as is the case with complainants and police officers. At the same time, respondents to these surveys will also most likely include people with a range of direct experiences with police, some positive and some adverse. All in all, there is a strong case for considering public views of police complaints systems as a means of enlarging democratic accountability.

Method

A systematic review was undertaken to identify published reports of public opinion surveys about the issue of who should process complaints against police. Databases searched up to August 2014 included Criminal Justice Abstracts, CINCH, Google Scholar, and Google Search. A diverse range of keyword combinations were employed, including *complaints against police*, *complaint investigation*, *public opinion*, and *police oversight*. The reference lists of publications identified by this means were also searched, as were the websites of police oversight agencies.

A short list was developed of public surveys that included questions about complaints against police. These surveys often involve outsourcing to private survey firms, and most are careful to engage in proper sampling and report on the demographics of respondents. Surveys were included in the final list if they had a question that essentially asked, "who should investigate complaints against police?" Surveys were also included if they asked questions about the disposition of complaints. For the main part of this report, surveys were excluded that asked questions about respondents' views of the agency in their jurisdiction because the questions were not sufficiently generic. However, some findings on agencies are reported as they relate to the primary question.

A number of limitations apply to these surveys. Responses are likely to be affected by contextual factors, which may be hard to identify, such as the nature of police–community relations or particular policing scandals. The wording of questions can also restrict the range of views. For example, questionnaires tend to polarize responses between external and internal investigations, excluding the option of mixed formats, and they usually do not ask for views about how different types of complaints should be handled. However, a few surveys were found that included these dimensions. Generic questions about preferred agencies for responding to complaints also are not usually followed by questions about reasons for different views. An attempt was made to probe this topic by examining demographic variation in responses and answers to associated questions.

Public Opinion: General Principles

After the search process, a final list of 11 public opinion surveys was established, which addressed the central generic question. Table 3.1 summarizes the main findings from two single surveys about the best agency to investigate complaints. Tables 3.2 and 3.3 show findings from repeated surveys. The first survey in Table 3.1 was sponsored by the Police Federation of England

Table 3.1 Summary Findings of Single Public Opinion Surveys on Who Should Investigate Complaints against Police

Location	Percentage Support				Source
	Independent	Both	Police	No View	
England and Wales	59.4	19.6	16.4	4.6	Electoral Reform Ballot Services, 1997, p. 7
New York City	75.8	N/A	18.9	5.3	McGuire Research Services, 2000, p. 11

Table 3.2 British Social Attitudes Survey: Percentage Response to "Serious Complaints against Police Should Be Investigated by an Independent Body, Not by the Police Themselves"

Year	Agree Strongly	Agree	(Total Agree Strongly/Agree)	Neither Agree nor Disagree	Disagree/ Disagree Strongly
1990	38.0	55.6	(93.6)	4.0	2.5
1994	40.0	52.6	(92.6)	3.6	3.8
1996	44.9	46.3	(91.2)	5.4	3.4

Source: www.britsocat.com.

Table 3.3   Queensland Surveys: "Complaints against the Police Should Be Investigated by an Oversight Body, Not the Police Themselves"

Survey Year	% Agree/Strongly Agree	% Neither Agree nor Disagree	% Disagree/Strongly Disagree
1995	89	2	9
1999	90	4	6
2002	84	6	10
2005	86	7	7
2008	92	3	5
2010	91	3	6

Source: CJC (1995, p. 10; 2000, p. 6), CMC (2003, p. 21; 2006, p. 27; 2009, p. 54; 2011c, p. 34). Used with permission.

and Wales, which has been unusually active on the topic of the investigation of complaints against police and unusually positive in supporting the principle of independence (see Chapter 5). In 1997, it commissioned the Market Research Department of the Electoral Reform Ballot Services (1997) to "conduct face-to-face interviews with members of the public across the two countries on their attitudes to the best means of handling complaints against police officers" (p. 3). Police officers were also surveyed (Chapter 5). In the *Police Review* magazine, the Federation vice chair stated that "having both its members" and the public's views on the issue would give it a rounder picture and clearer evidence to take to the Home Affairs Select Committee (Review of Police Disciplinary and Complaints Procedure) (Jenkins, 1997, p. 4). In relation to the public survey, the vice chair noted it was "important to test public opinion on the issue. 'The issue is one of perception. What we were trying to establish was whether our feelings about public perceptions were actually reflected in public opinion'" (in Jenkins, 1997, p. 4).

The questionnaire was developed through consultation between the Federation and the research agency. A total of 500 interviews were carried out, with a good match to the population in terms of gender, age, social class, and region. As Table 3.1 shows, in response to the question "In which of the following methods of investigations of complaints against police officers would you have the greatest confidence?" 59.4% supported "a body independent of the police," 16.4% supported "the police themselves (current system)," and 19.6% said they had "equal confidence in both."

The second finding was from a New York City Council survey of public satisfaction with the New York Police Department (NYPD) in the year 2000. The sample of 1500 residents reportedly reflected the ethnic and racial composition of the city and each borough. The results showed that 75.8% of respondents supported the statement "It is necessary to have an independent group to oversee and investigate the department"; 18.9% believed "The police department can oversee and investigate the conduct of its own officers";

and 5.3% were uncertain or did not answer (McGuire Research Services, 2000, p. 7).

Table 3.2 shows the results from three rounds of the British Social Attitudes Survey, conducted between 1991 and 1996, which included a question about the best body to investigate serious complaints against police. The face-to-face interviews, conducted in Great Britain, involved between 1197 and 970 respondents. The table shows consistently high levels of support for independent investigations, averaging 92%, including substantial numbers of respondents—averaging 41%—who strongly supported the proposition. Although there was a slight downward trend in overall support, strong support increased. Disagreement levels were extremely low. The immediate reason for introducing the question was not reported. In their summary of the three sets of findings, Tarling and Dowds (1997, p. 206) commented on the very high levels of support for independence:

> Such near-universal support for a new independent body is unusual and does suggest a degree of public concern, arising (almost certainly) from several recent high-profile cases in which evidence turns out to have been fabricated.

The cases presumably relate to the infamous English miscarriages of justice cases—including the Guildford Four, Maguire Seven, and Birmingham Six—in which terrorism suspects were wrongfully convicted on false evidence and coerced confessions by police (Graycar & Prenzler, 2013).

In Queensland, Australia, the Fitzgerald Commission of Inquiry, from 1987 to 1989, uncovered significant police corruption and a culture of denial, cover up, and deflection and intimidation of internal and external complainants (Fitzgerald, 1989). One of the major outcomes was the creation of an independent oversight body, the Criminal Justice Commission, later the Crime and Misconduct Commission (CMC). The Commission holds a mission for police reform, as well as complaints oversight, and it instituted a periodic public attitudes survey, beginning in 1991, to gauge perceptions and experiences with police integrity issues. The work has been outsourced to specialist private sector survey firms, with sampling based on state demographics. Response numbers in the telephone surveys have ranged between 900 and 1550 (CMC, 2009, p. 54; 2011c, p. 46). The third survey, conducted in 1995, introduced an item asking respondents' level of agreement with the statement "Complaints against the police should be investigated by an oversight body, not the police themselves." Unlike the British surveys, the word *complaints* was used without qualification. Results for the six surveys that included this topic are reported in Table 3.3. The results show consistently high support for the proposition, averaging 88.6%, but hitting 90% or slightly above in three surveys, including 91% in the most recent. In general, disagreement levels were very low, averaging 7.1%. (The two levels of strength of opinion within agreement and disagreement have not been reported.)

Public Opinion: Levels of Complaints

One set of repeat surveys and one other survey were identified that included questions about different types of complaints, based on a rough ranking according to presumed seriousness. Five of the Queensland surveys asked respondents "to which agency they would report the following hypothetical scenarios: 1. a police officer has been rude to them, 2. they had been assaulted by a police officer, 3. they suspected a police officer had taken a bribe" (CMC, 2011c, p. 35). The responses are shown in Table 3.4. They show some fluctuations over time, but with fairly consistent patterns overall. The idea of police management of rudeness complaints received support between approximately two-thirds and three-quarters. Support for the oversight agency, the CMC, fluctuated widely between a low of 4% and high of 39%, averaging 20%. For all external agencies, support ranged from 23% to 47%, averaging 31%. For assault, support for police varied between 26% and 64%, averaging 46%. Support for the CMC averaged 37%, and for all nonpolice agencies, support averaged 55%. For bribery, support for police averaged 33%, with support for the CMC averaging 53% and for all nonpolice agencies averaging 68%.

In 2014, the Independent Police Complaints Commission (IPCC) public confidence survey included a new question: "The public were asked who they felt should be responsible for investigating cases covering a range of scenarios" (Harvey, Shepherd, & Magill, 2014, p. 25). Four options were provided across nine scenarios. The scenarios included the subject officer's department, another police department, an "independent organization," and the new Police and Crime Commissioners (elected officials who oversee and partially manage police forces, see http://apccs.police.uk/role-of-the-pcc/). These four options were also combined as "police" and "nonpolice." It appears that this question was introduced in response to widespread and increasing dissatisfaction with the IPCC's detachment from the police complaints system and recurring police misconduct scandals (IPCC, 2014). The results are shown in Table 3.5, organized in order of support for a nonpolice agency. They show majority support for an external agency for seven of the nine scenarios.

Miscellaneous Surveys

Several other surveys were identified that asked questions relevant to the issue of who should investigate complaints against police. One used the term

Table 3.4 Public Opinion Surveys, Queensland (Percentage): "Agency Perceived to Be the Best to Deal with a Complaint Involving a Police Officer"

Survey Year/ Complaint/ Agency	CMC	QPS	Ombudsman	Local MP/ Councilor/ Mayor	Solicitor/ Lawyer/ Barrister	Media	Wouldn't Complain	Other Agency	Total Nonpolice
1999									
Rudeness	24	66	2	3	2	0	1	1	33
Assault	40	43	1	3	9	2	0	2	57
Bribery	65	27	1	3	2	1	1	1	74
2002									
Rudeness	19	78	1	1	1	0	0	1	23
Assault	52	43	0	1	4	0	0	1	58
Bribery	72	25	0	0	0	0	0	4	76
2005									
Rudeness	4	75	9	5	1	0	4	3	26
Assault	6	64	6	6	12	1	1	3	35
Bribery	15	54	5	12	4	1	2	7	46
2008									
Rudeness	12	67	8	4	2	0	2	4	32
Assault	20	52	4	4	13	1	1	5	48
Bribery	35	42	4	7	3	1	1	7	58
2010									
Rudeness	39	63	1	1	1	0	1	4	47
Assault	65	26	1	1	4	1	0	3	75
Bribery	80	15	1	0	1	1	1	2	86

Source: CMC (2011c, pp. 36, 37, 39). Used with permission.

Note: Not all totals sum to 100 due to rounding. CMC, Crime and Misconduct Commission; MP, Member of Parliament; QPS, Queensland Police Service.

Table 3.5 Public Opinion, England and Wales (Percentage): "Who Do You Think Should Be Responsible for Investigating the Following Cases Involving Police Officers?"

Scenario/Agency	Police Force	External Police Force	(Police)	Independent Organization	PCC	(Nonpolice)
Serious corruption	13	12	(25)	50	21	(71)
Dies after being restrained by police officers while detained in a cell	15	12	(27)	49	19	(68)
Dies from an existing illness while being detained	20	11	(31)	45	19	(64)
Dies in a road traffic incident after being pursued	21	14	(35)	41	20	(62)
Excessive use of force by a police officer	27	13	(40)	36	20	(56)
A police officer displaying racist behavior or attitudes	30	10	(40)	35	21	(56)
Failure by police officers to offer adequate protection to a vulnerable person	31	10	(41)	34	21	(55)
Being stopped and searched by police officers	42	9	(51)	26	19	(45)
A police officer being rude	52	8	(60)	21	15	(36)

Source: Harvey et al. (2014, p. 49; totals, p. 25). Used with permission.

Note: PCC, Police and Crime Commissioners.

monitor, as opposed to *investigate*, and two involved focus groups, without responses being precisely quantified. The following provides a summary:

- In Austin, Texas, interviews showed that 87% of respondents favored "the creation of a citizens' review board to monitor the Austin Police Department and study citizen complaints" (Schott, 2001, p. 5).
- A U.S. study, employing 10 focus groups, conducted in a midwestern city, reported that "a large majority of participants expressed deep cynicism about the (police-dominated) complaint process. Only a few believed that a complaint would produce results" (Walker, 1997, p. 219).
- In a focus group study in England and Wales, involving 20 main groups and mini-groups from social minorities, "the majority of participants—regardless of background—were in favour of an independent body being responsible for dealing with complaints against police" (Wake, Simpson, Homes, & Ballantyne, 2007, p. 27).

Finally, mention should be made of a 2007 survey in the United Kingdom. A report by the IPCC (2008), *Building on Experience: Taking Stock of the New Police Complaints System After Four Years of Operational Experience*, included a survey of approximately 5000 people. The results were not included in Table 3.1 because there was not a clear generic question about the type of agency that should investigate complaints. However, there was a closely related question concerning "the type of activity the IPCC (as opposed to the police) should be responsible for investigating" (IPCC, 2008, p. 9). The reportage combined "agreed" and "strongly agreed" but did not include the numbers for disagreed. The results are as follows (IPCC, 2008, p. 9):

- 47% agreed that "all complaints about the police should be dealt with by the IPCC no matter how minor";
- 49% agreed that "only the most serious complaints about the police should be dealt with by the IPCC";
- 77% agreed that "when someone dies after contact with the police, the IPCC should look into the case, not the police force"; and
- 87% agreed that "cases of serious corruption among police officers should be dealt with by the IPCC."

Disposition of Complaints

The surveys examined so far were limited to the concept of investigation—or "monitoring" in some cases. Investigation is, however, only one element of a range of possible responses to complaints, and it is possible that respondents conflate investigation and disposition. The latter includes both adjudication about culpability and then sanctioning or other responses to a finding about culpability. This shortfall was partially recognized and addressed in a 1992 survey sponsored by John Jay College of Criminal Justice in the United States, described as a "nationwide telephone survey of 1248 adults, conducted in early October by the polling organization of Louise Harris and Associates Inc." (Harris, 1992, p. 1). In response to the question "When police officers are charged with alleged misconduct, what kind of a committee do you think should judge them?" there was 80% support for "review boards with both police and civilian members," 15% for all-civilian boards, and 4% for all-police boards (Harris, 1997, p. 1). The immediate reasons for initiating the survey were not disclosed. Some very broad contextual information was provided in the introductory remarks and summary of the main findings (Harris, 1992, p. 1):

> Perhaps no issue in policing currently evokes more heated debate or frayed nerves than civilian review, which in city after city has driven wedges between political officials and the police rank and file. Police labor leaders insist that only a police officer can understand and judge the actions of another officer. Local officials, for their part, worry that justice may not be served if the police judge themselves.
>
> But while the issue simmers on the front burner of many an urban political agenda, where does the public stand?
>
> A new survey shows that an overwhelming majority of people, across a broad spectrum of demographic groups, believe that police officers accused of misconduct should have their cases reviewed by a committee composed of both civilians and other officers.

The commentary also noted the extremely low level of support for police-only review. The chief executive officer of the survey firm saw the results as evidence of a "broad public consensus" (in Harris, 1992, p. 1).

In 2014, the U.K. IPCC public confidence survey introduced a question about which agency should be responsible for disciplining officers, using five scenarios, with four types of agencies, also combined as "police" and "non-police." Table 3.6 shows the results organized in order of support for non-police agencies. They show support favoring external agencies in three of the scenarios, and police in one.

In addition, one survey was found regarding public opinion about the final disposition of complaints. The 2008 *Building on Experience* report by the IPCC included a question about how different types of complaints should be "dealt with." The results are shown in Table 3.7, indicating strong support in a number of cases for the nonpunitive responses of "receive an explanation" and "receive an apology" and limited support for punishment. (What is missing from this question, however, are options related to remediation, such as counseling, re-training, and close supervision of officers.) Of note is

Table 3.6 Public Opinion, England and Wales (Percentage): "Who Do You Think Should Be Responsible for Deciding How a Police Officer Should Be Disciplined if the Police Officer Was Found to Have....?"

Scenario/Agency	Senior Manager of Police Force	Senior Manager of Another Police Force	(Police)	Local Body Responsible for Overseeing Police	Independent Organization From Outside Police	(Nonpolice)
Been involved in serious corruption	16	11	27	25	44	69
Physically assaulted or used too much force	30	12	42	24	29	53
Displayed racist behavior or attitudes when dealing with a member of the public	36	11	47	22	26	48
Stopped and searched someone for no reason	50	10	60	18	18	36

Source: Harvey et al. (2014, pp. 26, 50). Used with permission.

Table 3.7   Public Opinion, England and Wales (Percentage): "Respondents Were Asked How They Wanted Different Sorts of Complaint Dealt with"

What Should Happen in These Circumstances	Officer Failed to Investigate Reported Burglary	Officer Rude When Asked for Help	Used Racist/Other Offensive Language	Physically Assaulted/Used Too Much Force at a Demo
Receive an explanation	60	32	24	22
Receive an apology from the officer/force	24	57	42	32
The officer should be punished	12	9	31	37
Receive some financial compensation	2	1	1	6
Don't know	2	2	2	3

Source: IPCC (2008, p. 10).

the fact that the same survey found that 61% of respondents said they would lodge a complaint with police (IPCC, 2008, p. 10). The report provided a nice summary of these issues as follows (IPCC, 2008, p. 10):

> The picture of public expectations seems clear. Most people expect the IPCC to investigate the most serious incidents and allegations of misconduct independently and they trust the IPCC to do so impartially and fairly. However, most people would expect to go to their local police station with a less serious complaint and want it to be resolved with an explanation, an apology or reassurance that the same thing will not happen again. Nevertheless, a significant minority of people would not make a complaint to the police, want the IPCC to do more and have more punitive attitudes.

Reasons

In most cases, the surveys summarized in previous sections did not explicitly ask follow-on questions about reasons for respondents' views on how complaints should be handled. One exception was the U.S. nationwide survey in Table 3.1, which reported 80% support for mixed civilian/police review. The survey also found that "Overall, 60 percent of respondents felt that police officers would be too lenient in judging officers accused of misconduct" (Harris, 1992, p. 1). Agreement with this view, and support for oversight, was fairly consistent across demographic groups. Contrary to expectations, Black respondents were no more likely to support all-civilian or mixed review, with Hispanics slightly more supportive of all-civilian boards. Older, more educated persons were slightly more supportive of mixed boards. Support for the idea that police treated people fairly was fairly high at 63% overall, but was only 38% among Blacks (Harris, 1992, p. 6).

In other cases, demographic variation and related questions provide some clues as to respondents' thinking on the issue—although this was not the case in the U.K. Police Federation survey, which showed no variation between respondents of any significance. The New York City Council survey, which showed 75.8% support for an independent body to "oversee and investigate" complaints, also found that "a majority of New Yorkers feel that the NYPD has a problem with police brutality (67%), and failing to respond appropriately to complaints of sexual assault or rape (62%) (and) significantly more Blacks and Hispanics believe that the NYPD has a problem with brutality (79% of Blacks, 66% of Hispanics)" (McGuire Research Services, 2000, pp. 2–3). The report concluded that "New Yorkers feel that the Police Department is not able to police itself" (McGuire Research Services, 2000, p. 3). The survey also found that approximately half the respondents felt that recent high-profile police brutality cases had been managed by the mayor and police commissioner in a way that worsened relations between police and the community. At the same time, 70% of respondents who had contact with police in the preceding year were satisfied with the experience (51% very satisfied; McGuire Research Services, 2000, p. 12). The British Social Attitudes surveys, which found extremely high levels of support for independent investigations of police, also found that, on average, only 48% of respondents thought police could be trusted "not to bend the rules...only some of the time (or) almost never" (Tarling & Dowds, 1997, p. 205).

The Queensland surveys produced particularly complex findings. As noted, support for the principle of independent investigations averaged 88.6%, but with several results above 90%. One might surmise this is a jurisdiction with low levels of trust in police. In fact, in the same surveys, confidence in police honesty averaged around 85% between 1995 and 2010, trending upward slightly (CMC, 2011c, p. 21). In the most recent survey, support for police honesty was at 90%, whereas support for independent processing of complaints against police was at 91%. Furthermore, support for the view that police "generally/mostly behave well" averaged around 90%, also trending upward slightly (CMC, 2011c, p. 19). Also of relevance was the fact that, in the most recent survey, 58% of those who had ever had contact with police said they were satisfied with these experiences and only 21% were dissatisfied, whereas 68% of those who had contact with police in the preceding 12 months were satisfied, and again, only 21% were wholly dissatisfied (CMC, 2011c, pp. 6–7). The 2008 survey included some demographic variables. Surprisingly perhaps, small but statistically significant higher levels of support for independent investigations were expressed by persons with lower levels of education and persons who had positive recent experiences of police (CMC, 2009, p. 57).

Referring back to Table 3.4, which described three levels of complaints, the CMC report noted the large shift in support away from police toward the CMC and other external agencies in the final survey. This coincided with several major scandals around that time, including revelations of inadequate internal investigations (CMC, 2011c). Public confidence in the police "properly investigating complaints" reduced from 62% in the 2008 survey to 57% in the 2010 survey, whereas confidence in the CMC increased from 71% to 74% (CMC, 2011c, p. 31).

The miscellaneous studies also provided some possible explanations for different views about which bodies should investigate complaints. The question in the Austin survey was part of a study concerned with improving race relations in the city. The results showed "overwhelming support for the creation of a citizens' review board across all ethnic groups. Minority groups support the board more heavily than Whites, but the difference is not great" (Schott, 2001, p. 45). The study also found that 71% of all respondents felt the police department did not treat all ethnic groups the same, with 83% of African Americans, 73% of Hispanics, 74% of Whites, and 53% of Asians holding to this view (Schott, 2001, p. 43). Satisfaction with police averaged 57%. Dissatisfaction averaged 15%, but 26% of African Americans were dissatisfied (Schott, 2001, p. 41). The study recommended the creation of a review board as a way of dealing with complaints more effectively and improving police services through complaint analysis.

The U.S. focus group study found that "cynicism about the complaint process" among participants "reflected the widespread belief that police departments cover up misconduct by their officers" (Walker, 1997, p. 220):

> One African-American male student in group 8 said that the police depart-ment "takes care of its own." Another, in group 7, explained that "everyone sticks to their own," and a third in group 9 said that "police officers protect each other just like doctors and lawyers." One African-American male in group 8 said that the officer's supervisor would probably laugh about the inci-dent and take the officer out for a drink...
>
> A few participants expressed fear of retaliation for complaining. One African-American woman in group 1 reported that she had been harassed for filing a complaint and "would never call in a complaint again because of that experience."

Overall, "the focus groups confirmed the powerful effect of race, ethnicity, and age on perceptions of police. There was deep hostility to the police among African-American adults and students and, to a slightly lesser extent, among white and Hispanic students" (Walker, 1997, p. 221). For some participants in the U.K. focus group study, support for independent investigations was linked "to fears of overt intimidation from the police or their inability to be impartial when handling a case against a colleague" (Wake et al., 2007, p. 27).

More generally, public opinion surveys that ask people why they would or would not complain against police tend not to produce results that bear directly on the issue of who should investigate complaints. A section of the British Crime Survey is one example. Over six surveys, on average, 19% of respondents had felt "really annoyed" with police in the previous 5 years, but only 9% of this group said they made a complaint (Grace & Bucke, 2009, p. 28). For persons who were annoyed but did not complain, the two most common reasons given over six surveys was "could see no benefit," averaging 64%, and "I was not the appropriate person to make the complaint/none of my business," averaging 15% (Grace & Bucke, 2009, p. 29). Only 4% stated "Worried about police response." (See also CMC, 2011c, p. 30.)

In 2014, the IPCC public confidence survey included a new question, "How confident are you that the *police* deal fairly with complaints made against the police?" The response was 58% agreed, and 35% disagreed, with slightly less support amongst younger and less affluent persons (Harvey et al.,

2014, p. 43). In addition, 44% said they would report misconduct directly to police, compared with 61% in 2007 (Harvey et al., 2014, p. 23). A preference to report to the IPCC was expressed by 15%, up from 10%. Support for all nonpolice agencies, including the IPCC, was 48%, up from 38%.

Views about Current Oversight Agencies

A systematic survey was not conducted for studies of public opinion of specific agencies, given the large number of these bodies and ambiguity surrounding levels of independent investigation and adjudication (Prenzler et al., 2013). However, surveys that were encountered during research for this study showed high levels of public confidence in existing agencies. For example, in the United Kingdom, the 2014 survey of public confidence in the police complaints system found that 77% of respondents were confident that the IPCC "would deal with complaints impartially" (Harvey et al., 2014, p. 45). However, a large proportion of respondents were misinformed about the Commission: 39% thought that it was responsible for "investigating all complaints about the police no matter how minor," 48% thought that it determined "whether officers should be prosecuted for criminal actions," and 44% thought that it determined "how police officers should be disciplined when misconduct has been found"—all of which were untrue (Harvey et al., 2014, p. 17). The same questions in an earlier survey in 2011 revealed an even wider gap between perception and reality: 69% thought the IPCC was responsible for investigating all complaints and 75% thought it was responsible for determining criminal prosecutions (Inglis, 2011, p. 17). In 2011/2012, 30,143 complaints were made against police in England and Wales, involving 54,714 allegations (IPCC, 2012, p. 5). In the same year, the IPCC commenced 126 investigations and completed 130 (IPCC, 2014, p. 17). It does appear, however, that the IPCC is finally responding to evidence about dissatisfaction with the system. The 2013/2014 *Annual Report* announced that, "we are preparing for a significant increase in the number and type of investigations we undertake, together with an increased capacity to ensure our findings influence policing and complaints handling more generally" (IPCC, 2014, p. 4).

As noted, in the Queensland surveys, public confidence in the CMC "properly investigating complaints" increased from 71% to 74% between 2008 and 2010 (CMC, 2011c, p. 31). An omnibus agency with a special mission to support police integrity, the CMC states that "we receive and investigate allegations of misconduct to ensure that Queensland's public institutions are accountable for their conduct" (CMC, 2013, p. 2). However, the Commission has no adjudicative nor disciplinary authority and it investigates a tiny fraction of complaints. In 2012/2013, there were 2190 complaints involving 5240 allegations against police. The CMC "conducted 43 investigations into 192 allegations [3.6%]" (CMC, 2013, p. 27).

By way of contrast, in Northern Ireland, the Police Ombudsman investigates all complaints against police and has significant authority in adjudication (Chapters 1 and 2). Over the 5 years from 2008/2009 to 2012/2013, on average (PONI, 2013, pp. 38–39, 41, 42):

- 79% of respondents in public awareness and opinion surveys expressed confidence in the Ombudsman dealing with complaints impartially;
- 85% were confident of being treated fairly if they made a complaint;
- 83% viewed the Ombudsman as being independent of police; and
- 85% believed the Ombudsman would "help ensure that the police do a good job."

An earlier survey of "Black and minority ethnic communities" found that 76% believed the Ombudsman was "necessary" and 59% believed that it "can help change the police" (Radford, Betts, & Ostermeyer, 2006a, p. 102). However, a survey of the lesbian, gay, and bisexual community found much lower levels of confidence (around 51%) and considerable uncertainty (with support around 40%) regarding the impartiality and independence of the Ombudsman (Radford, Betts, & Ostermeyer, 2006b, p. 90).

Discussion

This review of the available survey literature on public views of police complaints and discipline systems produced a number of valuable findings. The results should be incorporated into the design of systems to strengthen their legitimacy. Unfortunately, as shown here and in other chapters in this book, most systems fall far short of the democratic ideal. A system that more accurately reflects public opinion should also be more effective in reconciling complainants and police, improving police–community relations, and reducing misconduct (Porter & Prenzler, 2014). The surveys reported on in this chapter show clearly that there is very high and consistent support for the basic principle of independent processing of complaints against police— subject to a number of qualifiers related to less serious matters and alternatives to the investigate-and-prosecute model.

The reasoning behind public opinion on this issue was somewhat less clear. There was some limited evidence that upward trends in support for independence were related to recent policing scandals (cf. Brown & Benedict, 2002). There was also some evidence that support for independence was strengthened in some locations by dissatisfaction with how a complaint was managed and by elevated levels of distrust of police and negative experiences with police—particularly among minority groups. However, the study also revealed a significant paradox. In many cases, high levels of support for independence were associated with high levels of trust and confidence in police.

What might appear at first glance as a contradiction is perhaps not so difficult to explain. It is simply the case that the public recognizes that due process needs to be followed when an allegation of wrongdoing is made, and that entails an institutional separation between the accused person and the investigator. It is not enough for the investigator to be a senior police officer or an officer from another area or department. In these cases, there is also the chance, or the possible perception, of bias toward a colleague. The idea of clear divide between a complainant and an accused person is in fact the major rationale behind the creation of modern public sector detective units and modern court systems (Prenzler & Sarre, 2012). The rule of law requires independence, and this applies across the professions, as argued in Chapter 1. For example, in the Queensland public opinion surveys, the question about who should investigate complaints against police was extended to public servants and local government for the first time in 2010. The responses mirrored those for police: 90% supported the statement "Complaints about public service employees should be investigated by an oversight body, not by the Government," with 90% agreeing in relation to local government (CMC, 2011a, p. 35; CMC, 2011b, p. 38).

An associated irony in this issue is that while there is a strong public preference for investigations by an external agency, most people also express a preference for lodging a complaint at a police station. One way to interpret this is that police stations are more visible and accessible. Most oversight agencies usually only have one office, typically in a central business district of a capital city. Decentralizing agency offices and making them more visible and accessible is one possible implication. Two of the most independent and successful agencies in the world—the Northern Ireland Police Ombudsman and the Hong Kong Independent Commission Against Corruption—have regional offices (Graycar & Prenzler, 2013). The Hong Kong Independent Commission Against Corruption's main office has a discrete point of access open 24/7 (Graycar & Prenzler, 2013). It is also possible that the preference for lodging complaints with police provides some complainants with a means of making police aware of their complaint while expecting police to refer it on to the independent agency. The fact that many complainants have, at best, conflicted feelings about police makes it imperative that an alternative to a police station (or police website or telephone line) is always available. One way to achieve this on an economical basis is to include police matters within a public-sector-wide anticorruption agency that has sufficient resources to establish regional offices (Graycar & Prenzler, 2013).

This study has been focused on the issue of who should "investigate" complaints against police. Some limited findings were also made on the disposition of matters, largely supporting an independent adjudicative function and nonpunitive restorative responses to most types of complaint matters. The following two chapters, which examine complainant and police views, address this issue in greater depth. Taking all these into account, one option that is likely to significantly enhance the legitimacy and flexibility of systems is to make allowance for negotiation with complainants about how their complaint should be processed.

Negotiation with complainants need not entail complete complainant control. For example, more serious matters—especially those involving potential criminal actions—initially should be investigated and adjudicated independently. Mediation or informal resolution might then be possible after the formal inquisitorial process. At the same time, there is a valid argument that minor matters should also be dealt with externally—through an investigation or externally managed mediation—if this is particularly important to a complainant who is highly distrustful of police. For example, the IPCC (2009) has conceded that what may appear as a lower-level complaint, suitable for in-house police processing, "may be a serious, unique and often frightening event for a citizen" (p. 7).

Finally, it should be noted that all the surveys covered in this chapter were conducted in relatively wealthy western democracies: Britain, the United States, and Australia. At present, it appears that these are the only surveys available. There are few reasons to suspect the results would not have wider application. However, it would be good to see more countries and/or police jurisdictions implement their own surveys to assess local levels of support for different types of systems.

Conclusion

This chapter canvassed the results of public opinion surveys that asked questions about respondents' views on the most appropriate institution to deal with complaints against police. The results are strongly supportive of an independent agency. This is consistent with the general principle of independence in justice processes. Police should investigate allegations from the public against alleged criminals without any conflicts of interest—real of apparent. This principle also applies to allegations against police. The more serious the allegation, the more important it is that impartiality is underwritten by institutional separation between the accused and the investigator. For many police oversight agencies or public sector anticorruption commissions, this means they need to expand their investigative capacity and their outreach to the public through regional offices and services. At the same time, there is a case for complainants to be given a choice about who should investigate minor complaints, given they may be highly distrustful of any police officers. Overall, the idea of formal investigations, findings, and sanctions needs to be heavily qualified in light of the variety of alternative responses—including mediation—developed in more detail in the following chapters.

References

Brown, B., & Benedict, W. R. (2002). Perceptions of the police. *Policing: An International Journal of Police Strategies and Management, 25*(3), 543–580.

CJC. (1995). *Public attitudes towards the Queensland Police Service.* Brisbane: Criminal Justice Commission.

CJC. (2000). *Public attitudes towards the QPS.* Brisbane: Criminal Justice Commission.

CMC. (2003). *Public perceptions of the Queensland Police Service.* Brisbane: Crime and Misconduct Commission.

CMC. (2006). *Public perceptions of the Queensland Police Service.* Brisbane: Crime and Misconduct Commission.

CMC. (2009). *Public perceptions of the Queensland Police Service.* Brisbane: Crime and Misconduct Commission.

CMC. (2011a). *Public perceptions of local government.* Brisbane: Crime and Misconduct Commission.

CMC. (2011b). *Public perceptions of the public service.* Brisbane: Crime and Misconduct Commission.

CMC. (2011c). *Public perceptions of the Queensland Police Service.* Brisbane: Crime and Misconduct Commission.

CMC. (2013). *Annual report, 2012–13.* Brisbane: Crime and Misconduct Commission.

Electoral Reform Ballot Services. (1997). *Survey of attitudes to police discipline and complaints.* London.

Fitzgerald, G. (1989). *Report of a commission of inquiry pursuant to orders in council.* Brisbane: Government Printer.

Goldsmith, A. (1991). *Complaints against police: The trend to external review.* Oxford: Clarendon.

Grace, K., & Bucke, T. (2009). *Public annoyance and complaints about the police: Findings from the 2006/07 British Crime Survey.* London: Independent Police Complaints Commission.

Graycar, A., & Prenzler, T. (2013). *Understanding and preventing corruption* (pp. 1–161). Houndmills: Palgrave-Macmillan.

Harris, L. (1992). Public solidly favors mixed police/civilian review boards. *Law Enforcement News, XVIII*(367), 1 & 6.

Harvey, P., Shepherd, S., & Magill, T. (2014). *Public confidence in the police complaints system.* London: Independent Police Complaints Commission.

Hopkins, T. (2009). *An effective system for investigating complaints against police.* Melbourne: Victoria Law Foundation.

Inglis, G. (2011). *Confidence in the police complaints system: A survey of the general population in 2011.* London: Independent Police Complaints Commission.

IPCC. (2008). *Building on experience: Taking stock of the new police complaints system after four years of operational experience.* London: Independent Police Complaints Commission.

IPCC. (2009). *IPCC investigations: A survey seeking feedback from complainants and police personnel.* London: Independent Police Complaints Commission.

IPCC. (2012). *Police complaints: Statistics for England and Wales 2011/12.* London: Independent Police Complaints Commission.

IPCC. (2014). *Annual report and statement of accounts 2013/14.* London: Independent Police Complaints Commission.

Jenkins, C. (1997). Independent body to investigate police has public support. *Police Review, 17*, 4.

Knapp, W. (1972). *Report of a commission to investigate allegations of police corruption and the city's anti-corruption procedures.* New York: The City of New York.

McGuire Research Services. (2000). *Public satisfaction survey: New York City Police Department.* New York: The New York City Council.

PONI. (2013). *Annual Statistical Bulletin 2012/13.* Belfast: Police Ombudsman for Northern Ireland.

Porter, L. E., & Prenzler, T. (2014, in press). Improving police behaviour and police–community relations through innovative responses to complaints. In S. Lister & M. Rowe (Eds.), *Accountability in policing: Contemporary debates.* Abingdon: Routledge.

Prenzler, T., Mihinjac, M., & Porter, L. (2013). Reconciling stakeholder interests in police complaints and discipline systems. *Police Practice and Research: An International Journal, 14*(2), 155–168.

Prenzler, T., & Sarre, R. (2012). The criminal justice system. In H. Hayes & T. Prenzler (Eds.), *An introduction to crime and criminology* (pp. 243–257). Sydney: Pearson.

Radford, K., Betts, J., & Ostermeyer, M. (2006a). *Policing, accountability and the black and minority ethnic communities in Northern Ireland.* Belfast: Institute for Conflict Research.

Radford, K., Betts, J., & Ostermeyer, M. (2006b). *Policing, accountability and the lesbian, gay and bisexual community in Northern Ireland.* Belfast: Institute for Conflict Research.

Schott, R. L. (2001). *Ethnic and race relations in Austin, Texas.* Austin: Lyndon B. Johnson School of Public Affairs, University of Texas at Austin.

Stone, C., & Ward, H. (2000). Democratic policing: A framework for action. *Policing and Society, 10*(1), 11–45,

Tarling, R., & Dowds, L. (1997). Crime and punishment. In R. Jowell J. Curtice, A. Park, L. Brook, K. Thomson, & C. Bryson. (Eds.). *British social attitudes.* Aldershot: Ashgate.

Wake, R., Simpson, C., Homes, A., & Ballantyne, J. (2007). *Public perceptions of the police complaints system.* London: Independent Police Complaints Commission.

Walker, S. (1997). Complaints against the police: A focus group study of citizen perceptions, goals, and expectations. *Criminal Justice Review, 22*(2), 207–225.

Complainants' Views of Police Complaint Systems
The Gap between Aspiration and Experience

4

LOUISE PORTER
TIM PRENZLER

Contents

This chapter explores the views of complainants regarding their experiences with police complaint handling systems. While early police complaints systems relied on police agencies themselves to investigate and manage complaints made against their members, dissatisfaction and mistrust of these systems have led to the establishment of varying levels of external independent oversight, management, or control of the process. There is now a variety of police complaint models across different jurisdictions, but each should fundamentally see the complainant as its key stakeholder. This chapter reviews 46 surveys conducted with complainants regarding their experiences of these differing systems, broadly described as police dominated, independent, and mixed systems. While the surveys do show that the majority preference is for independence, with such systems attracting greater satisfaction regarding process and outcomes, complainants' experiences are affected by the quality of treatment by the agency, perceptions of bias, and administrative inefficiencies regardless of which system they engage. Informal resolution and mediation are discussed as mechanisms for improving the complainant experience, at least for less serious grievances.

Background

Policing has long been recognized as a high-risk area for corruption and misconduct. Further, with the effectiveness of democratic policing lying in the balance between enforcement and public consent, a high degree of responsibility rests on officers to carry out their duties with professionalism and legitimacy. One of the key accountability mechanisms for police is the ability for those aggrieved or affected by police behavior to voice their issues and have them investigated impartially and with due diligence. Responding to complaints with appropriate and timely action should build confidence in the system and the police as a professional agency, improve service delivery, and provide a deterrent for future deviance (Maguire & Corbett, 1991). Weak accountability mechanisms (or such perceptions) undermine the legitimacy of the police and can reduce public support and cooperation.

Historically, police complaints were dealt with internally by "internal affairs" departments, who typically received criticism from both the public and fellow police. Complainants viewed them as biased toward police officers, whereas police officers rejected investigators as betraying the police culture of solidarity. With growing recognition of the public as significant stakeholders in the police accountability process, public satisfaction and confidence have increasingly been formalized as key performance indicators for police service delivery. To increase public confidence in police, the introduction of "oversight" has provided improved independent scrutiny of police complaint handling. However, while the fundamental issue of independence has been the driver of external complaint handling bodies, most systems around the world do not represent full independence. Indeed, many agencies have powers limited to review rather than independent investigative and adjudication functions (Porter & Prenzler, 2012). The evolution of oversight has therefore been patchy rather than strategic and has left systems with differing powers and functions, many of which seem to go through cycles of devolution, rather than moving toward a model system.

As central stakeholders in the complaints process, complainants represent a key source of information on the effectiveness of complaints handling systems. In recognition of this, as agencies evolve, some have utilized complaint data and sought feedback from their client base to understand why people complain (or choose not to), what complainants seek from engaging the complaint process, and how they experience the complaint process, to improve their systems and services. This body of work informs us of the complainant experience of different complaint handling systems and allows us to consider which systems may evoke more satisfaction for complainants.

What Complainants Want

Although it might be expected that people complain about police officers because they want them to be dismissed or charged for their behavior, this is not supported by research. In Denver, De Angelis and Kupchick (2006) reported that fewer than a third of surveyed complainants desired an outcome that severely sanctioned the subject officer. Commonly, complainants instead sought an apology or for the subject officer to receive counseling/training to improve his/her behavior. Indeed, a study by the Criminal Justice Commission (CJC, 1994) in Queensland, Australia, highlighted that many complain to prevent the same from happening to others in the future or to "let the officer know how I felt" (p. 65). Further, Ridgeway et al. (2009) reported that Cincinnati complainants "may not have been happy with the complaint process but acknowledged that the process allowed them to tell their side of the story" (p. 134). Unfortunately, complainants' experiences of complaints handling systems can leave them feeling neither listened to nor that their complaint has achieved any result.

Many external complaints handling agencies, including Ombudsman Offices, are set up to receive appeals by complainants who are unsatisfied with the way their matter has been initially handled by a police agency. For example, in England and Wales, "If complainants are dissatisfied about the outcome of a local resolution, about the process followed during a local investigation, or about the non-recording of their complaint, then they have a right of appeal to the Independent Police Complaints Commission (IPCC)" (Hagger Johnson & Hipkin-Chastagnol, 2011). This independent review function offers a layer of oversight and accountability to police internal investigations, while still expecting the majority of matters to be dealt with at that internal level.

The utilization of such external complaint review services clearly infers dissatisfaction with internal complaint handling systems. The outcomes of appeals further shed light on the inadequacies of internal systems. For example, in England and Wales, the IPCC upheld 21% of the appeals it investigated in 2009/2010 (Hagger Johnson & Hipkin-Chastagnol, 2011). Appeals were upheld most frequently (41%) based on inadequacies of the original investigation, such as police complaint investigations failing to gather sufficient evidence or not reaching reasonable conclusions from the evidence. Just over a quarter of appeals (27%) were upheld due to insufficient information being shared with the complainant regarding the findings or outcome of their complaint. In the majority of cases, the result of these appeals was to recommend the police reinvestigate the complaint or release information to the complainant. However, under the Police Reform Act 2002, the IPCC does have the power to direct that a recommended action is implemented by the police agency, for example, bringing disciplinary proceedings against an officer. Such powers are rare, though, among oversight agencies, with most merely having the power to recommend rather than direct action, potentially leaving the complainant with further disappointment after a lengthy process of investigation and reinvestigation (Porter & Prenzler, 2012).

In many jurisdictions, however, complainants now have a choice of agency with which to initially file their complaint. They can complain directly to the police agency or approach an external complaint handling body. Studies show that complainants often have concerns regarding approaching police directly with their complaint, for example, feeling intimidated, fearful that they will be harassed by police as retribution for complaining, or that they will not be treated fairly (e.g., Ethical Standards Department [ESD], 1999; Hagger Johnson, 2010). Complainants also approach an external agency because of the difficulty in lodging a complaint directly with police, reporting that attempts to complain are ignored or discouraged (Hagger Johnson, 2010; McDevitt, Farrell, & Andresen, 2005). Thus, there is clearly a demand for external agencies that have the power to receive complaints about police and investigate matters independently. The question remains whether the degree of independence positively affects the complainants' experiences of complaint handling systems.

Experiences of Complaints Systems

As with the previous chapter, this section details results from a systematic search of surveys of complaint systems, focusing on those that surveyed the experiences of complainants. A total of 46 surveys were identified where it was evident whether respondents were being questioned about a system that was police dominated (e.g., respondents being asked their experience of the police's handling of their complaint), an independent system (where complainants who engaged a fully independent investigative agency were surveyed), or a "mixed" system (where respondents were questioned generally about "the system" and that system comprised an external complaint handling body that may investigate complaints, manage investigations or refer complaints to police to investigate, and review or audit internal investigations or respond to appeals). A small number of surveys of informal resolution and mediation were also identified and are discussed separately.

The majority of surveys reported here involved direct sampling of persons who had made formal complaints. A smaller number involved general surveys of public opinion about police with a subset of questions asking whether respondents had complained about police and their satisfaction with the response. One report excluded from the study involved interviews with "street-involved" persons in British Columbia, Canada (Strathcona Research Group, 2006). Although 91 of the 209 persons interviewed were considered complainants, in that they reported having "raised their concerns with someone," only 18 said they had lodged a formal complaint and 8 said they received a reply (Strathcona Research Group, 2006, p. 14).

Police-Dominated Complaints Systems

Findings from 25 surveys on police-dominated complaints systems were found from 13 jurisdictions across the United Kingdom, United States, Canada, and Australia (the largest number [nine] being from England and Wales). Whereas 14 surveys reported overall satisfaction and/or dissatisfaction ratings for the system, 11 provided results for satisfaction and/or dissatisfaction with the process and the outcome. Results are summarized in Table 4.1.

Overall, on average, 71.3% of complainants in police-dominated systems were dissatisfied. There did not seem to be any particular pattern of satisfaction over time or by jurisdiction. Results for the formal complainant surveys (14) and general surveys (11) were very similar—71.1% and 72.5% dissatisfaction, respectively. There was some variation in relation to satisfaction with process and outcome. Where dissatisfaction in the process was reported, this ranged from 44% of complainants (in Oakland and Berkeley) to 82% of complainants (in Boston), whereas dissatisfaction with the outcome ranged from 53% in Scotland to 97% in England and Wales (Maguire & Corbett, 1991). On average, where both numbers were available, 23.2% were satisfied and 69.1% were dissatisfied with the outcome, whereas 26.6% were satisfied and 65.8% were dissatisfied with the process.

Some surveys reported that satisfaction was related to whether the complaint had been substantiated, particularly that the proportion of complainants satisfied with the outcome reflected the general rate of substantiation for complaints (e.g., Calgary Police Commission, 1999, p. 93). However, other surveys showed that satisfaction was not always related to the outcome. For example, the report by the Victoria Police ESD (1999) noted that the proportion of satisfied complainants was higher than the substantiation rate for complaints, "which means that satisfaction for complainants is not directly related to substantiation" (p. 32). Indeed, it is likely that those who do not obtain the desired outcome can still see value in the process and those whose complaints are substantiated can still be dissatisfied with the process.

Although, clearly, not all complainants have negative experiences of police-dominated systems, across the surveys, it was evident that particular

Table 4.1 Summary of Complainant Experience Surveys of Police-Dominated Systems

Location	% Satisfied			% Dissatisfied			% Supporting Independence	Source (and Survey Year Where Relevant)
	Process	Outcome	Overall	Process	Outcome	Overall		
Albuquerque					78			Luna & Walker, 1997, p. 28
Boston	4	7	14	82	82	71		McDevitt et al., 2005, pp. 60–61
Calgary				68	80			Calgary Police Commission, 1999, p. 92
Cincinnati	36	36		64	64			Ridgeway et al., 2009, p. 134
Denver	8		12		86	75	68 "investigate" 94 "monitor"	De Angelis & Kupchick, 2006, pp. 23–24, 32
England and Wales								
			20			60		Brown, 1987, p. 37
		3	17		97	82	90	Maguire & Corbett, 1991, pp. 162, 164, 180
		20			71	67	67	Waters & Brown, 2000, pp. 629, 631
			29			71		Grace & Bucke, 2009, p. 28, 2001/2002
			36			64		Grace & Bucke, 2009, p. 28, 2002/2003
			20			80		Grace & Bucke, 2009, p. 28, 2003/2004
			24			76		Grace & Bucke, 2009, p. 28, 2004/2005
			19			81		Grace & Bucke, 2009, p. 28, 2005/2006
			20			80		Grace & Bucke, 2009, p. 28, 2006/2007

(Continued)

Table 4.1 (Continued) Summary of Complainant Experience Surveys of Police-Dominated Systems

Location	% Satisfied			% Dissatisfied			% Supporting Independence	Source (and Survey Year Where Relevant)
	Process	Outcome	Overall	Process	Outcome	Overall		
Oakland and Berkeley				44			77	Perez, 1994, p. 112
Pasadena				78				Bobb et al., 2006, p. 80
Queensland	40	28	48	60	72	52		CJC, 1994, pp. 60–62
			39			56		CJC, 1995, p. 9
				65				CJC, 2000, p. 7
				71				CMC, 2009, p. 47
	45			50				CMC, 2011, p. 29
Scotland		12			53			Fraser, 2009, p. 36
Toronto			16			84	73	Landau, 1994, pp. 63–64
Victoria (Australia)	23	21		62	55			ESD, 1999, p. 32
	30	24		59	62		78	Prenzler, Allard, Curry, & Macintyre, 2010, pp. 8, 11

dissatisfaction with outcomes stems from feeling that the investigators are "going through the motions" rather than taking issues seriously, or that nothing has been achieved and the system is a waste of time. Criticisms of the process typically include protracted timeframes and lack of communication, including not being informed of the outcome or how it was decided. Feelings of intimidation or lack of impartiality in relation to the complaint process are also common issues, particularly, criticism that investigators side with police and that police attempt to dissuade complainants or refuse to take complaints (e.g., ESD, 1999, p. 29; McDevitt et al., 2005, p. 56).

Interestingly, where positive experiences of police-dominated systems were reported in the surveys, qualitative comments detailed that complainants viewed the complaint handing process, particularly investigators, as impartial and unbiased in their treatment of involved parties. For example, in Boston, "The officer receiving the complaint didn't try to talk me out of it or defend his fellow officer nor did he take my side. He was respectful, courteous, professional" (in McDevitt et al., 2005, p. 56), and in Denver, "Internal Affairs...were fair, professional, [and] unbiased" (in De Angelis & Kupchick, 2006, p. 26).

In an early survey of the police complaints system for England and Wales, Brown (1987, p. 37) noted that "Nearly two-thirds of the sample was dissatisfied because they felt it was wrong in principle for the police to investigate complaints against their own number." Indeed, six of the surveys of police-dominated systems provided information on respondents' opinions regarding independence within the complaints system; the majority of survey respondents (over two thirds) supported independent complaints investigations or independent monitoring of police.

Mixed Complaints Systems

Nine surveys of mixed systems were reviewed, representing six different jurisdictions across the United States, England and Wales, Israel, and the Philippines. All of these surveys involved persons who had lodged complaints. Survey results are summarized in Table 4.2. As with the police-dominated systems described in the previous section, in all but one of the surveys, rates of dissatisfaction outweighed satisfaction. Only in the Philippines were the majority (over two-thirds) of respondents satisfied with the system, although in New York City, 42% were satisfied with the process. Where measured, respondents showed particular dissatisfaction with outcomes; as many as 96% were dissatisfied with the outcome in the England and Wales survey (Maguire & Corbett, 1991). This had reduced to 70% in the more recent IPCC (2009) survey for the same jurisdiction.

Interestingly, a report from the IPCC in 2010 separately asked respondents about their experience with the IPCC and their experience with the

Table 4.2 Summary of Surveys of Complainant Experiences of Mixed Complaints Systems

Location	% Satisfied			% Dissatisfied			% Supporting Independence	Source
	Process	Outcome	Overall	Process	Outcome	Overall		
Denver	11	10	15		87	74	88 "monitor"	De Angelis, 2008. pp. 13, 16
		7						Schaible, De Angelis, Wolf, & Rosenthal, 2013, p. 640
England and Wales		4	26		96	74	82	Maguire & Corbett, 1991, pp. 162, 164, 180
		10			70			IPCC, 2009, p. 11
Israel					77	89.2	97	Herzog, 2000, pp. 134, 136
Kansas City	22	18	7	59	75	90	64	Perez, 1994, pp. 180, 183
New York City	43	32	36			64		Sviridoff & McElroy, 1989, pp. 45, 47
			32					Bartels & Silverman, 2005, p. 627
Philippines			69			32		De Guzman, 2008, p. 131

police regarding the complaints system (Hagger Johnson, 2010). The report notes that 61% of their 732 respondents had previously attempted to make their complaint directly to police before approaching the IPCC. The report states that this "suggests that many people who complain via the IPCC would rather their complaints were dealt with at force level" (Hagger Johnson, 2010, p. 10). Indeed, the mixed system provided to complainants includes the IPCC "act(ing) as a gateway to the complaints system by accepting complaints and passing them to the relevant appropriate authority" (Hagger Johnson, 2010, p. 15). The report notes that, in the 2009/2010 financial year, 74% of complainants agreed for their complaint to be forwarded in this manner. However, the results of the survey show that 72% of respondents were dissatisfied with police complaint handling. Further, the survey shows that only 37% of respondents who consented to their complaint being forwarded by the IPCC were satisfied with the way the IPCC handled the complaint. This would suggest that, although it might appear that complainants wish their complaint to be handled by police, in practice, they are not satisfied when this is done. However, for those respondents who did not allow the IPCC to forward their complaint to police, an even smaller proportion (20%) were satisfied with the IPCC's complaint handling. For all respondents, negative feedback highlighted issues over communication and customer service, with the level experienced not meeting expectations.

As noted, the IPCC has the ability to act as a "gateway" agency that handles complaints by forwarding them to the subject agency to investigate. The 2010 IPCC report cited previously includes data from a subset of interviews completed with survey respondents. The report highlights the disparate viewpoints of complainants who agree or disagree with their complaint being forwarded to the police to investigate. Quotes taken from the report (Hagger Johnson, 2010, p. 17) illustrate how "consenting" complainants understand that the subject agency must take responsibility for their complaint in order to improve (e.g., one respondent stated "Unless you [the IPCC] approach them [the police], how do they know?"), whereas "nonconsenting" complainants fear their complaint will not be handled objectively (e.g., a respondent stated that "No organisation, whether it be the police or anything else, should investigate itself when there's been a complaint. They should be independent").

Indeed, four of the surveys of mixed systems, representing the United States, Israel, and England and Wales, asked respondents their opinion regarding the independence of complaint investigations. All four surveys reported over 60% of respondents in support of independence. This was as high as 97% in the Israeli survey.

A further interesting comparison between views of internal and external police complaints handling systems is available from the jurisdiction of Portland, Oregon, in the United States. After the Independent Police Review

(IPR) Division of the Auditor's Office was established in 2001, complainant satisfaction surveys were sent to complainants who had experienced the former complaints handling of the Internal Affairs Division of the Portland Police Bureau and those who had filed complaints with the IPR (2003, 2009). Before the creation of the IPR, Portland's complaint handling system could be characterized as police dominated, whereas the IPR complaints handling system can be described as a mixed system. The IPR surveys showed improvement in satisfaction levels, with the movement away from the police-dominated system. Particularly, the proportion satisfied with the complaints process in general increased from 18.7% for the pre-IPR process to around one quarter of complainant respondents experiencing the IPR process in its first years. However, the proportion dissatisfied overall did not change substantially across the pre- and post-IPR samples. Complainants were also asked how satisfied they were with the fairness of the outcome received; whereas the proportion satisfied actually reduced slightly with the introduction of the IPR, the proportion dissatisfied did decrease from 73% pre-IPR to 65% and 67% in the 2002 and 2003 IPR process years, respectively (a larger proportion opted for the neutral "neither satisfied nor dissatisfied" response in relation to the IPR process than did for the pre-IPR process). The proportion of satisfied complainants increased for the IPR process, compared with the pre-IPR process, for all other measures, including the quality of interviews and communication, explanations about the complaints process, thoroughness, and efficiency.

Dissatisfaction with the IPR was detailed with qualitative survey responses in the IPR (2003) report. Issues raised tended to relate to the police handling of the complaint (once referred by IPR) and included perceptions of bias and not treating complaints seriously. Criticisms of the IPR process generally highlighted the lack of power of the system to produce change, particularly in police behavior, including the inability to enforce outcomes. Indeed, the report was able to highlight that satisfaction was linked to complaint outcome and noted several planned strategies for improving performance in this area, including greater communication with complainants regarding likely outcomes and increasing informal resolution options (discussed later in this chapter). The IPR continued to collect complainant survey data until 2009. Figure 4.1 shows that, over the full time period, satisfaction with both process and outcome increased, with process consistently showing higher levels of satisfaction than outcome (IPR, 2009). After 2009, the IPR decided that the response rate to the survey (less than 20%) was too low to justify its continuance (IPR, 2010, p. 22).

Independent Complaints Systems

Only one system, the Police Ombudsman for Northern Ireland (PONI), was considered to be fully independent for the purposes of this study. The

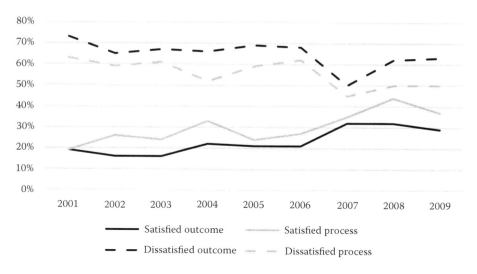

Figure 4.1 Summary of complainant satisfaction with process and outcome in Portland, pre-IPR (2001) and post-IPR (2002 onward).

PONI conducts annual surveys of complainants, 12 of which were available to review for this research and are summarized in Table 4.3. In comparison with the police-dominated and mixed systems, the independent system of the PONI receives consistent majority satisfaction. Over 50% of respondents express satisfaction with the system overall each year, although this has reduced somewhat in recent years, from 65% satisfied in 2009/2010 to a low of 50% in the most recent reporting period. The PONI (2012b) annual report

Table 4.3 Summary of Complainant Experiences in Independent Complaints Systems (Northern Ireland)

% Satisfied			Dissatisfied	
Process	Outcome	Overall	Overall	Source (and Survey Year)
		56		PONI, 2011, pp. 18–19, 2002/2003
		67		PONI, 2011, 2003/2004
70	40	58		PONI, 2011, 2004/2005
67	38	58		PONI, 2011, 2005/2006
74	40	62		PONI, 2011, 2006/2007
70	37	57		PONI, 2011, 2007/2008
68	42	59		PONI, 2011, 2008/2009
73	47	65		PONI, 2011, 2009/2010
69	41	59	31	PONI, 2011, 2010/2011
61	39	52	37	PONI, 2012a, p. 17, 2011/2012
62	37	52	39	PONI, 2014, pp. 22, 25, 2012/2013
60	39	50	38	PONI, 2014, pp. 22, 25, 2013/2014

for 2011/2012 notes contextual issues for the decrease in satisfaction in the form of public criticism and scrutiny of the independence of the governance and operations of the office.

> During the year its [PONI's] reputation and credibility became the subject of intense public scrutiny and saw its operational independence, its governance arrangements and its leadership openly questioned...The Senior Management team acknowledge that these events have damaged the confidence of some stakeholder groups; a fact clearly demonstrated in falling levels of complainant satisfaction. (PONI, 2012b, p. 4)

Respondents who offered comments in the latest survey on how the PONI service could be improved largely highlighted perceptions of bias in favor of police in complaint investigations, inadequate communication to complainants, and inadequate outcomes (PONI, 2014, pp. 12–13). Indeed, consistent with the results of other surveys of complaints systems previously noted, satisfaction with the outcome has been lower than satisfaction with the process. Satisfaction with the outcome of complaints has remained largely stable over the years, with a peak of 47% satisfied in 2009/2010. Satisfaction with the process has seen a particular decline since 2009/2010, when 73% of respondents were satisfied, to around only 60% in recent years. Satisfaction with the process has been calculated here from seven separate questions, which are detailed in Table 4.4. Consistently, the aspects that complainants find less satisfaction with are the overall time taken to resolve the complaint, the seriousness with which the complaint was treated, and the frequency of progress updates. Overall, though, the majority experience of the PONI seems to be

Table 4.4   Percentage of Complainant Satisfaction with Aspects of the Complaint Process in Northern Ireland

Aspect	2009/2010	2010/2011	2011/2012	2012/2013	2013/2014
How easy to understand correspondence	86%	84%	73%	75%	74%
Length of time to respond after incident reported	82%	78%	72%	71%	69%
Clarity of explanation of process	77%	72%	63%	66%	60%
Advice provided by staff	72%	68%	61%	59%	60%
Frequency of progress updates	67%	63%	55%	58%	54%
Seriousness with which complaint was treated	66%	63%	55%	55%	54%
Overall time to resolve complaint	60%	58%	53%	51%	49%

Source: PONI, 2014, p. 22.

a positive one, particularly when compared with those of police-dominated and mixed systems discussed previously.

Informal Resolution and Mediation

A consistent criticism of the systems described in the previous sections relates to the protracted nature of complaints investigations, particularly the unnecessary time and resources spent on formal investigations of relatively minor matters. Indeed, complainant satisfaction has been linked to the process of complaint handling; for example, the IPR Division in Portland noted that complainants were more satisfied with both process and outcome when their complaints were handled managerially as "service complaints" (IPR, 2003, p. 131). In response to these findings, IPR increased the number of matters dealt with as informal "service complaints" and implemented a mediation program (IPR, 2003). Although they did not formally survey the effects of this, the results of their annual complainant satisfaction surveys show that the proportion of satisfied complainants has increased since that time, particularly in relation to satisfaction with the outcome of their complaints (see Figure 4.1).

Eight surveys of complainants' experiences with informal resolution or mediation were identified. Informal resolution typically refers to a process of complaint handling that avoids a formal investigation, instead dealing with the matter with an administrative or managerial approach. This is usually adopted for less serious complaints, for example, behavior that would not result in disciplinary action even if proved or where allegations are unlikely to be substantiated. Complainants involved in informal resolution likely have contact with the subject officer's supervisor, who may offer an apology or explain that the officer will be counseled for his/her behavior. In comparison, mediation is a more formal process of resolution involving a trained mediator in a face-to-face meeting with, usually, both the complainant and subject officer present to discuss the issues and how it should be resolved (although, in practice, the subject officer's supervisor might appear in place of the officer himself/herself). Similar to informal resolution, such complaints would typically be less serious and result in an apology or some form of developmental management action.

Four of the identified surveys concerned informal (local) resolution with mixed results. Two of the surveys showed majority dissatisfaction. In England and Wales, just over half (51%) of complainants were dissatisfied with the police-managed "local resolution" program, compared with 41% who were satisfied (May, Hough, Herrington, & Warburton, 2007, p. 23). In Victoria, Australia, almost three-quarters (72%) of complainants whose matter was dealt with under a "Management Intervention Model" "rated the process as unsatisfactory" (Office of Police Integrity, 2008, p. 47). Interestingly, in Victoria, the majority (78%) of respondents reported that they did not actually have contact with the subject officer during the process, with many of them (51%) stating that they would have liked to have had contact. When asked to comment on potential improvements, survey respondents most frequently noted that complaints should be handled by an independent person, that the process could be quicker, and that complainants should be informed of the outcomes.

Although not a survey, a report by Hagger Johnson and Hipkin-Chastagnol (2011) looked at cases where complainants appealed to the IPCC in the United Kingdom after having been through the process of informal resolution. They similarly identified that, most commonly, complainants are dissatisfied with the informal resolution process or the outcome, particularly the amount of information provided in relation to these. For example, appellants stated that they had not been informed whether the agreed outcome of the resolution had actually taken place.

Positive results were found in the remaining two surveys, conducted in Northern Ireland and Queensland, Australia. A PONI evaluation of "police-led informal resolution" found that over half (52%) of complainants were satisfied that their complaint had been "successfully resolved" (PONI, 2005, p. 29). In Queensland, a survey by the CJC explored complainant satisfaction of "informal resolution" that used police officers trained by civilian Alternative Dispute Resolution specialists. Almost twice as many complainants were satisfied with the informal resolution process compared with formal investigation (76% compared with 40%, respectively), and more than twice as many were satisfied with the outcome (60% compared with 28%; CJC, 1994, pp. 60–62). Exploration of the reasons for the increased satisfaction rates for informal resolution highlighted that resolution allows a broader range of possible outcomes and that these are more achievable due to the lower standard of proof required. Resolution was also "quicker than formal investigation, the complainant is kept more informed and has more opportunity to express his or her views" (CJC, 1994, p. 62).

Four surveys of mediation were identified. In Calgary, Canada, perceptions of mediation were negative, reporting that "The majority of complainants offered mediation refused it and cited…a lack of faith that mediation would result in a positive outcome for them" (Calgary Police Commission, 1999, p. 93). Unfortunately, the report does not detail the experiences of those who accepted mediation. The remaining three studies of mediation showed positive outcomes. Bartels and Silverman (2005) highlighted the positive experience of complainants regarding the quality of treatment in mediation compared with standard investigation. Their survey of persons whose complaint was either investigated or mediated by the New York City Civilian Complaint Review Board showed that "Eighty-one percent of the complainants felt that the real issues of their complaint were discussed in their mediation session, compared with 32 percent of those who participated in regular full investigation" (Bartels & Silverman, 2005, p. 627).

In the United Kingdom, a study by Young, Hoyle, Cooper, and Hill (2005) compared complainants' perceptions of informal resolution with "restorative" cases involving "a face-to-face meeting between complainant(s) and police officers(s) in the presence of a trained facilitator" (p. 285). Although most often the facilitator was a police officer, in a few cases where complainants objected to this, an external person was used (Young et al., 2005, p. 291). Almost twice as many complainants were satisfied with the restorative approach compared with the informal resolution (61% compared with 33%, respectively). Whereas fewer than a third of complainants in the restorative group were dissatisfied (28%), in the informal resolution group, more complainants were actually dissatisfied (45%) than were satisfied (Young et al., 2005, p. 303). Finally, in Denver (United States), mediation conducted through "an independent mediation vendor" showed even greater success, with seven times more complainants satisfied with mediation compared with the "nonmediation" sample (79% compared with 11%, respectively), and nine times more complainants satisfied with the outcome in mediated cases than in nonmediated cases (63% compared with 7%, respectively; Schaible, De Angelis, Wolf, & Rosenthal, 2013, p. 640).

Discussion

This chapter reviewed 46 surveys of complainants' views and experiences of complaints systems, which can be differentiated as police dominated, independent, or mixed. The results of the surveys have been contextualized with additional research of complainants' opinions of complaints handling. It is clear from the results that two main factors affect the experience of complainants when making a complaint: the degree to which the handling of the complaint is seen to be independent of the body complained about—and thus impartial—and the quality of the treatment received or level of customer service.

The surveys detailed in this chapter provide a strong case that agency/investigator independence (or complainant perceptions of independence) affects complainant satisfaction. Comparisons across surveys of different types of complaint handling systems show consistently higher rates of satisfaction for the independent system of the PONI compared with both mixed and police-dominated systems. Further, within the surveys of the PONI, a drop in satisfaction rates was attributed to a reduction in confidence regarding the office's independence following public criticism of the way it handled historic cases related to "The Troubles" (PONI, 2012b). In addition, surveys that provided complainants with the opportunity to voice their thoughts on whether police complaints should be handled by an independent body most frequently showed support for the idea, and dissatisfaction with systems often stemmed from feeling that investigators were biased toward police.

As noted earlier, the main driver of the establishment of independent complaints handling bodies or oversight agencies was the perception that internal complaint handling would be biased, and thus, to achieve fairness and adequate scrutiny, investigators should be independent. The results here therefore support the view that this driver is indeed valid as it directly affects the experience of a key stakeholder group—complainants. Thus, the results may be unsurprising but nevertheless raise questions as to why not all complaint handling systems have achieved true independence; only the PONI could be described as truly independent, with all others still relying on internal complaint handling to some extent.

Perceptions of bias in the system affected complainants' experiences of both the process and the outcome, which, although linked, were clearly separate issues. Interestingly, complainants could be dissatisfied with the outcome but more satisfied with the process, particularly if they felt they had been treated fairly. However, if complainants perceive the process to be biased, then they will likely view the outcome as biased too. In some systems, complainants have the option of appealing to an independent body if they believe this to be the case (e.g., in England and Wales). However, this cannot be described as ideal, as it draws out an already lengthy process, with independent reinvestigations often concluding that the original body should further investigate the matter (Hagger Johnson and Hipkin-Chastagnol, 2011).

Related to the independence of the agency, but distinct from it, is the second area of importance to complainants' experiences—the quality of treatment received. As noted previously, perceptions of treatment can be related to general perceptions of agency independence. However, specific experiences of treatment by individual investigators are often more directly important for the complainants' overall satisfaction with the process. Consistent problems noted in the surveys involved communication, timeliness, and neglect or apathy.

The surveys show that communication is particularly crucial to complainants' satisfaction with the process, both the extent of communication and the manner with which they are dealt. Complainants were often dissatisfied that they received little response to their complaint, few or no updates throughout the often lengthy time taken to investigate the complaint, and often no communication as to the outcome. Complainants were therefore largely left in the dark as to whether their complaint was being taken seriously or ignored. With most complainants wanting to either be heard or for action to be taken so that their complaint is not repeated in the future (CJC, 1994), it is clear that this experience would fall well below the standard expected.

The quality of treatment of the complainant by the complaint handling agency sends a strong message as to the authenticity of the process. Complainants who perceived that their complaints were not taken seriously had little respect for the seriousness of the system, whereas complainants appreciated staff who were polite, helpful, and respectful, and this seemed to temper disappointing outcomes. The aspects of treatment that complainants' comments highlighted as important echo the concept of "procedural justice." Procedural justice is demonstrated by the fairness of decision making and the fairness of treatment received from a decision maker (Murphy, 2015; Sunshine & Tyler, 2003), particularly where decision makers demonstrate neutrality, respect, and trustworthy motives and give the recipient "voice" (Lind & Tyler, 1988). Interestingly, police use of procedural justice in their encounters with members of the public has been linked to public trust in police (Murphy, Mazerolle, & Bennett, 2014) and intentions to cooperate with police (Sunshine & Tyler, 2003). Extending the use of procedural justice to encounters with members of the public who make complaints is therefore likely to be particularly important for maintaining good public relationships. Demonstration of procedural justice in the complaints handling context would entail the complaint investigator demonstrating that they are not biased to either the complainant or subject officer (neutrality), being polite and respectful of all parties, demonstrating the independence of the system (trustworthy motives), and providing complainants with the opportunity to discuss their complaint issue and their thoughts regarding the outcome. The positive effects of procedural justice in complaint handling are also likely to apply to the treatment of the subject officers (see the next chapter) as well as complainants.

It is clear that procedural justice plays an important role in the complainants' experience of the police complaints systems, regardless of which agency is handling their complaint. Thus, although *who* investigates the complaint is important, in terms of their reputation for independence, *how* agencies handle complaints is crucial to achieving complainant satisfaction. Mediation, at least for less serious complaints, seems to provide a possible optimum solution to both the question of who should deal with complaints and how. The few surveys of mediation experiences available suggest that mediation can offer complainants an experience that more greatly reflects their expectations and can deliver procedural justice, particularly providing voice to complainants. Negative experiences of mediation tended to reflect distrust of the process (or motives of the mediator). To produce maximum satisfaction, mediation should involve an independent trained facilitator who can demonstrate impartiality and who provides the opportunity for both complainants and subject officers to voice their issues in a neutral and respectful environment.

Conclusion

Key issues for ensuring complainant satisfaction with complaint handling lie in the independence of the system and the quality of treatment received by the complainant. Complainants want to know that they are heard, taken seriously, and treated impartially and that the process has an effect, particularly that things will be improved in the future. Often, it is about who is handling the complaint as much as how, with a general perception that complaints must be handled independently to ensure integrity of the process and the outcome. Regardless of agency, or system, though, fairness of treatment was important. Mediation, at least for less serious complaints, seems to provide a possible optimum solution to complaint handling, providing both independence, through a trained mediator, and a procedurally fair process.

References

Bartels, E. C., & Silverman, E. B. (2005). An exploratory study of the New York City Civilian Complaint Review Board mediation program. *Policing: An International Journal of Police Strategies and Management, 28*(4), 619–630.

Bobb, M. J., Buchner, B. R., DeBlieck, S., Jacobson, M. P., Henderson, N. J., & Ortiz, C. W. (2006). *Assessing police–community relations in Pasadena, California.* New York: Vera Institute of Justice.

Brown, D. (1987). *The police complaints procedure: A survey of complainants' views.* London: Home Office.

Calgary Police Commission. (1999). *Report.* Calgary: Citizen Complaints Review Committee.

CJC. (1994). *Informal complaint resolution in the Queensland Police Service: An evaluation.* Brisbane: CJC.

CJC. (1995). *Ethical conduct and discipline in the Queensland Police Service: The views of recruits, first year constables and experienced officers.* Brisbane: Criminal Justice Commission.

CJC. (2000). *Public attitudes towards the QPS.* Brisbane: CJC.

CMC. (2009). *Public perceptions of the Queensland Police Service: Findings from the 2008 Public Attitudes Survey.* Brisbane: Crime and Misconduct Commission.

CMC. (2011). *Public perceptions of the Queensland Police Service.* Brisbane: Crime and Misconduct Commission.

De Angelis, J. (2008). *Assessing the impact of the Office of the Independent Monitor on complainant and officer satisfaction.* Denver: Office of the Independent Monitor.

De Angelis, J., & Kupchik, A. (2006). *Measuring complainant and officer satisfaction with the Denver police complaint process.* Denver, CO: Office of the Independent Monitor.

De Guzman, M. C. (2008). Complainants' views about civilian review of the police: A study of the Philippines. *Asian Journal of Criminology, 3*(2), 117–138.

Ethical Standards Department. (1999). *Client satisfaction survey.* Melbourne: Victoria Police.

Fraser, O. (2009). *Complainants' satisfaction research report.* Glasgow: Police Complaints Commissioner for Scotland.

Grace, K., & Bucke, T. (2009). *Public annoyance and complaints about the police: Findings from the 2006/07 British crime survey.* London: Independent Police Complaints Commission.

Hagger Johnson, H. (2010). *Direct complaints survey: A survey seeking feedback from people who complain directly to the IPCC.* London: IPCC.

Hagger Johnson, H., & Hipkin-Chastagnol, C. (2011). *Learning from appeals: A statistical and thematic analysis of appeals upheld in 2009/10.* London: IPCC.

Herzog, S. (2000). Evaluating the new Civilian Complaints Board in Israel. In A. Goldsmith & C. Lewis (Eds.), *Civilian oversight of policing.* Oxford: Hart.

IPCC. (2009). *IPCC investigations: A survey seeking feedback from complainants and police personnel.* London: IPCC.

IPR. (2003). *Annual report 2003.* Portland: Office of the City Auditor.

IPR. (2009). *Annual report 2009.* Portland: Office of the City Auditor.

IPR. (2010). *Annual report 2010.* Portland: Office of the City Auditor.

Landau, T. (1994). *Public complaints against the police: A view from complainants.* Toronto: University of Toronto.

Lind, E. A., & Tyler, T. R. (1988). *The social psychology of procedural justice.* New York: Plenum Press.

Luna, E., & Walker, S. (1997). *A report on the oversight mechanisms of the Albuquerque Police Department.* Omaha: Albuquerque City Council.

Maguire, M., & Corbett, C. (1991). *A study of the police complaints system.* London: HMSO.

May, T., Hough, M., Herrington, V., & Warburton, H. (2007). *Local resolution: The views of police officers and complainants.* London: IPCC.

McDevitt, D. J., Farrell, A., & Andresen, W. C. (2005). *Enhancing citizen participation in the review of complaints and use of force in the Boston Police Department.* Boston, MA: Institute on Race and Justice.

Murphy, K. (2015). Does procedural justice matter to youth? Comparing adults' and youths' willingness to collaborate with police. *Policing and Society, 25*(1), 53–76.

Murphy, T., Mazerolle, L., & Bennett, S. (2014). Promoting trust in police. *Policing & Society, 24*(4), 405–424.

Office of Police Integrity. (2008). *Improving Victorian policing services through effective complaint handling.* Melbourne: Office of Police Integrity.

Perez, D. W. (1994). *Common sense about police review.* Philadelphia, PA: Temple University Press.

PONI. (2005). *An evaluation of police-led informal resolution of police complaints in Northern Ireland: The complainants' perspective.* Belfast: Police Ombudsman for Northern Ireland.

PONI. (2011). *Annual report on complainant satisfaction with services provided by the Police Service Ombudsman's Office in Northern Ireland 2010/11.* Belfast: Police Ombudsman for Northern Ireland.

PONI. (2012a). *Annual Statistical Bulletin 2011/12.* Belfast: Police Ombudsman for Northern Ireland.

PONI. (2012b). *Annual report and accounts for the year ended 31 March 2012*. Belfast: Police Ombudsman for Northern Ireland.

PONI. (2014). *Annual report on complainant satisfaction with services provided by the Police Service Ombudsman's Office in Northern Ireland 2013/14*. Belfast: Police Ombudsman for Northern Ireland.

Porter, L. E., & Prenzler, T. (2012). *Police integrity management in Australia: Global lessons for combating police misconduct*. Boca Raton, FL: CRC Press—Taylor & Francis.

Prenzler, T., Allard, T., Curry, S., & Macintyre, S. (2010). Complaints against police: The Complainants' experience. *The Journal of Criminal Justice Research, 1*(1), 1–18.

Ridgeway, G., Schell, T. L., Gifford, B., Saunders, J., Turner, S., Riley, K. J., & Dixon, T. L. (2009). *Police–community relations in Cincinnati*. Santa Monica, CA: RAND Corporation.

Schaible, L. M., De Angelis, J., Wolf, B., & Rosenthal, R. (2013). Denver's citizen/police complaint mediation program: Officer and complainant satisfaction. *Criminal Justice Policy Review, 24*(5), 626–650.

Strathcona Research Group. (2006). *Appendix F: Report on the core area awareness survey conducted for the review of the police complaint process in British Columbia*. Vancouver, BC: Author.

Sunshine, J., & Tyler, T. (2003). The role of procedural justice and legitimacy in shaping public support for policing. *Law and Society Review, 37*, 513–547.

Sviridoff, M., & McElroy, J. E. (1989). *Processing complaints against police in New York City: The complainant's perspective*. New York: Vera Institute of Justice.

Waters, I., & Brown, K. (2000). Police complaints and the complainants' experience. *British Journal of Criminology, 40*(4), 617–638.

Young, R., Hoyle, C., Cooper, K., & Hill, R. (2005). Informal resolution of the complaints against the police: A quasi-experimental test of restorative justice. *Criminal Justice, 5*(3), 279–317.

Police Views on Processing Complaints against Police

5

TIM PRENZLER

Contents

This chapter examines the views of police about how complaints should be managed. Police have an obvious stake in the complaints and discipline process as the subject of complaints. At the same time, police can also act as complainants (see Chapter 4), and they frequently serve as investigators and adjudicators of complaints. Outside any personal stake they have in complaints, they have both direct and indirect insider experiences, with knowledge and insights that should be considered in system design. This chapter covers 37 studies of police attitudes and experiences. The findings challenge a conventional notion of police opposition to the independent investigation of complaints. In particular, the chapter highlights the achievements of the independent Police Ombudsman for Northern Ireland in generating high satisfaction rates from police participants, particularly in officer views of the fairness and impartiality of the process. The chapter also highlights the potential value to police of mediation as an alternative to both formal adversarial processes and informal resolution.

Background

In 1997, in the United States, two police union leaders and a political consultant published a book titled *Police Association Power, Politics, and Confrontation: A Guide for the Successful Police Labor Leader*. There was little in the book on civilian oversight of police, except for the inclusion of a case study of union action in challenging moves toward oversight. In one chapter, "The 1992 Police Civilian Review Board Controversy in San Jose," the past-president of the San Jose Police Officers' Association described how his union fought down moves by the local Bar Association, a student group, and other activists to introduce a civilian review board in the wake of the Rodney King beating in Los Angeles and mounting concerns about police violence in the United States (Fehr, 1997). The proposal was for a board that would investigate excessive force complaints, hold open hearings, and have subpoena powers to compel testimony by officers.

The Association considered the proposal "a clear threat to the well-being of the Police Association membership" (Fehr, 1997, p. 260). It aligned itself with the police chief in total opposition to the proposal and to an alternate proposal for an auditor. The chief reputedly believed that "the department's internal affairs process was beyond reproach, and that if there was civilian review of department procedure, policy and discipline, then there would be no need for a police chief" and threatened to resign if a board were put in place (Fehr, 1997, p. 262). The Association also initiated a campaign, informing all officers of the need for action, lobbying community leaders for support, and promoting their viewpoint in the press. The council held an all-day public meeting to determine the issue, and approximately 100 police officers attended in a show of force. The president argued that the department had successfully policed itself for many years and that there was absolutely no case for change. He also argued that the proposed inquisitorial model violated officers' rights to the confidentiality of their personnel records. The Council supported the appointment of an auditor with no real powers. The president's verdict was that, "In summary, we came out ahead of the curve in the civilian review fight" (Fehr, 1997, p. 265).

The uncompromising nature of the San Jose Police Association's campaign on the issue of civilian oversight has been repeated many times in police history. Police opposition—including court action, rallies, and demonstrations—has contributed to the closure of review boards at different times, including in New York City, Philadelphia, and Rochester in the United States and Victoria, Australia (de Guzman, 2004; Freckelton, 1991). Police opposition has also helped weaken oversight, as in the San Jose case, with review boards or auditors often so enfeebled they are essentially doomed to failure, adding to their lack of credibility (de Guzman, 2004; USCCR, 2000).

Opposition has been apparent across all police ranks. One of the most high-profile peak bodies, The International Association of Chiefs of Police (IACP), has offered, at best, a grudging accommodation of civilian review subject to levels of public support and perceived or real police misconduct (IACP, 2000).

Wells and Schafer (2007) describe four main objections by police to external oversight: "(1) citizen oversight is not needed, (2) citizen involvement in this intimate police matter contradicts police professionalism, (3) citizens are not qualified for oversight responsibilities, and (4) citizen oversight uniquely compromises police work" (p. 15). The IACP (2000) has also listed concerns of police executives in more detail, as follows (p. 6):

- Officers become wary of review and avoid conflict in order to reduce potential allegations.
- When citizen review first begins there may be a marked increase of complaints, especially from critics of a police agency.
- Citizen members of a review board may not have a law enforcement background and fail to understand proper police policy and procedure. Accordingly, they may not judge officer actions correctly.
- Citizen review may lead to a chief losing control over the agency discipline process.
- Citizen review/recommendations may promote police policies that cannot or are too difficult to be implemented. Inability to implement recommendations could degrade the public view of the agency.
- Citizen review may create animosity between the officers and the public.
- The often political nature of citizen review may introduce partisan politics into law enforcement decision-making.
- Costs of review mechanisms, both financial and human, may burden the department.

Despite what may appear as police solidarity on this issue, there is evidence of contrary views, and some of the more sophisticated arguments, at a policy level, come from police industrial associations. Police unions and members can be concerned about public opinion, and they can be motivated to support independent processes where there is scandal and significant mistrust of police. Hence, in New South Wales, during the large-scale royal commission into police corruption (1994–1997), the Police Association (1995) developed a policy of complete externalization of investigations as a way of removing any doubt about bias and cover-ups. Within a two-tiered scheme of complaints, the Association recommended that lower-level disciplinary matters be returned to police once the credibility of police management was reestablished. In another example, after the Ramparts Scandal in Los Angeles, in a move described as "remarkable," the Los Angeles Police Protective League alleged that the reform program did not go far enough in regard to independent investigation and adjudication of complaints (Barry, 2000, p. 1; LAPPL, 2000). The Police Federation of Australia has also advocated the view that "external review of police agencies is absolutely essential" (Alexander, 1999, p. 2). However, this was qualified by claims that existing oversight agencies were overly legalistic, in that they allegedly focused excessively on individual guilt or innocence without due regard for the need to understand the provocations of police work. Consequently, the Federation expressed a preference for responses focused on improving behavior, with adequate avenues of appeal regarding decisions against police. Police unions have also indicated support for external investigations subject to the same standard being applied across public sector agencies (Prenzler, 2011). Of course, self-interest may be part of the equation if unions and rank-and-file officers see external processes as potentially weaker and more easily subverted than internal processes.

Chapter 3 in this book included the results of a public opinion survey on internal and external complaints mechanisms sponsored by the Police Federation of England and Wales. The survey included police officers and was designed to test support for the Federation's policy, established in 1981, of support for independent investigations. Public confidence had been put forward as a major criterion, given the many scandals besetting British policing. In a 1997 statement, the Federation argued that the complaints system must be:

> seen by the public to be wholly independent of the police service... The fact that police officers undertake the investigations, albeit under the direct supervision of PCA (Police Complaints Authority) members, lays the system open to allegations of partiality and cover-up. (Police Federation, 1997, p. 5; see also http://www.polfed.org/aboutus/179.aspx)

The editor of the Federation's journal also pointed to unfairness and a number of ironies in the limited review model in operation at the time, and proposed independence for all-round improvement:

> This is not the first time that the Police Federation has called for a wholly independent complaints system. In 1983, when the Police and Criminal Evidence Legislation was going through Parliament, we sought such a change, arguing that tinkering with the system by grafting on an independent supervisory arm while retaining police investigators, would not satisfy the critics. What was needed, we said, was a root and branch change involving complete openness and fairness to police and complainants alike. The chief officers, and most of those who had been inveighing against the complaints system, said

that the Federation was simply trying to protect the villains in the service, because they would be able to pull the wool over the eyes of outside investigators. Today's chief officers, including those who are wringing their hands over their alleged impotence in the face of corruption, would still defend the retention of the police-only investigations. The Police Complaints Authority baulks at such a change, perhaps because it knows that it would then have to take full responsibility, instead of constantly complaining that it is obstructed by manipulative lawyers.

The current demands of the Association of Chief Police Officers (ACPO), for shifting the burden of proof to the lower standard of civil cases, and for powers of summary dismissal, in our view strengthens the case for taking the system out of the hands of chief officers and putting it with a new, publicly accountable, independent authority. Conceding ACPO's demands might well result in speedier justice in a small number of cases, but the risk of injustice towards innocent police officers would be increased considerably. (Editorial, 1997, p. 5)

The statement clearly demonstrates a degree of self-interest, albeit reasonable, regarding the potential for oppressive use of dismissal powers by senior officers. An external agency might offer greater procedural fairness. The view is, nonetheless, unusual historically. As Reiner (1991, p. 215) observed:

In 1981 the Police Federation, the rank-and-file representative body, came out in support of a completely independent system for the investigation of complaints against police. This was a remarkable *volte face* after years of opposing such a scheme, and found the Federation uniting with the Law Society and the National Council for Civil Liberties ... Since then the Federation has been able to maintain the stance of support for completely independent investigation, while vigorously attacking the half-a-loaf of independence which exists in the shape of the PCA.

Reiner (1991) went on to confirm that it was opposition from the ACPO that was "crucial to maintaining the status quo by preventing independence from being the favoured policy of the major bodies of professional opinion" (p. 215).

The examples given in the previous paragraphs indicate that "police officers are more open to the idea of independent investigation than may have been previously thought" (Liberty, 2000, p. 5). The remainder of this chapter is concerned with examining police opinion on complaints and discipline, and civilian oversight, in greater depth. Police are key participants in the complaints process, with a great deal at stake, including their livelihoods, careers, and reputations. As noted, many have direct experience of complaints and discipline systems, and others have opinions informed from insider sources of evidence. Their views should therefore be given serious consideration.

As with the previous two chapters, keyword searches were conducted of criminological databases and the Internet, with a view to identifying as many surveys as possible of police officers concerning their views and experiences of different systems. Three areas of focus were developed: (1) general views about what type of agency should investigate or manage complaints; (2) experiences across three types of systems—police dominated, mixed, and independent; and (3) experiences with alternative dispute resolution formats.

General Views on the Best Agency to Investigate Complaints

As with the previous chapters, this part of the study focused on surveys concerned with the concept of complaint "investigation," keeping in mind that "investigate" appears to imply the key function of gathering evidence as well as adjudication. Four sets of results were identified from three surveys that included a general question about views across the spectrum of internal, external, and mixed systems. The results, all from England and Wales, summarized in Table 5.1, showed a general preference for internal systems, but with some solid support for external and also strong support for mixed in one case.

In England and Wales, Reiner (1991) interviewed 40 of 43 chief constables across a range of issues, including complaints and discipline. Under the system at the time, chief constables had primary responsible for adjudicating complaints, occasionally sitting "alongside two Police Complaints Authority

Table 5.1 Police Views Across the Internal–External Spectrum for Investigations of Complaints

Location	% Support			Qualifier	Source
	Internal	External	Mixed/Both[a]		
England and Wales	0	30	70	Chief constables	Reiner, 1991, p. 215
England and Wales	"Just over half"	"Almost half"	[b]	Investigated officers	Maguire & Corbett, 1991, p. 70
England and Wales	"A majority"	"About one-third"	[b]	Investigating officers	Maguire & Corbett, 1991, p. 71
England and Wales	44.8	33.3	19.9		Electoral Reform Ballot Services, 1997, p. 9

[a] Review or oversight body.
[b] Categories not asked.

members in those rare instances where the PCA directs that a disciplinary tribunal be held" (Reiner, 1991, p. 214). The large majority of interviewees also had extensive experience in managing the complaints investigation process in their previous roles as deputy chief constables. In addition, the group constituted the ACPO which, as noted in the Background section, successfully opposed Police Federation support for independent processing of complaints. It was not surprising, therefore, that Reiner found that 70% of chief constables supported the existing mixed system—although one largely dominated by police. Some expressed the view that the system worked because it was tough on police misconduct and that Federation support for independence was motivated by a perceived easier process for unethical police.

In Reiner's (1991) study, the 30% of chief constables who saw problems in the existing system and favored external investigations were divided equally between those concerned about the lack of public confidence and those concerned that complaints management generated excessive bureaucracy and distraction from core tasks. "Despite this strong vote of confidence in existing arrangements, only a bare majority (52 per cent) rejected the idea of a completely independent system… Nearly a third (30 percent) supported a completely independent system, while 18 per cent were undecided, seeing strong arguments either way" (Reiner, 1991, p. 215).

Also in Britain, the study by Maguire and Corbett (1991) of the police complaints system at the time, with oversight by the PCA, included 50 interviews with police who had experienced the system and 19 officers who conducted investigations. Support for internal investigations—"just over half" and "a majority," respectively—was related to beliefs about the importance of insider knowledge in having sympathy for the difficulties of police work. At the same time, many of the "almost half" of investigated officers supporting external investigations felt that independence would give the system greater credibility, as did the third of investigating officers. In addition, among investigated officers, "about 60 per cent admitted the existence of something like a 'code of silence' among junior officers" (Maguire & Corbett, 1991, p. 71).

Table 5.1 includes a survey sponsored by the Police Federation of England and Wales. (As noted in Chapter 3, the survey included citizen views.) The Federation had campaigned in favor of independent investigations but sought to clarify its stance by surveying the public and officers. The Market Research Department of the Electoral Reform Ballot Service was contracted to conduct the survey in 1997. A key question was, "In which of the following methods of investigation of complaints against police officers would *you, as a police officer*, have the greatest confidence" (Electoral Reform Ballot Services, 1997, p. 9). A questionnaire was posted to approximately 16,000 officers across 43 police forces, with a response rate of 57%. The sample of 9,109 officers was made up of 75% constables, 17% sergeants, and 8% inspectors and chief inspectors, with 50% having 15 or more years of service. The results showed that 44.8% of respondents expressed "greatest confidence" in "police them-selves," and 33.3% in "an independent body," with 19.9% reporting "equal confidence" and 1.9% holding "no view" (Electoral Reform Ballot Services, 1997, p. 9). Responses were fairly evenly distributed across respondents, with longer serving officers having slightly greater confidence in an independent body. For example, 39.1% of those with 15 or more years of service expressed faith in an independent body and 39.9% of the same group expressed faith in police (Electoral Reform Ballot Services, 1997, p. 10).

In addition, the survey asked officers, "Which of the following methods of investigation of complaints against police officers do you believe would give greater *public confidence*?" (Electoral Reform Ballot Services, 1997, p. 12). Investigation by "an independent body" was supported by 84.6%, with only 6.9% expressing support for "police themselves," 7.0% reporting "equal confidence in both," and 1.5% having no view (Electoral Reform Ballot Services, 1997, p. 12). Again, the results were fairly evenly distributed, but with a trend toward independence by rank. An independent body was sup-ported by 82.7% of constables, 89.4% of sergeants, 91.8% of inspectors, and 93.6% of chief inspectors. Increased age and years of service showed a similar upward trend in support for independence.

Police Views Limited to Civilian Review

Six surveys were located that asked about police views on civilian oversight without including a fully external option. A U.S. survey of 65 officers across a range of police departments put forward the statement, "A good means of regulating police conduct is using citizen review boards" (Hunter, 1999, p. 162). The results showed that 41.5% of respondents agreed, 41.6% dis-agreed, and 16.9% were neutral. Also in the United States, a national study of police attitudes to abuse of authority, based on a telephone survey, included a question about how to reduce the problem (Weisburd, Greenspan, Hamilton, Williams, & Bryant, 2000, p. 7):

> When asked about the effectiveness of different institutional procedures for addressing abuses of authority, most considered internal affairs units effec-tive (78.6 percent). A much smaller percentage (37.8 percent) considered citi-zen review boards an effective way to prevent police misconduct. [Multiple responses were included.]

Results by race showed that 69.8% of Black officers, compared with 33.3% of White officers, saw citizen review boards as effective (Weisburd et al., 2000, p. 10). The researchers interpreted this as evidence, along with other results, of Black officers' "faith in their community" (Weisburd et al., 2000, p. 9).

In an Israeli survey, Herzog (2001) surveyed police accused of excessive force and investigating officers in the oversight agency the Machash. For the present study, the agency was categorized as mixed, although it was border-line police dominated, because investigators were seconded, or "on loan," from the police. Herzog called it "an intermediate model" (p. 444). A questionnaire was developed about accused officers' experiences with the system, including a question about the "desirability of civilian review" (Herzog, 2001, p. 451). A random sample of officers accused of excessive force (300 of approximately 1,000) was mailed a questionnaire, with a response rate of 46%. Of these, 62.3% considered civilian review "desirable" in dealing with excessive force complaints, whereas 30.7% deemed it "undesirable" and 6.9% were uncertain. Herzog also surveyed all 37 investigating officers, with a 100% response rate. Of this group, 94.6% expressed support for civilian review in excessive force cases, 89.2% thought it was more efficient than the previous purely internal system, and 81.1% believed it provided a deterrent to excessive force (Herzog, 2001, p. 451).

In another U.S. study, Wells and Schafer (2007) surveyed officers in the Carbondale (Illinois) Police Department and the Southern Illinois University Carbondale campus police in 2003. Results were not disaggregated at the request of the two organizations. The survey was initiated as part of the establishment of a new Human Relations Commission to oversee police after years of conflict with students and minorities. Self-complete anonymous questionnaires were distributed to 90 officers, with 76 (84%) responding. Only 1% supported the view that "a citizen oversight committee should investigate citizen complaints against officers" (Wells & Schafer, 2007, p. 13). Furthermore, only 3% supported a committee recommending sanctions, 13% supported a committee reviewing findings of police investigations, and 11% thought they helped prevent misconduct, whereas 88% agreed that citizen oversight committees "do little to improve the quality of complaint investigation," 78% agreed that they "make it harder for officers to do their job," 83% agreed they are "biased against officers," and 82% felt "they allow citizens to review matters they do not understand" (Wells & Schafer, pp. 13 and 15–17).

A 2009 survey of police in Los Angeles found that approximately 29% of "nonsupervisors" and 39% of supervisors agreed that "the Inspector General gives the (police) disciplinary system greater integrity" (Stone, Foglesong, & Cole, 2009, p. 57). This had changed slightly from a 1999 survey, which found support at 34% and 35%, respectively.

Kang and Nalla (2011) asked South Korean police officers their views about civilian oversight as part of a larger survey conducted during the officers' attendance at national officer training courses in 2008. A return rate of 62% was achieved, with 406 completed questionnaires obtained from

650 distributed. The main findings were as follows (Kang & Nalla, 2011, p. 184):

- 36.3% agreed that "overall, the idea of a citizen oversight program is good," whereas 27.1% disagreed and 36.6% were not sure;
- 35.1% agreed that "the existence of Civilian Review Boards will increase more positive opinion among citizens," whereas 22.2% disagreed and 42.7% were unsure; and
- 37.2% agreed that "the existence of CRBs will fortify more positive police relationships with local community members," with 37.2% disagreeing and 40.3% unsure.

Police Experiences of Complaint Investigations

This section is concerned with how police have experienced different types of agency investigations: police dominated, mixed, and independent (see Chapter 4 on complainants). Surveys were included if it was evident that the respondents had, in general, been subject to a formal investigative process. Experiences of informal resolution and mediation are covered in the section following this.

Police-Dominated Systems

There were seven surveys regarding police experiences in police-dominated complaints and discipline systems, as shown in Table 5.2. The results were highly variable. Three surveys showed high satisfaction rates between 70% and 76%—two surveys in Queensland and one in Pasadena. The remaining four surveys showed fairly divided results—around the 30%–45% mark for both satisfied and dissatisfied.

Only two surveys included answers to additional questions that provided clues about reasons for satisfaction rates. In the first Queensland study, with high satisfaction rates, only 15.7% of officers in the sample reported the complaint as substantiated (Criminal Justice Commission, 1994, pp. 69–76). In addition:

- 34.9% felt the time taken to complete the investigation was either "very quick" or "reasonable";
- 64.5% thought it took "a little too long" or "much too long";
- 83.7% felt the investigator was thorough;
- only 15.8% thought the investigation was superficial or deliberately aimed at avoiding the truth;

Table 5.2 Summary of Police Experiences in Police-Dominated Complaints Systems

Location	% Satisfied			% Dissatisfied			Source
	Process	Outcome	Overall	Process	Outcome	Overall	
Queensland[a]	76.0	67.6		23.9	31.9		Criminal Justice Commission, 1994, p. 76
Queensland[a]			70.4			29.6	Criminal Justice Commission, 1995, p. A-2
Victoria (Australia)	39	38		42	41		Ethical Standards Department, 1999, pp. 22–23
Boston	45.5	27.3	36.3	45.4	45.5	63.7	McDevitt, Farrell, & Andresen, 2005, p. 69
Denver	45.9	48.6	11.6	29.9	34.8	63.7	De Angelis & Kupchik, 2006, p. 19
Pasadena			75			18	Bobb et al., 2006, p. 50
Victoria (Australia)	36.4	25.9		39.3	36.2		CAPPE, 2008, p. 17

[a] Officers with complaints "investigated by Queensland Police Service."

- 42.6% felt very or fairly informed and 57.3% felt fairly or very uninformed; and
- 85.7% felt they were given "sufficient opportunity" to express their views compared with 14.3% who disagreed.

The negative results in the Denver survey were reflected in more detailed views about the system, as follows (De Angelis & Kupchik, 2006, pp. 18–19):

- 72.8% of officers with complaints believed "the complaint process is biased in favour of citizens";
- 93.8% believed that "most citizen complaints are frivolous";
- Only 20.3% felt that "officers' basic rights are well protected within the complaint process";
- 65.9% felt the final decision was not made within a reasonable time frame;
- 46.6% were satisfied that sufficient information was obtained; and
- only 28.0% were satisfied that the police department considered their views.

Reference should also be made to a 2014 report, *Perspectives on the Disciplinary System of the LAPD*, based on focus groups involving more than 500 sworn and unsworn staff. Results were not quantified, but overall, the feedback was extremely negative. Focus group participants alleged that there was an excessive concern with complaint investigations, and a key downside was that supervisors were overly engaged in investigations and distracted from frontline management. A lack of transparency was also alleged, particularly in regard to reasons for disciplinary decisions. Leaking of information by investigators was identified as a major problem. The main fault, however, lay in an alleged double standard favoring senior officers and their associates, for example (Special Assistant for Constitutional Policing, 2014, p. 7):

- The higher the rank, the more misgivings are overlooked by the Department
- Patrol officers are disciplined and treated differently than the rest of the Department
- Friends and family members of higher ranking officers are protected from discipline …
- People who sit on Board of Rights hearings are beholden to the Chief of Police, which means they cannot be fair or impartial.

Mixed Systems

Six sets of results were identified in mixed systems, showing considerable variance (Table 5.3). The Queensland survey also found high levels of

Table 5.3　Summary of Police Experiences in Mixed Complaints Systems

Location	% Satisfied			% Dissatisfied			Source
	Process	Outcome	Overall	Process	Outcome	Overall	
Queensland[a]			79.3			20.6	Criminal Justice Commission, 1995, p. A-2
Israel					78.7	89.8	Herzog, 2000, p. 134
Philippines	82.4	80.5	80.0	17.4	19.5	20.0	de Guzman, 2004, pp. 372–373
Denver		55.9	36.7		24.6	42.5	De Angelis, 2008, p. 15
England and Wales		55	39		23	31	IPCC, 2009, pp. 15–16
Denver	12.0	48.9					Schaible, De Angelis, Wolf, & Rosenthal, 2012, p. 641

[a] Officers with complaints "investigated by Criminal Justice Commission."

satisfaction of just under 80%. In the latter case, complaints were said to be investigated by the oversight body, the Criminal Justice Commission. However, the survey was categorized as mixed because the commission was heavily reliant on seconded police for investigations and it has no disciplinary authority. It could have been categorized as police dominated. In contrast, the Israeli system, also reliant on ex-police, produced very high levels of dissatisfaction—between approximately 80% and 90%. The mixed system in the Philippines produced very positive responses: 80.0% expressed satisfaction overall. Of some note is the change in experiences of the complaint process by Denver Police before and after the introduction of the Office of the Independent Monitor (OIM). Officer satisfaction with the outcome increased from 45.9% to 55.9%, and overall satisfaction increased from 11.6% to 36.7%. Finally, the system in England and Wales generated a peak satisfaction level with outcomes of 55%, but with an overall satisfaction rate of 39%. The system involved variable levels of input by the Independent Police Complaints Commission depending on the seriousness of complaints.

The following surveys included information about possible reasons for satisfaction rates. Herzog's (2000) survey of officers deemed "suspects" in excessive force complaints found very high levels of dissatisfaction overall and for outcomes. High dissatisfaction was also found in relation to "involvement in the investigation" (74.6%), "updating during the investigation" (76.9%), "updating on the outcome" (68.5%), length of the investigation (63.8%), and "investigator impartiality towards the adversarial side" (63.8%; Herzog, 2000, p. 134). In a subsequent study, Herzog (2001, p. 451) also found that:

- 61.4% of "suspects" believed offenders were "out to slander police officers";
- 89.8% agreed that "events occurred but details [were] presented in an exaggerated/distorted way" and 8.6% stated the events did not occur at all; and
- 63.8% thought investigators were "antipolice."

In the Philippines case, de Guzman (2004) reported that, in the development phase, "officers openly rallied against the establishment of a civilian review and a civilian dominated police commission" (p. 360). The survey was conducted a decade after the establishment of the People's Law Enforcement Board in 1991. According to de Guzman, the positive findings "did not conform to what was expected" (p. 370), with very high levels of satisfaction with both processes and outcomes. Despite the fact that 51.0% of officers with a complaint against them were dissatisfied with the Board's composition (pp. 370 and 373):

- 64.1% were satisfied with the investigators;
- 82.4% were satisfied with "the overall fairness of the investigation";

- 76.2% were satisfied with the thoroughness of the investigation;
- 78.3% were satisfied with the "fairness of the hearing";
- 76.4% were satisfied with the "thoroughness" of the decision;
- 65.2% were satisfied with its objectivity; and
- 80.5% were satisfied with its fairness.

Unfortunately, however, de Guzman's account did not include a description of how the Board operated. Consequently, the level of independent input cannot be identified.

A similar problem is apparent in the first Denver study in Table 5.3, which showed an improvement from the police-dominated system (Table 5.1) after the introduction of the OIM. The OIM is a "hybrid monitor/auditor oversight agency" that "monitors and participates in the investigation of citizen complaints, internal complaints, and critical incidents" (Schaible et al., 2012, p. 632). It makes disciplinary recommendations to the police chief and reports on outcomes. The study was also limited in that detailed questions about process were not asked in the follow-up survey of officers with complaints, with the exception of timeliness—which increased from 20.0% (64.0% dissatisfied) to 33.9% (43.0% dissatisfied; De Angelis, 2008, p. 15).

In addition, of note is a study that did not use satisfaction as a criterion but asked two relevant questions. Walker (1999) conducted a survey of 58 officers in Minneapolis who had been subject to a citizen complaint "reviewed" by the Civilian Review Agency. Approximately 90% felt they had been treated fairly and "had a chance to tell their story" and 85% felt the outcome was "fair" (Walker, 1999, p. 5). Of additional note is independent, but limited, work by the York Civilian Complaint Review Board. In a series of focus groups, police officers subject to investigation reported that they felt "mistreated" by the Board, without sufficient opportunity to prepare a defense (Sviridoff & McElroy, 1989, p. 48).

Independent Systems

There were eight results for independent systems, all from the Northern Ireland Police Ombudsman (Table 5.4). All officers subject to an investigation by the Ombudsman were posted a confidential questionnaire with a return envelope once the complaint was closed. Overall satisfaction averaged 70.3%, with a fairly stable trend over time. Officer satisfaction with outcomes was higher: averaging 81.5%, also at a fairly stable rate. An average of 71.1% of investigated officers agreed that the complaints system "makes police more accountable." There were a large number of questions related to reasons for satisfaction, with some variation in results. There were some relatively low scores for "frequency of updates" (averaging 55.7%) and "time taken to investigate the complaint" (53.0%). A better score of 73.0% was obtained for

Table 5.4 Percentage Investigated Police Officer Satisfaction Levels, Police Ombudsman for Northern Ireland

Criterion/Year	2006/2007	2007/2008	2008/2009	2009/2010	2010/2011	2011/2012	2012/2013	2013/2014
Overall	70	70	68	68	74	72	73	67
Outcome	84	86	81	80	86	81	80	74
Fairness	83	85	83	82	85	83	85	80
Timeliness	47	50	47	52	56	57	61	54
Frequency of updates	53	58	48	57	58	56	60	56
Staff polite	97	98	98	96	96	98	96	97
Staff manner during interview	85	87	81	80	81	77	80	78
Explanation of process	75	74	69	69	76	78	73	70
Quality of documentation	72	74	63	65	72	72	72	64
Staff professional	93	95	93	92	93	94	92	92
Staff knowledgeable	88	91	92	88	94	92	88	87
Staff not interested	9	8	8	9	8	3	5	5
Staff impartial	92	92	91	88	93	93	91	91
Ombudsman deals with complaints impartially	75	81	78	77	84	79	79	74
System makes police more accountable	72	73	69	68	68	69	73	69

Source: Police Ombudsman for Northern Ireland (2012, pp. 28–29; 2014, pp. 17–18).

"explanation of process" and 69.2% for "quality of documentation." High scores were obtained for "manner of staff during interview" (81.1%), staff professionalism (93.0%), staff knowledge (90.0%), and staff politeness (97.0%). On the crucial question of impartiality, staff were given an average score of 91.3%, and the Ombudsman itself, a score of 78.3%. The fairness of the process was supported by 83.2% of officers on average.

Informal Resolution and Mediation

A number of surveys were also identified that asked about officers' experiences of some type of alternative dispute resolution, which normally involves nonpunitive outcomes. It was often difficult to identify the exact nature of the process regarding informal resolution—although most cases appear to involve an explanation or apology to a complainant by a senior officer, rather than the more formal process of face-to-face mediation between a complainant and the subject officer. The survey results are subject to a degree of bias in that there is no random allocation of cases. Normally, with mediation, cases are preselected according to suitability criteria, complainants have to agree to the process, and then officers have to agree. At the same time, there is some pressure on police to participate in mediation, given that nonmediation can mean the process reverts to a more formal investigation with possible sanctions.

Informal Resolution

Informal resolution showed mixed results among police. In a Queensland study, 75.8% of officers who experienced "informal resolution" were satisfied with the outcome, compared with 67.6% who experienced a "formal investigation," and 83.4% were satisfied with the process, compared with 76.0% subject to formal investigation (Criminal Justice Commission, 1994, p. 76; cf. Table 5.1). Officers who experienced informal resolution were more likely to feel they were kept informed during the case compared with those with "investigated" cases (77.3% compared with 42.6%) and were not stressed or only a little stressed (69.8% compared with 44.5%; Criminal Justice Commission, 1994, pp. 73 and 75). At the same time, opinions about the thoroughness of the process and opportunities to have a say were almost the same for both groups.

In contrast, in one U.K. study, only 25% of police were satisfied with informal resolution (Warburton, May, & Hough, 2003, p. 22). In another, 27% were satisfied and 54% were dissatisfied with "local resolution" (May, Hough, Herrington, & Warburton, 2007, p. 20). A Cincinnati study found officers fairly evenly divided over their experiences with a complaint resolution procedure. A small majority were positive: 56.5% believed the outcome was fair, whereas 43.4% disagreed; 42.1% were satisfied with the process, whereas 47.8% were dissatisfied (Ridgeway et al., 2009, p. 134). Across the studies, reasons for dissatisfaction were largely related to perceptions of bias in favor of the complainant, alleged triviality of complaints, delays, and lack of information.

Mediation

Satisfaction levels were consistently high where police experienced mediation. In a Calgary study, 78% of officers accepted the offer of mediation, and of these, 83% were satisfied with the outcome (Calgary Police Commission, 1999, p. 92). A U.K. study of "restorative" and "conciliation" cases found high levels of complainant satisfaction with police experiences of both responses. In relation to how the complaint was handled, 61% of police in the restorative group were fairly or very satisfied, compared with 77% who experienced conciliation, and 34% in the restorative group were dissatisfied compared with 15% in the conciliation group (Young, Hoyle, Cooper, & Hill, 2005, p. 306). However, 86% of the restorative group were satisfied with the outcome and 10% were dissatisfied, whereas 54% of the conciliation group were satisfied with the outcome and 39% were dissatisfied. Overall, 85% of the restorative group were satisfied and 5% were dissatisfied, whereas 69% of the conciliation group were satisfied and 15% were dissatisfied. The reasons for these differences were not apparent.

A Portland, Oregon, study of mediation did not compare mediation with other responses. Nonetheless, the responses of police (and complainants—see Chapter 4) are worth noting. Of a sample of approximately 21 police who experienced mediation, 70.0% felt the complaint was resolved to their satisfaction (Independent Police Review Division, 2003, p. 105). In addition, 95.5% felt that they had the opportunity to explain themselves, 100.0% felt the mediator was "fair to both sides," and 85.7% said they would recommend mediation to other police. The following statements by officers provided more insight into the success of the process (Independent Police Review Division, 2003, p. 107).

- Instead of just hearing what the sergeant or IA tell you about some complaint, we get to understand what the complainant's concerns really were—and they get to really hear and understand our side.
- I felt the line of communication opened up.
- We all learned something.
- The citizen and I got to explain our actions in a friendly manner. I was able to see both sides of the situation and see how it escalated.
- What brought us here were misunderstandings. We cleared those up.

- This process gives both sides an opportunity to understand what they did/said and why.
- I was able to ask questions of the other side that I was not able to ask at the time of the incident. I could feel for the situation they were in as maybe they were also victims... [I would change] the way the original situation was handled.
- The process worked well and the mediators did a good job at leading the discussion and defusing some hostilities that arose.

Nonetheless, the following statements indicate some of the limits to mediation from the officers' perspective (Independent Police Review Division, 2003, p. 107):

- [The complainant] never would admit what they said to me that day. That was what I wanted.
- The mediators were talented. They did their very best. But no matter how skilled or motivated...you can't squeeze blood out of a turnip! I got to explain myself in more ways than I thought possible. The complainant still didn't get it.
- Even if I did not agree with everything said by the other party, I did hear it.... Maybe emphasize at the beginning (a bit more) that all portions of this conflict or disagreement may not be resolved.
- My only issue is that a fair amount of resources and time were spent to clarify his assumptions.

In a Denver study of mediation, 81% of police participants were satisfied with the process, compared with 12% in the nonmediation sample, and 73% were satisfied with the outcome compared with 49% with nonmediated cases (Schaible et al., 2012, p. 16; see Chapter 4 for complainant responses). Mediation cases were selected across a range of allegation types, with 80% related to issues of courtesy, compared with 66% in the overall complaints profile, but with a number of cases related to alleged racial discrimination (5%) and excessive force (6%). Mediation was conducted by an independent specialist mediation firm. The nonmediation sample appears to have included officers who experienced either informal resolution or formal investigations. The study involved large samples, with 299 officers who experienced mediation providing responses and 368 without mediation. The Denver study included some additional questions with clues to reasons for the large differences in responses (Schaible et al., 2012, p. 146):

- 46.4% of officers with nonmediated complaints were satisfied with the fairness of the process compared with 96.0% with mediated complaints;

- 39.7% of respondents in nonmediated cases were satisfied with the information provided, compared with 85.5% with mediated cases; and
- 59.2% were satisfied with "motives" in nonmediated cases compared with 97.0% in mediated cases. (In nonmediated cases, respondents were asked if they were satisfied that "Denver is serious about investigating police misconduct" and the mediation sample was asked if they were satisfied "That the mediator was genuinely interested in resolving the complaint." (Schaible et al., 2012, p. 636))

It should also be noted that a focus group study in New York City of officers who had been subject to an investigation (the section on "Mixed Systems") found that "the overwhelming majority of officers claimed that they would prefer some procedure which would permit face-to-face interaction between officers and complaints" (Sviridoff & McElroy, 1989, p. 36). Reasons included the ability to counter false and malicious complaints. In the Carbondale survey (section on "Police Views Limited to Civilian Review"), 27% of officers supported mediation by oversight committees (Wells & Schafer, 2007, p. 13).

Discussion

This section summarized the findings of 37 studies of police opinions and experiences with different complaints and discipline systems. The findings confirmed what was suggested by the preliminary discussion of qualitative sources: Police are not 'rusted on' with regard to in-house processes. When it comes to investigation and adjudication, some feel they might receive a fairer response from outsiders, and officers can also see benefits in terms of greater public confidence in police accountability. Police are not oblivious to the fact that even the best internal investigations lack credibility in the eyes of complainants and general public because of a perceived intrinsic conflict of interest.

Personal experiences of different systems were highly variable, with considerable variation in satisfaction rates in both police-dominated and mixed systems. Perceptions of impartiality, fairness, and professionalism by investigators appear to influence overall satisfaction. In terms of review-type oversight agencies, as Perez observed in relation to the Berkeley Board and de Guzman observed in relation to the Philippines Board, "police officers developed confidence in the board once they perceived fairness in its operations" (2004, p. 374). However, what was most outstanding were the very high levels of officer satisfaction across almost all aspects of complaints investigations by the only fully independent police complaints and discipline system in the study, the Police Ombudsman for Northern Ireland. Experience there shows that police fears about civilian investigators not understanding their situation and favoring complainants are likely to be unfounded in a system that both is independent and puts a high premium on procedural justice. It could be argued that this is merely an outcome of the lack of evidence on police complaint matters. But it is a crucial point in favor of independence nonetheless when also considering the strength of complainant and community support for independence (Chapters 3 and 4).

The chapter also showed compelling evidence when it came to different forms of alternative dispute resolution. Informal resolution can attract high rates of police satisfaction, but there are also some poor ratings on the record. Informal resolution can serve as a superficial response that seeks to appease complainants through an apology or a meeting with a senior officer in a way that is administratively expeditious. Complainants can often see through this (Chapter 4), and it would seem that police can also feel cheated if informal resolution prevents them from providing their view on allegations and there is no real due process in the final outcome. It should be no surprise then that the few studies available show extremely high rates of officer satisfaction with mediation. Mediation, almost by definition, satisfies the criterion of independence—with the management of the face-to-face meeting by an independent chairperson. In addition, it allows both parties to have their say in a controlled environment where the mediator, as a trained professional, ensures that each side is able to express its views and provide a reply. Even if mediation does not lead to one or both parties admitting fault and apologizing, it would seem that, in most cases, a reconciliation of sorts can be reached and much of the bitterness and rancor taken out of the grievance. There is little, perhaps no systematic, evidence that mediation leads to improved police conduct or better police–community relations. But it is possible to achieve these outcomes when mediation is part of a system that uses complaints as a learning tool (Chapters 11 and 12).

Conclusion

The final chapter of this book follows up on the question of police perceptions and experiences of complaints and discipline systems by comparing them more systematically with public and complainants' views, outlined in preceding chapters. It would seem that there is considerable scope for a win–win outcome for all parties through a much more developed independent complaints management process. When it comes to mediation, the scope for both parties to a dispute being satisfied appears to be greatly magnified through an independently managed face-to-face encounter.

References

Alexander, P. (1999). PASA president states police case in WA Parliament House. *Police Journal (SA), 80*(3), 12–13.

Barry, D. (2000). LA Police Union calls for civilian oversight. *APBnews.com*. Retrieved November 12, 2014, from http://www.ipsn.org/2000-10-06.htm.

Bobb, M. J., Buchner, B. R., DeBlieck, S., Jacobson, M. P., Henderson, N. J., & Ortiz, C. W. (2006). *Assessing police-community relations in Pasadena, California*. New York: Vera Institute of Justice.

Calgary Police Commission. (1999). *Report*. Calgary: Citizen Complaints Review Committee.

CAPPE. (2008). *An integrity system for Victoria Police: Police members' and complainants' perceptions, survey results*. Melbourne: Centre for Applied Philosophy and Public Ethics, University of Melbourne.

Criminal Justice Commission. (1994). *Informal complaint resolution in the Queensland Police Service: An evaluation*. Brisbane: Criminal Justice Commission.

Criminal Justice Commission. (1995). *Ethical conduct and discipline in the Queensland Police Service: The views of recruits, first year constables and experienced officers*. Brisbane: Criminal Justice Commission.

De Angelis, J. (2008). *Assessing the impact of the office of the independent monitor on complainant and officer satisfaction*. Denver, CO: Office of the Independent Monitor.

De Angelis, J., & Kupchik, A. (2006). *Measuring complainant and officer satisfaction with the Denver police complaint process*. Denver, CO: Office of the Independent Monitor.

de Guzman, M. C. (2004). One for all? Philippine police officers' perceptions of civilian review. *Policing: An International Journal of Police Strategies & Management, 27*, 358–379.

Editorial. (1997). Independence is the only answer. *Police: The Voice of the Service, XXIX*(13), 5.

Electoral Reform Ballot Services. (1997). *Survey of attitudes to police discipline and complaints*. London: Author.

Ethical Standards Department. (1999). *Client satisfaction survey*. Melbourne: Victoria Police.

Fehr, M. (1997). The 1992 Police Civilian Review Board controversy in San Jose. In J. Burpo, R. DeLord & M. Shannon (Eds.), *Police association power, politics, and confrontation: A guide for the successful police labor leader* (pp. 259–266). Springfield, IL: Charles C. Thomas.

Freckelton, I. (1991). Shooting the messenger: The trial and execution of the Victorian Police Complaints Authority. In A. Goldsmith (Ed.), *Complaints against police: The trend to external review* (pp. 63–114). Oxford: Clarendon Press.

Herzog, S. (2000). Evaluating the new Civilian Complaints Board in Israel. In A. Goldsmith & C. Lewis (Eds.), *Civilian oversight of policing* (pp. 125–146). Oxford: Hart.

Herzog, S. (2001). Suspect police officers investigated by former police officers: Good idea, bad idea? *Law & Policy, 23*, 441–467.

Hunter, R. D. (1999). Officer opinions on police misconduct. *Journal of Contemporary Criminal Justice, 15*(2), 155–170.

IACP. (2000). *Police accountability and citizen review: A leadership opportunity for police chiefs*. Alexandria, VA: International Association of Chiefs of Police.

Independent Police Review Division. (2003). *Independent Police Review Division annual report*. Portland, Oregon: City of Portland, Office of the City Auditor.

IPCC. (2009). *IPCC investigations: A survey seeking feedback from complainants and police personnel*. London: IPCC.

Kang, W., & Nalla, M. K. (2011). Perceived citizen cooperation, police operational philosophy, and job satisfaction on support for civilian oversight of the police in South Korea. *Asian Journal of Criminology, 6*, 177–189.

LAPPL. (2000). Los Angeles Police protective league offers 15 recommendations for improving DOJ consent decree. Press release. Retrieved November 12, 2014, from http://www.thefreelibrary.com/Los+Angeles+Police+Protective+League+Offers+15+Recommendations+for...-a065746191.

Liberty. (2000). *An Independent Police Complaints Commission*. London: Liberty, The National Council for Civil Liberties.

Maguire, M., & Corbett, C. (1991). *A study of the police complaints system*. London: HMSO.

May, T., Hough, M., Herrington, V., & Warburton, H. (2007). *Local resolution: The views of police officers and complainants*. London: Independent Police Complaints Commission.

McDevitt, D. J., Farrell, A., & Andresen, W. C. (2005). *Enhancing citizen participation in the review of complaints and use of force in the Boston Police Department*. Boston: Institute on Race and Justice.

Perez, D. W. (1994). *Common sense about police review*. Philadelphia, PA: Temple University Press.

Police Association. (1995). *Submission to the Royal Commission into the NSW Police Service*. Sydney: Police Association of NSW.

Police Federation. (1997). *Where we stand: Police accountability*. Police Federation of England and Wales. Retrieved August 21, 2001, from http://www.polfed.org.uk/wherewes.html.

Police Ombudsman for Northern Ireland. (2012). *Statistical Bulletin 2011–12*. Belfast: Author.

Police Ombudsman for Northern Ireland. (2014). *Annual report on police officer satisfaction provided by the Police Ombudsman's Office in Northern Ireland 2013–14*. Belfast: Author.

Prenzler, T. (2011). The evolution of police oversight in Australia. *Policing and Society, 21*(3), 284–303.

Reiner, R. (1991). Multiple realities, divided worlds: Chief constables' perspectives on the police complaints system. In A. Goldsmith (Ed.), *Complaints against the police: The trend to external review* (pp. 211–231). Oxford: Clarendon.

Ridgeway, G., Schell, T. L., Gifford, B., Saunders, J., Turner, S., Riley, K. J., & Dixon, T. L. (2009). *Police–community relations in Cincinnati*. Santa Monica, CA: RAND Corporation.

Schaible, L. M., De Angelis, J., Wolf, B., & Rosenthal, R. (2012). Denver's Citizen/Police Complaint Mediation Program: Officer and complainant satisfaction. *Criminal Justice Policy Review, 24*(5), 626–650.

Special Assistant for Constitutional Policing (Los Angeles Police Department). (2014). *Perspectives on the disciplinary system of the LAPD*. Los Angeles: LAPD.

Stone, C., Foglesong, T., & Cole, C. M. (2009). *Police in Los Angeles under a consent decree: The dynamics of change at the LAPD.* Cambridge, MA: Program in Criminal Justice Policy and Management, Harvard Kennedy School.

Sviridoff, M., & McElroy, J. (1989). *The processing of complaints against police in New York City: The perceptions and attitudes of line officers.* New York: Vera Institute of Justice.

USCCR. (2000). *Revisiting who is guarding the guardians? A report on police practices and civil rights in America.* Washington, DC: United States Commission on Civil Rights.

Walker, S. (1999). *Citizen and police officer evaluations of the Minneapolis Civilian Review Authority.* Minneapolis, MN: Minneapolis Civilian Review Authority.

Warburton, H., May, T., & Hough, M. (2003). *Opposite sides of the same coin: Police perspectives on informally resolved complaints.* London: Police Foundation.

Weisburd, D., Greenspan, R., Hamilton, E. E., Williams, H., & Bryant, K. A. (2000). *Police officer attitudes toward abuse of authority: Findings from a national study.* Washington, DC: National Institute of Justice.

Wells, W., & Schafer, J. A. (2007). Police skepticism of citizen oversight: Officers' attitudes toward specific functions, processes, and outcomes. *Journal of Crime & Justice, 30*(2), 1–25.

Young, R., Hoyle, C., Cooper, K., & Hill, R. (2005). Informal resolution of the complaints against the police. A quasi-experimental test of restorative justice. *Criminal Justice, 5,* 279–317.

Regional, National, and Jurisdictional Accounts of External Oversight

Civilian Oversight of Police in Africa
Trends and Challenges

JULIE BERG
SIMON HOWELL

Contents

In taking seriously the complexity of policing in the African continent, and the resulting challenges and roles of/for civilian oversight, this chapter aims to provide an overview of the context(s) in which the civilian oversight of the police becomes important and necessary for consideration. To sharpen focus on this concern, this chapter will draw attention to some of the issues impacting on civilian oversight in the continent, focusing on those that emerge in practice and as a result of the frequent dissonances between policy and practice. In discussing these issues or challenges, we make use of specific examples of civilian oversight in select African countries to illustrate the point being made. However, the aim of this chapter is not to provide an audit of civilian oversight mechanisms in Africa. Albeit dated, detailed audits of African police accountability and/or reform have already been conducted (see African Policing Civilian Oversight Forum, 2008; Berg, 2005a,b; Lumina, 2006; Rauch & van der Spuy, 2006). Ultimately, the purpose of this chapter is to give a pragmatic overview of civilian oversight mechanisms in the African continent in light of the issues or challenges that impact on their functioning and effectiveness. In doing so, we separate out the operational issues (such as lack of resources) and systemic issues (such as political will) that impact on civilian oversight in the continent.

Preliminary Methodological Difficulties

Two primary methodological difficulties frequently arise in studying civilian oversight bodies in Africa. The first concerns gaining access to primary data and information. This information is desperately needed in attempting to paint a reliable picture of their activities, successes, and failures. The second, as Berg (2005a, pp. 2–3) has argued, concerns accurately understanding how policy and legislation are implemented at a local/practical level: "as an analysis of a piece of legislation, for instance, does not reveal the manner in which the legislation is interpreted and applied."

Speaking to the first concern, it must be remembered that much of the data and information gathered by these bodies are sensitive in nature. It may also be classified, especially when dealing with ongoing cases. When the political fragility of many African states is also taken into account—in which the police are never exempt and often deeply implicated—the right information can become a potent tool with which to question the legitimacy of the state, as a whole, and the police specifically. As such, many organizations are loathe to provide accurate data or may provide data that have been manipulated in some form to protect vested interests, whether they be political or economic. There is also a frequent dissonance between the legislative paradigm that individual countries may adopt and the effective implementation of that framework in practice. Simply because an individual country may be party to an international treatise or have as a legal requirement for specific oversight mechanisms does not mean that these measures will actually be implemented. Moreover, and even if the measures do translate into actual action, this in no way guarantees that these measures will be followed correctly or in full or that they will be effective. Attempting to understand the impact of civilian oversight bodies on the continent then requires that one look beyond political rhetoric and attempt to understand the reality of policing and oversight using information drawn from reliable primary sources. The result, as we briefly demonstrate, is that a rhetorically rosy environment may often only serve political ends, with the reality telling a very different story. As such, engaging with these measures requires that one maintain a critical stance, one that takes into account the context and environment in which policing and oversight are individually constituted in each country.

We now turn to the resulting issues or challenges confronting civilian oversight bodies on the African continent. In doing so, as mentioned, we draw on country-specific examples to illustrate the congruent failures and successes achieved by individual agencies. However, the importance of understanding the context in which civilian oversight mechanisms are deployed remains pivotal to both interpreting their actions and analyzing their results.

Impacts on Civilian Oversight in Africa

In light of the range of challenges that civilian oversight mechanisms may encounter in the African continent, the following overview will subdivide these into the operational and the systemic, in line with our concern with the importance of contextual specificities. Operational issues, as the name suggests, are those that hinder the daily procedures driving the civilian oversight mechanisms and as such include capacity and resource constraints, issues of independence, mandate and power, and legislative frameworks. Systemic issues include those that impact on the broader system of accountability—including civilian oversight—and encompass historical legacies, political traditions, and broader reform efforts. Finally, it must be remembered that the operational and systemic issues impact on each other and should not be viewed as a discrete or analytically independent set of issues.

Operational Issues Confronting Civilian Oversight Bodies

Independence and/or Power

One of the key issues confronting the effective operation of civilian oversight bodies is their ability (or inability) to conduct activities independently and with the necessary (legal and material) tools to do so. Lack of independence and power is tied into many other issues, as discussed below—including the effects of political manipulation and underresourcing. However, this is one of the most prominent challenges facing civilian oversight bodies in their day-to-day activities. To illustrate this point, consider how the lack of independence and power impacts on civilian oversight in Lesotho. Lesotho has a Police Complaints Authority that is legally demarcated as an independent, civilian oversight body tasked with monitoring or overseeing instances of police abuse or crime (Hendricks & Musavengana, 2010). The Police Complaints Authority's powers are, however, severely limited in that it cannot receive complaints concerning the police from the public but is mandated to investigate only complaints referred to it by the Police Commissioner. Similarly, it can make recommendations to the police only on the basis of the outcomes of its investigations—it is only ever a reactive rather than a proactive agency. It does not have peace officer powers and so cannot, for instance, empower its agents to make arrests. As a result, although Lesotho may make provision for a civilian oversight body, the reality is that the Police Complaints Authority's powers are severely limited. Indeed, they are entirely dependent on police discretion and cooperation and are subject to the Police Commissioner's direction (Hendricks & Musavengana, 2010). Thus, an effective system of civilian oversight in Lesotho is constrained by the authority of the Police Commissioner.

In contrast to this, consider the South African case, where legal powers are specifically granted to the civilian oversight body for the purposes of being able to perform effectively and as independently as possible. South Africa's main civilian oversight body is the Independent Police Investigative Directorate (IPID). The IPID derives its powers from the Independent Police Investigative Directorate Act (2011)—hereafter the IPID Act—which, as discussed in Chapter 7, compels the South African Police Service (SAPS) to report any of its offenses "immediately after becoming aware" of them and also submitting a written report to the IPID within 24 hours (IPID Act, 2011, Section 29, 1). In 2013, the IPID investigated 6,728 individual cases. Similarly, the IPID Act compels the SAPS to cooperate with the IPID in other ways, through giving identity parades, making officers available for taking affidavits, giving evidence or producing any document, and providing any other information or documentation required for IPID to investigate (IPID Act, 2011). The most important provision in the IPID Act is the fact that the National Commissioner of the Police is compelled to initiate disciplinary recommendations made by the IPID within 30 days, submit a quarterly report on progress regarding disciplinary matters to the Minister of Police, and similarly, report to them when a disciplinary matter is finalized and report on the outcome thereof (IPID Act, 2011). The IPID Act also explicitly mentions that police officers who fail to comply with the requests of the IPID will be liable for conviction (IPID Act, 2011). Yet, despite these extensive powers, the executive director of the IPID is still appointed by the Minister of Police and the IPID still housed within the same Ministry, which has possible implications for independence (IPID Act, 2011).

With this in mind, one can see that independence and power deficits or strengths manifest in different ways in the above countries—where Lesotho lacks independence and power due to lack of legal mandate, this is the opposite experience in South Africa, at least in terms of legal mandates.

Cooperation from Police

In light of the above, a lack of cooperation from the police is particularly problematic for those civilian oversight bodies that are dependent on it in the fulfillment of their mandate. Yet lack of police cooperation may be just as problematic for those countries less dependent on the police to achieve their mandate, such as in South Africa, where, as mentioned, the IPID Act legally empowers the IPID to such an extent that it has considerable power to investigate and influence the police as an institution—even so far as laying criminal charges against all police officers failing to report to it ("IPID to take action against unjust cops," 2012). In practice, these powers may not translate into a cooperative relationship on the ground and the IPID may not have the resources to pursue criminal cases against defaulting police. Consider also the situation in Nigeria, where an antagonistic relationship exists between civilians and the police, the ultimate effect of which is the sustainment of an environment of distrust that may lead to outbreaks of violence. Furthermore, Alemika (2003, p. 8) claims "police fear that external review board can be used by citizens as a platform for vendetta, revenge for arrest and prosecution, and for frustrating prosecution." Moreover, that "police officials are usually hostile to an external review board" (Alemika, 2003, p. 8). Therefore, those who do not fully understand the complex nature of police work may view a civilian oversight body as an unnecessary intrusion. With this in mind, effective civilian oversight mechanisms would need to be supplemented with substantive support mechanisms for individual officers, ranging from psychological to social support. Such antagonistic relationships may also escalate, with the police using their resources as a means of intimidating complainants. All of these processes eventually have the effect of delegitimizing the police and the services they offer, while making ineffective civilian oversight mechanisms.

Capacity and Resources

The issue of capacity and resource constraints is as problematic for civilian oversight mechanisms as it is for the police. Neither can perform their functions efficiently, effectively, and democratically without the capacity or resources to do so. In many African countries, including Nigeria and South Africa (the continent's two largest economies), the police are underfunded. In this environment of limited funding, civilian oversight mechanisms are simply not seen as essential.

For instance, a number of African countries (such as Liberia, Sierra Leone, and South Sudan) maintain police forces that are underpaid, paid sporadically, or not paid at all (Akech, 2005; Baker, 2010). They may also have to function with very limited resources and equipment and may not receive sufficient training (Abatneh & Lubang, 2011; Baker & Scheye, 2007). As Baker (2010) explains with respect to policing in Liberia:

> ...police can only be paid an unattractive US$90 per month; there are few handcuffs, batons, torches, radios, stationery supplies, or vehicles for the officers; and the police stations are often without electricity, filing cabinets, and toilets.... There is only one forensic laboratory for the entire country. There are few fingerprint kits. Its chemistry laboratory is empty. The photographic section has one digital camera, but the computer is down. There is no crime scene van. There are no specialists—no pathologists, toxicologists, ballistics specialists, fingerprint specialists, forgery experts.... (pp. 187–188)

This is by no means the case for all African countries, yet it serves to illustrate the immense challenges faced by civilian oversight bodies in overseeing police forces that, in many respects, are products of the contextual conditions in which they operate. For instance, consider the widespread problem of corrupt practices and the use of problematic operational strategies, such as the extraction of confessions through torture (due to lack of investigative training and/or forensic facilities). These problems are especially endemic in countries such as Zimbabwe and Libya, who have only the most rudimentary of oversight mechanisms.

Even at the international level, and with respect to civilian oversight bodies, there is a tendency for governments to "ignore their need for adequate resources" (Clarke, 2009, p. 3). For instance, South Africa's IPID (then known as the Independent Complaints Directorate [ICD]) began operations without a budget and had to rely on the resources and support from the South African Police Service (Manby, 2000). Even though it eventually acquired its own independent budget (which increased eightfold from 1997 to 2011) and its own skilled staff (which tripled in the same period), it has never reached its full staff complement. Thus, there has always been a greater demand for its services than it can adequately deal with (Hendricks & Musavengana, 2010). This has therefore impacted on its ability to effectively deal with its total cases, to deliver quality investigations, and to engage with broader issues which may be more pressing (such as corruption and torture; Bruce, 2006; Du Plessis & Louw, 2005; Pigou, 2002). It is also ironic that the IPID's extensive powers and mandate, as mentioned above, essentially translates into a large mandatory caseload requiring more specialized skills, more time devoted to crime scenes and testifying in court, and more access to resources (such as forensic support), as well as a bigger caseload per investigator (Faull, 2012; Prenzler & Ronken, 2001). It remains to be seen whether its budget will be able to keep pace with the range of cases, which the IPID is compelled to investigate in light of its more far-reaching powers (e.g., as mentioned, laying criminal charges against all police officers failing to report to it; "IPID to take action against unjust cops," 2012).

Legislative Frameworks

Civilian oversight mechanisms, if created and sustained by the government, need to be informed by legislation that is implementable. Similarly, the police need to be guided by clear and relevant legislation that takes into account the challenges of policing new global risks and the way in which human rights should inform police practices. However, it has been found that some countries have retained their colonial-era legislation, while making incremental amendments rather than rewriting their legislation (Abatneh & Lubang, 2011; Isima, 2011; Lumina, 2006). Other countries have no legislation at all with which to mandate the civilian oversight over their police (Abatneh & Lubang, 2011; Gompert, Davis, & Stearns Lawson, 2009). The challenge of reforming police in practice is thus compounded when there is nothing on paper to inform what these practices should entail. In other words, legislation is a means by which the normative aspiration of having a democratic, accountable, and nonpartisan police service can be formalized.

A further challenge is that legislation often remains "on paper," without becoming part of the institutional culture of the police. This is to differentiate between "accountability in action" versus "accountability in the books" (Reiner, 1995, p. 91). In other words, new legislation may need time to "filter down" to police rank-and-file (Abatneh & Lubang, 2011). However, the formal laws and regulations may never filter down. It has been found, for instance, that police will continue to be guided by informal rules and institutional culture in their daily operations despite reforms in legislation—which is not necessarily a desirable state of affairs (Hornberger, 2010; Marks & Shearing, 2005). Contemporarily, many African countries now draw on a variety of legal traditions and histories, ranging from the colonial to the customary (Joireman, 2001).

However, given these challenges, the introduction of new legislation may be a positive development. For instance, despite the political pressure to resolve high crime rates through tougher policing, South Africa seems to have entered a new phase with respect to how civilian oversight is envisaged. The appointment of a new Minister of Police in 2009, emphasizing the need for a strengthened civilian oversight system, seems to have been the catalyst for the enactment of a tranche of new legislation aimed at tightening up the accountability framework. The new phase reflects a desire to balance police effectiveness and accountability rather than allowing one to trump the other. This shift in focus has meant that the IPID (created to replace the ICD) has its own legislation. In other words, whereas the ICD was created through the South African Police Service Act of 1995, the IPID is mandated through the IPID Act and the Regulations for the Operation of the IPID, 2012. This is a move toward ending the "uncomfortable connection to the SAPS Act" (Faull, 2011, p. 5).

Lesotho likewise provides an interesting example of the means by which legislation can facilitate reform. For instance, Lesotho's Police Service Act specifically states that the Police Complaints Authority "shall have sufficient staff to enable it effectively to carry out its functions" (Police Service Act, 1998, Section 22.4). Notwithstanding the limitations of legislation with respect to it being enacted and taking effect, the use of legislation in this instance may be a way in which deliberate underresourcing of civilian oversight bodies can be challenged through legal means.

Systemic Issues Confronting Civilian Oversight Bodies

Historical Legacies

As has been noted in numerous fields and studies, a vast number of African countries have complex histories, including having experienced varied forms of colonialism, racial/ethnic discord, violence, civil wars/conflict, and autocratic leadership (Abatneh & Lubang, 2011; Abbay, 2004; Alemika, 2011; Baker, 2007, 2010; Ebai, 2011; Griffiths, 2011; Loden, 2007). Although the nature of these forms of violence and conflict may vary, many contemporary African countries still experience the long-term effects of their histories and are often understood to be lawless, with major deficits in resources and infrastructure (Baker, 2003, 2010; Loden, 2007; Tankebe, Hills, & Cole, 2014).

These historical narratives have had systematic impacts on the police and policing. Colonial policing, as an example, aimed to maintain remote systems of exploitation, resource extraction, and protection, all in the name of the interests of the colonial power (Alemika, 2009; Tankebe, 2008). Minimally, these systems did not take seriously accountability or democratic governance. Consequently, many scholars have emphasized the lasting legacy of colonial policing, which is often characterized by hostility between communities and the police. This, in turn, has a profound impact on present policing systems and their reformation to more democratic mechanisms (Alemika, 2009).

Notwithstanding some prominent exceptions, it may reasonably be argued that much of the African populace experiences forms of policing that are pluralized and/or frequently contested. In many of the frequently fragile, transitional, or postconflict African countries, the tainted narrative of state policing—exhibited through frequent bouts of violence and corruption—is all too familiar. Rather than a source of safety and security, a number of African police forces may be viewed as the primary sources of insecurity, criminality, and human rights violations. Indeed, they are frequently articulated as abusive, "predatory," corrupt, and/or ineffective (Akech, 2005; Alemika, 2013; Anderson, 2012; Auerbach, 2003; Baker, 2010; Ebai, 2011; Isima, 2011; Marenin, 2009; Neild, 2003; Oluwaniyi, 2011; Ruteere, 2011; Tankebe, 2008). They may also be considered as irrelevant or absent, either in their inability to cater to the needs of the populace or as a result of their lack of physical reach and capacity. This is often the result of resource constraints, a lack of training, and corruption (among many other localized concerns; Baker, 2010; Baker & Scheye, 2007; Griffiths, 2011; Marenin, 2013). Many police forces have also been accused of lacking accountability to the public, particularly in democratic African states, where this is a normative prescription or expectation (Ebai, 2011; Isima, 2011).

Consequently, the state police may not be considered a legitimate source of security for the populace. At the very least, their legitimacy is often fragile and highly contested. Into this vacuum, other sources of security may become powerful and relied upon; these include, for instance, community organizations, private sector policing forces, and vigilante groupings (Alemika, 2009; Anderson, 2012; Baker, 2010; Baker & Scheye, 2007; Marenin, 2009). In light of this, when one considers the state of policing in many parts of Africa (and the many unique challenges to police reform), the role and function of civilian oversight of the police become complex. Many of the challenges experienced by higher-income countries—who generally have far more rigorously defined, well-equipped, and better funded forces—may be exacerbated in African countries, as a function of the lingering complexity of multiple historical, political, and socio-economic factors. This is not to say, however, that all of these concerns are isolated or unique, with many finding resonance in other developing contexts (such as countries in Latin America; Hinton, 2006).

The state of the police system after the end of an autocratic system or conflict will also determine to what extent a regulatory system (or the state itself) needs to be "fixed"—whether it has to be rebuilt "from scratch" and/or whether an existing police force needs to be reformed to align with democratic principles (Baker, 2003, p. 145; 2007). Doing so will require the consolidation of, and place emphasis on, the importance of nonstate systems of governance. It will also require shifts from autocratic to democratic systems of governance and the import of global economic and political understandings that emphasize the need for systems of accountability and oversight.

Politics

Attendant to these structural legacies are ongoing concerns with political stability and accountability. For instance, Hills (2000, 2007) argues that, historically, police forces have been used as a political tool for those in power. As Akech (2005) explains,

> The need for regime maintenance also explains why the police in Africa have been deprived of resources. For example, according to Alice Hills, the police could threaten the political order of the day if they do their job well. For example, if they were truly independent, they could investigate regime officials suspected of violating the law. (p. 236)

The result is the political manipulation of the police, through such avenues as funding, as a means of limiting their effectiveness and thus limiting their ability to investigate political crimes (Hills, 2000, 2007). The result is disparate forms of policing that lack cohesiveness and broader strategic goals. Ironically, this often serves to increase the levels of antagonism between the state and the population, making effective rule and the development of democratic systems even harder. The police, it must be remembered, are often the first (if not only) representative of the state in isolated or distant communities. Violence or unjustified actions by these forces serve to directly undermine the legitimacy of the state, the result of which is an environment in which political instability is the order of the day. Such scenarios have been seen in numerous African countries, ranging from South Africa to Egypt. In the process, forms of civilian oversight are completely forgotten, preventing the public from voicing their concerns and anger at ineffective policing measures.

To further illustrate the politicization of accountability, consider the case of Kenya. Kenya's civilian oversight body, the Independent Policing Oversight Authority, is "responsible for providing civilian oversight, investigating excessive use of force, and handling complaints from the public" (Noyes, 2013, p. 39). It only began operating in November 2012. Thus far, it has failed to achieve substantive reforms (Noyes, 2013). Indeed, and as a function of the specific political environment in Kenya, which has witnessed high levels of corruption and manipulation, the "police are often used by the government in power to advance partisan political interests at the expense of citizen protection and service" (Ruteere, 2011, pp. 11–12).

As noted above, the most pressing challenge to civilian oversight in Kenya is that of political manipulation and/or interference. The Kenyan police have been described as having "no autonomy from the executive branch of government" with its "policies and operations...determined by the interests of the political regime of the day" (in Ruteere, 2011, p. 15). While "the reintroduction of multiparty politics in Kenya has lessened the political dimension in policing by opening up the force to more criticism and public scrutiny" (Ruteere & Pommerolle, 2003, p. 592), individual acts of violence, corruption, and the misuse of authority continue to define the public image of the police. The police force has not undergone any substantive restructuring process since the colonial era, and therefore, civilian oversight is predominantly limited to criticisms by those specifically mandated to perform the role of oversight, such as the national press. The result, it has been argued, is that acts of "scrutiny and criticism...have not led to accountability" (Ruteere & Pommerolle, 2003, p. 592). Thus, the Kenyan example demonstrates the problem of civilian oversight falling prey to manipulation, itself a product of a highly contested and frequently violent political atmosphere.

Similarly, in Nigeria, "[d]espite the many mechanisms of police oversight in Nigeria, police corruption, brutality, arbitrary arrest and detention, and excessive use of force remain commonplace, according to recent U.S. State Department human rights country reports" (Gompert et al., 2009, p. 8). There are significant levels of corruption, at all levels, in the force. These endemic levels of corruption, driven by an institutional culture that often actively legitimates fraudulent behavior, have sustained deep-seated relationships with criminal entities and groups. In turn, this has undermined the police force's legitimacy.

In South Africa too, many of the interventions or recommendations made with respect to accountability have also been characterized by political interpretations, which, as we note, intersect with still-meaningful understandings of history, culture, and (especially in South Africa) race. As such, oversight bodies have only had limited success, with a lack of cooperation between agencies and other key stakeholders (such as, e.g., the South African Human Rights Commission) rarely delivering sustainable interventions. Indeed, in measuring any intervention's success, its long-lasting effects are an important marker. In point of fact, the SAPS have undergone three national restructuring programs yet continue to be blighted by officers committing brutal acts of violence and coercion that dominate the news nearly every week. Liability, rather than reform, continues to be the order of the day. Much like in Nigeria, corruption in South Africa has become de jure, with the public expecting (and thus not reporting) corrupt officers and processes.

Broader Reform Efforts

Civilian oversight and police accountability need to be considered in the light of broader attempts to reform the security and justice apparatus of transitional or postconflict countries, such as in Latin America and Africa. The shift to a democratic system of security governance is all the more complex in light of the "inherent contradictions between the police role and the ideals of democracy" (Hinton, 2006, p. 3) and the context of high crime/violence accompanying a transition from an authoritarian to democratic system (Barolsky & Pillay, 2009). Considering that the police are the face or symbolic front-end of state legitimacy, or "the public face of government" on the streets, means that police reform cannot be divorced from broader reform efforts (Bayley & Perito, 2010, p. 151; Hinton, 2006; Hornberger, 2010). In other words, how does one conceptualize and align civilian oversight with respect to broader security sector reform (SSR) efforts taking place in postconflict/transitional African countries?

Although SSR has been the subject of considerable discussion (and critique) among scholars and policy makers, it is not within the ambit of this chapter to engage with those debates (for an overview on SSR developments and critique thereof, see Baranyi & Salahub, 2011). In terms of its normative role, SSR is a coordinated, "comprehensive [and] holistic" effort to "depoliticize, professionalize, and establish democratic civilian oversight of the state security apparatus in post-conflict and democratizing states" (Noyes, 2013, p. 29; Wilén, 2012, p. 1326). The purpose of SSR is thus to align state security structures (including the police) to "democratic standards of good governance" (Wilén, 2012, p. 1326). In reality, the story is different, as SSR has been accused of, among other things, being too ambiguous and vague, ineffectively applied, and state-centric, thereby ignoring the very systems of security that have the most potential, it is argued, to be reformed—the non-state sector (Baker & Scheye, 2007; Baranyi & Salahub, 2011; Wilén, 2012). This is in light of the accusation that police institutions are the most resistant or resilient when it comes to reformation (Hills, 2008).

Discussion

In light of the above, how then does civilian oversight fit into broader reform efforts? There seem to be two positions in this regard. On the one hand, civilian oversight is viewed as the potential to be a "catalyst by which democratic principles are reinforced and readapted"; that is, civilian oversight perpetuates and encourages broader reform of the state (police) (Hryniewicz, 2011, p. 80). On the other hand, it is argued that civilian oversight can only be effective once "organizational climates," which perpetuate abuse of authority, are transformed (Bayley, 1995, p. 94), the rationale being that simply engaging on an individual case-by-case basis (which many oversight mechanisms do) will not get to the heart of the deeper problems underlying newly democratized state institutions, such as the police. In fact, civilian oversight systems have generally been criticized because of this fact—punishing individual transgressors on a case-by-case basis rather than focusing on deeper, systemic organizational problems (Bayley, 1995; Goldsmith, 1995). There have thus been calls to "fix the police barrel" or the rotten orchards rather than simply focusing on the rotten apples (Bayley, 1995, p. 96; Punch, 2003). As noted by Harris (2012, p. 241), "[t]he causes of complaint are, it is argued, the product (or at least influenced by) wider, systemic policies and practices within the police service." Indeed, systemic concerns with civilian oversight are neatly summed up by Goldsmith (1995):

> Even with the indications of some complaints bodies exhibiting a more systemic approach to the analysis of complaints, the structural location of these bodies and the degree of political influence they can exercise, which are the product of their resources as well as their constitutional and legal status, constrain the degree to which they can highlight, let alone have an impact on, the wider considerations that frame the debates on police accountability. (pp. 126–127)

What is essentially at stake here is a paradigm shift from a deterrence approach to an opportunity-focused approach. A deterrence approach is how many criminal justice systems operate, focusing on individual offending through a case-by-case basis to punish individuals to deter would-be offenders. It operates in a reactive way, focusing on breaches of the law after they have occurred (Reiss, 1984). An opportunity-focused model focuses on opportunities for offending rather than just on individual offenders and will ask a different set of questions. For instance, instead of asking who is to blame, it will ask questions about how offenses can be prevented from recurring in terms of the conditions that were present to allow the problem to take place (Berg & Shearing, 2011). It is a more proactive strategy focused on controlling opportunities for breaching the law and it is more reflective, in terms of problem solving (Shearing & Stenning, 1982). It also requires a more networked approach to uncover deeper issues (Wood & Shearing, 2007). An optimal system would be one in which there is a balance between the two paradigms, as both have benefits and harms (Braithwaite, 2002). Civilian oversight and broad reform efforts should be complementary, mutually supporting, and mutually constitutive. In other words, one should avoid a "wholesale reliance" on civilian oversight (characterized by independent complaints bodies) but also find a way in which broader reform efforts can be operationalized and not remain at the level of rhetoric (Goldsmith, 1995, p. 112).

However, this is a tall order, especially in developing contexts. In addition to the issue of political will, there is also the challenge for civilian oversight mechanisms to penetrate police institutions "given the strength of the police culture and police knowledge of how to evade prosecution" (Prenzler & Ronken, 2001, p. 168). Linked to this concern is the age-old problem of resources; no matter how strong a legislative framework, enforcement relies on capacity, expertise, and resources (Clarke, 2009). Undertaking systemic overviews and/or analyses of entire police forces (or even simply clusters of stations) requires resources that are often not available to poorly funded civilian oversight bodies (Stone & Bobb, 2002). Moreover, such work requires skills that often require external consultation, which are again often limited by resources. This is not to say that these skills cannot be developed, but that civilian oversight bodies may frequently find themselves caught between the need to undertake this broader work and the requirement of addressing individual concerns on an ad hoc basis. Ultimately, and in nearly all African countries, civilian oversight bodies require far more funding and need to be embedded far more deeply in the legal structures on which they draw to complete their work.

There are multiple factors that may have a detrimental effect on the successful deployment of civilian oversight mechanisms in African countries. As previously mentioned, many of these are not unique to Africa, although they may be compounded by historical and contextual factors specific to individual countries. Indeed, some may be unique to developing contexts and thus not be factors regularly experienced in or by developed countries. The issues or challenges listed above are common to most, if not all, African countries. This being said, their pragmatic realization will be contextually specific; both South Africa and Nigeria, for instance, have troubled histories that impact on civilian oversight, yet the way in which those histories are felt is very different. Moreover, these challenges can affect civilian oversight at every stage of its development—from inception to its daily operations. Civilian oversight may, for example, be hampered at the very outset by the inability or unwillingness of the government to legislate for it. Alternatively, even if the relevant legislation is drafted and promulgated correctly, it may not be the case that the legislation and/or regulations grant sufficient detail defining what civilian oversight should entail. Legislation may, in other words, be flawed (containing legal loopholes, for instance) or be nonimplementable in light of the contextual realities of resource constraints and a lack of infrastructure or skill. Therefore, if established, civilian oversight mechanism may also be subject to deeper resource constraints, a lack of cooperation or oversight, and a lack of real power to undertake their mandate and/or may lack the independence to be effective. These logistical, commonplace issues are intermeshed with the broader challenges that impact on the effectiveness of civilian oversight. For instance, historical legacies may hinder civilian oversight as a function of the continuing salience of cultures of militarization, corruption, and/or brutality. The politico–historical context in which a country is developed and understood may also have an impact, whether in a new or an established democracy or one facing threats of war or conflict. In other words, one needs to consider whether practices of reform and accountability are underdeveloped or already entrenched, and of course whether there is a police force yet to be overseen (DiBenedetto, 2007). Trends in political rhetoric, such as frequent measures to be "tough on crime," may inadvertently yet seriously undermine lingering concerns with human rights and accountability. Civilian oversight may also be affected by the nature of broader reform efforts, such as SSR (Berg, 2005a,b). As Abatneh and Lubang (2011, p. 97) argue, "the wider criminal justice sector reforms—in terms of modernising laws, training judges, making courts more effective and improving correctional facilities—must be undertaken in tandem with other security sector reform initiatives."

Conclusion

In conclusion, the civilian oversight of the police in Africa is a necessary requirement of effective policing and governance. However, and although there have been numerous attempts to set up and sustain effective institutions, many have met very difficult challenges. These difficulties emerge from the structural conditions in which they are deployed, which are, in turn, often a product of specific contextual factors, such as individual historical narratives and unstable political climates. The importance of civilian oversight is often lost in the milieu of concerns that may seem, especially to impoverished citizens, far more immediate. However, we do not wish to present these challenges as yet another African "failure." We instead urge that these challenges need to be understood within the specific contexts in which they arise. Indeed, it is precisely these more nuanced understandings that can act as a springboard for both further research and practices. Many of these challenges are not insurmountable but require systemic implementation. In turn, their importance needs to be highlighted and fought for—civilian oversight mechanisms need to be shown to be an effective means by which individuals and groups can engage with the police and the state. Such conversations increase participation and legitimacy, allowing the police to carry out their duties more effectively, without having to resort to heavy-handed operational protocols or methods. Therefore, many of these initiatives will need to be "homegrown," and the result of local community efforts to make accountable those who are tasked with serving them. Such efforts have already begun. What is needed now is the political recognition and drive to make them sustainable and effective.

References

Abatneh, A., & Lubang, S. (2011). Police reform and state formation in Southern Sudan. *Canadian Journal of Development Studies, 32*(1), 94–108.

Abbay, A. (2004). Diversity and state-building in Ethiopia. *African Affairs, 103*(413), 593–614.

African Policing Civilian Oversight Forum (APCOF). (2008). *An audit of police oversight in Africa.* Cape Town: African Minds.

Akech, A. (2005). Public law values and the politics of criminal (in)justice: Creating a democratic framework for policing in Kenya. *Oxford University Commonwealth Law Journal, 5*, 225–256.

Alemika, E. E. O. (2003). Police accountability in Nigeria: Framework and limitations. In E. E. O. Alemika & I. Chukwuma (Eds.), *Civilian oversight and accountability of police in Nigeria* (pp. 45–94). Lagos: Centre for Law Enforcement Education and the Police Service Commission (CLEEN).

Alemika, E. E. O. (2009). Police practice and police research in Africa. *Police Practice and Research, 10*(5–6), 483–502.

Alemika, E. E. O. (2011). Police internal control systems in West Africa: An introduction. In E. E. O. Alemika & I. Chukwuma (Eds.), *Police internal control systems in West Africa* (pp. 7–18). Lagos: CLEEN.

Alemika, E. E. O. (2013). *Criminal victimization, policing and governance in Nigeria* [Monograph]. CLEEN Monograph Series, (Serial No. 18). Lagos: CLEEN.

Anderson, D. (2012). Vigilantes, violence and the politics of public order in Kenya. *African Affairs, 101*(405), 531–555.

Auerbach, J. (2003). Police accountability in Kenya. *African Human Rights Law Journal, 3*(2), 75–313.

Baker, B. (2003). Policing and the rule of law in Mozambique. *Policing and Society, 13*(2), 139–158.

Baker, B. (2007). Post-war policing by communities in Sierra Leone, Liberia, and Rwanda. *Democracy and Security, 3*(2), 215–236.

Baker, B. (2010). Resource constraint and policy in Liberia's post-conflict policing. *Police Practice and Research: An International Journal, 11*(3), 184–196.

Baker, B., & Scheye, E. (2007). Multi-layered justice and security delivery in post-conflict and fragile states. *Conflict, Security & Development, 7*(4), 503–528.

Baranyi, S., & Salahub, J. (2011). Police reform and democratic development in lower-profile fragile states. *Canadian Journal of Development Studies/Revue Canadienne d'Études du Développement, 32*(1), 48–63.

Barolsky, V., & Pillay, S. (2009). A call for comparative thinking: Crime, citizenship and security in the Global South. *SA Crime Quarterly, 27*, 15–21.

Bayley, D. (1995). Getting serious about police brutality. In P. Stenning (Ed.), *Accountability for criminal justice: Selected essays* (pp. 93–109). Toronto: Toronto University Press.

Bayley, D., & Perito, R. (2010). *Police in war: Fighting insurgency, terrorism, and violent crime.* London: Lynne Rienner.

Berg, J. (2005a). *Audit of police oversight bodies in the East African region.* Research document prepared for the African Policing Civilian Oversight Forum, Cape Town.

Berg, J. (2005b). *Overview of plural policing oversight in select Southern African Development Community (SADC) countries.* Paper prepared for the Open Society Foundation for inclusion on the Republic of South Africa's government Police Accountability Website, Cape Town.

Berg, J., & Shearing, C. (2011). The practice of crime prevention: Design principles for more effective security governance. *SA Crime Quarterly, 36*, 23–30.

Braithwaite, J. (2002). *Restorative justice and responsive regulation.* New York: Oxford University Press.

Bruce, D. (2006, February). *Staggering under the burden: ICD policies on the receipt of complaints and on investigations and their negative impact on the ICD, on public confidence, and on police discipline.* Paper presented at the meeting of the Independent Complaints Directorate, Pretoria.

Clarke, S. (2009). Arrested oversight: A comparative analysis and case study of how civilian oversight of the police should function and how it fails. *Columbia Journal of Law and Social Problems, 43*(1), 1–49.

DiBenedetto, C. (2007, Spring). Policing the police: A Nigerian NGO teaches human rights to local law enforcement agencies. *Stanford Social Innovation Review*, 68–69.

Du Plessis, A., & Louw, A. (2005). Crime and crime prevention in South Africa: 10 years after. *Canadian Journal of Criminology and Criminal Justice, 47*(2), 427–446.

Ebai, E. (2011). Police internal control system in Cameroon. In E. E. O. Alemika & I. Chukwuma (Eds.), *Police internal control systems in West Africa* (pp. 112–137). Lagos: CLEEN.

Faull, A. (2011). *Oversight agencies in South Africa and the challenge of police corruption* (ISS Paper 227). Retrieved from http://www.issafrica.org/uploads/Paper227.pdf.

Faull, A. (2012, March). *Setup to fail? South Africa's Independent Complaints Directorate's 2011/12 budget is cause for concern.* Retrieved from http://www .issafrica.org/iss-today/setup-to-fail-south-africas-independent-complaints -directorates-201112-budget-is-cause-for-conce.

Goldsmith, A. (1995). Necessary but not sufficient: The role of public complaints procedures in police accountability. In P. Stenning (Ed.) *Accountability for criminal justice: Selected essays* (pp. 110–134). Toronto: Toronto University Press.

Gompert, D., Davis, R., & Stearns Lawson, B. (2009). *Oversight of the Liberian National Police.* RAND, National Defense Research Institute, occasional paper OP-230-OSD. Retrieved from http://www.rand.org/pubs/occasional_papers /OP230.html.

Griffiths, C. (2011). Internal control system in Liberian police. In E. E. O. Alemika & I. Chukwuma (Eds.) *Police internal control systems in West Africa* (pp. 83–100). Lagos: CLEEN.

Harris, F. (2012). Holding police accountability theory to account. *Policing, 6*(3), 240–249.

Hendricks, C., & Musavengana, T. (2010). *The security sector in Southern Africa* [Monograph]. ISS Monograph Series, (Serial No. 174). ISS: Johannesburg.

Hills, A. (2000). *Policing Africa: Internal security and the limits of liberalization.* Boulder, CO: Lynne Rienner.

Hills, A. (2007). Police commissioners, presidents and the governance of security. *Journal of Modern African Studies, 45*(3), 403–423.

Hills, A. (2008). The dialectic of police reform in Nigeria. *Journal of Modern African Studies, 46*(2), 215–234.

Hinton, M. (2006). *The state on the streets: Police and politics in Argentina and Brazil.* Boulder, CO: Lynne Rienner.

Hornberger, J. (2010). Human rights and policing: Exigency or incongruence? *Annual Review of Law and Social Science, 6,* 259–283.

Hryniewicz, D. (2011). Civilian oversight as a public good: Democratic policing, civilian oversight, and the social. *Contemporary Justice Review, 14*(1), 77–83.

Independent Police Investigative Directorate Act, 1 R.S.A. § 34298 (2011).

IPID to take action against unjust cops. (2012, June 4). *News24.* Retrieved from http://www.news24.com/SouthAfrica/News/IPID-to-take-action-against -unjust-cops-20120604.

Isima, J. (2011). Police internal control systems in Nigeria. In E. E. O. Alemika & I. Chukwuma (Eds.), *Police internal control systems in West Africa* (pp. 38–62). Lagos: CLEEN.

Joireman, S. (2001). Legal systems and effective rule of law: Africa and the colonial legacy. *The Journal of Modern African Studies, 39*(4), 571–596.

Loden, A. (2007). Civil society and security sector reform in post-conflict Liberia: Painting a moving train without brushes. *The International Journal of Transitional Justice, 1*(2), 297–307.

Lumina, C. (2006). Police accountability and policing oversight mechanisms in the Southern African Development Community. *African Security Review, 15*(1), 92–108.

Manby, B. (2000). The South African Independent Complaints Directorate. In A. Goldsmith & C. Lewis (Eds.), *Civilian oversight of policing: Governance, democracy and human rights* (pp. 195–222). Oxford: Hart.

Marenin, O. (2009). The futures of policing African states. *Police Practice and Research: An International Journal, 10*(4), 349–363.

Marenin, O. (2013). *Policing reforms and economic development in African states: Understanding the linkages: Empowering change* (Working Paper No. 2013/013). Helsinki: UNU-WIDER.

Marks, M., & Shearing, C. (2005). Reconceptualising reform practice in South African policing. *South African Review of Sociology, 36*(2), 131–140.

Neild, R. (2003). Human rights NGOs, police and citizen security in transitional democracies. *Journal of Human Rights, 2*(3), 277–296.

Noyes, A. (2013). Securing reform? Power sharing and civil–security relations in Kenya and Zimbabwe. *African Studies Quarterly, 13*(4), 27–52.

Oluwaniyi, O. (2011). Police and the institution of corruption in Nigeria. *Policing & Society, 21*(1), 67–83.

Pigou, P. (2002, April). *Monitoring police violence and torture in South Africa.* Paper presented at the meeting of the Mexican National Commission for Human Rights, Merida.

Police Service Act, 7 Government of Lesotho § 29 (1998).

Prenzler, T., & Ronken, C. (2001). Models of police oversight: A critique. *Policing and Society, 11*(2), 151–180.

Punch, M. (2003). Rotten orchards: 'Pestilence,' police misconduct and system failure. *Policing and Society, 13*(2), 171–196.

Rauch, J., & van der Spuy, E. (2006). *Recent experiments in police reform in post-conflict Africa: A review.* Pretoria: Institute for Democracy in South Africa.

Reiner, R. (1995). Counting the coppers: Antinomies of accountability in policing. In P. Stenning (Ed.), *Accountability for criminal justice: Selected essays* (pp. 74–92). Toronto: Toronto University Press.

Reiss, A. (1984). Selecting strategies of social control over organisational life. In J. Hawkins & J. Thomas (Eds.), *Enforcing regulation* (pp. 23–35). London: Kluwer-Nijhoff.

Ruteere, M. (2011). More than political tools: The police and post-election violence in Kenya. *African Security Review, 20*(4), 11–20.

Ruteere, M., & Pommerolle, M. (2003). Democratizing security or decentralizing repression? The ambiguities of community policing in Kenya. *African Affairs, 102*(409), 587–604.

Shearing, C., & Stenning, P. (1982). Snowflakes or good pinches? Private security's contribution to modern policing. In R. Donelan (Ed.), *The maintenance of order in society* (pp. 96–105). Ottawa: Canadian Police College.

Stone, C., & Bobb, M. (2002, May). *Civilian oversight of the police in democratic societies.* Paper presented at global meeting on Civilian Oversight of Police, Los Angeles.

Tankebe, J. (2008). Colonialism, legitimacy, and policing in Ghana. *International Journal of Law, Crime and Justice, 36*(1), 67–84.

Tankebe, J., Hills, A., & Cole, B. (2014). Emerging issues of crime and criminal justice in Sub-Saharan Africa. *Criminology and Criminal Justice, 14*(1), 3–7.

Wilén, N. (2012). A hybrid peace through locally owned and externally financed SSR-DDR in Rwanda? *Third World Quarterly, 33*, 1323–1336.

Wood, J., & Shearing, C. (2007). *Imagining security.* Cullompton: Willan.

Police Accountability and Citizen Oversight in Emerging Democracies in Asia

7

MAHESH K. NALLA

Contents

While many developed nations have ensured public participation in matters of police oversight, particularly as they relate to police misconduct and accountability issues, interest in such oversight among the new Asian democracies has been noticeable in recent decades. More specifically, the development of governance and democratic institutions with special emphasis on the civil society's role in matters related to law and criminal policies is more prominent (Lu & Liang, 2011). Credit for this can be attributed partly to citizens' awareness and desire for responsiveness, accountability, transparency, and overall efficiency (Rahman & Robinson, 2006) in matters of governance, including policing. Consider the fact that a few decades ago, police organizations across the United States, one of the oldest democracies, had overwhelmingly rejected proposals for citizen participation but have now set an example by introducing some form of citizen supervision in many of its law enforcement agencies (Walker, 2005).

A survey of most developed democracies shows that more than 60% of the top 20 democracies in the world (Economist Intelligence Unit [EIU], 2011) have citizen supervision in their policing system, suggesting a congruence among nations that value idealistic democratic notions and social regulatory mechanisms that reflect democratic policing, police legitimacy, and procedural justice to ensure a sound foundation for democratic governance. Police oversight mechanisms can range from measures that provide for police personnel who oversee and assess citizen complaints to boards comprising government-appointed civilians as well as police personnel or even boards constituted entirely of civilians (see Chapter 1 in this volume).

In the post-World-War-II era, many former colonies established themselves as newly independent democratic countries. They are not, however, identical in the manner in which they govern their citizens, nor do their political institutions reflect the core mission of their national constitutions. Identifying as democratic republics, many of them claim to hold the values of political freedom, civil liberties, and freedom of the press. However, it is unclear to what extent the policing cultures in these countries reflect these prime democratic indicators in real terms, as is the extent to which a civilian role in police accountability is allowed. Thus, in this chapter, we examine the various forms of police oversight mechanisms in Asia and whether the degree of democratic principles applied in the design of these mechanisms relates to the respective democratic rankings of these countries. In other words, one would expect that countries that are ranked high in the overall democracy rankings would have in place a higher degree of citizen participation in police accountability programs, reflecting a greater degree of transparency, accountability, and effectiveness.

Maturing Democracies and Democratic Policing in Asia

The basic objective of civilian complaint procedures and citizen review boards (CRBs) is to handle complaints against the police and monitor police organizations independently beyond internal oversight mechanisms. That is, ideally, democratic states cannot ignore democratic values if they ensure citizens' participation in matters that affect their lives, judicious application of rule of law, protection of human rights, and transparency in governance. Does citizens' participation in police accountability processes indicate the maturity of a developed democracy? Many countries have internal review mechanisms including written departmental policies for police accountability.

There is wide-ranging diversity among many of the Asia-Pacific developing countries in terms of economic, political, and social structures. Despite their diversity, many countries in this region share in a common history of colonial rule and are in various stages of transition from autocratic to democratic rule. In addition, a growing population is another common thread that runs through many countries in this region, along with overcrowded cities, a rural and urban divide, poverty, and the concentration of political and economic power in fewer hands. Further, many countries that achieved independence after World War II have witnessed a transition from regime-style policing to varying degrees of what is called democratic policing (Nalla & Mamayek, 2013). Given this context, the role of police and social regulation in Asia is examined in this chapter.

The maturity of a democracy is judged by indicators such as free citizen participation in the political process, human rights protection, the effectiveness and independence of the civil service, and the equal application of rule of law, among others. Based on these measures, countries are categorized as full democracy, flawed democracy, hybrid regime, and authoritarian regime (EIU, 2011). Nalla and Mamayek (2013), in a study of 24 Asian countries, compared various measures of democracy with provisions for civilian participation in police accountability processes. They found that democracy rankings are not good indicators of the presence or absence of developed citizen-driven police oversight mechanisms, which is the highest form of civilian representation in police oversight. Although their work does not suggest that CRBs are the most effective police oversight mechanism relative to forms such as a human rights commission (HRC) or national ombudsman, among others, findings suggest that when it comes to issues of policing in former colonies, standard measures of democracy are poor predictors of democratic policing.

The scope of this chapter is less ambitious but more comprehensive. Drawing data from World Governance Indicators (2013), first we rank countries in South, Southeast, and East Asia (with the exception of three countries, Brunei, Maldives, and Macao, as democratic rankings were not available for these countries) on various democratic parameters, including government effectiveness, rule of law, corruption control, and voice and accountability. We used the categories outlined by the EIU (2011): full democracies, flawed democracies, hybrid regimes, and authoritarian regimes. Although full democracies (e.g., South Korea and Japan) and flawed democracies (e.g., Thailand, India, Indonesia, Malaysia, and the Philippines) ensure political and civil freedom, satisfactory government functioning, governmental checks and balances, independent media and judiciary, and enforcement of judiciary rulings (EIU, Democracy Index, 2012), the latter have weaknesses in governance that contribute to an underdeveloped political culture and minimal political participation. Hybrid regimes (e.g., Singapore, Pakistan) are those that interfere with free and fair elections and reflect a weak political culture, ineffective governance, poor citizen participation, rampant corruption, weak civil society, ineffective rule of law, media hindrance, and a nonindependent judiciary.

Finally, authoritarian regimes (e.g., China, North Korea) restrict political pluralism, manipulate elections, own the media, and crush civil liberties. Justice is either denied or delayed, and there are dire consequences for criticizing the government.

Nalla and Mamayek (2013) caution that the descending order of country democracy rankings may not reflect their actual rankings on different parameters of democracy. For instance, India (39th) and Malaysia (64th) are more democratic than the Philippines (79th) in rank. But the Philippines exceeds India in government effectiveness and Malaysia in voice and accountability. Similarly, Singapore, a hybrid regime, although holding a low ranking of 81, nonetheless has very high percentile rankings on various measures even when compared with those highest on the democracy rankings. In addition, these rankings are fluid and move across categories over the years. Compared with 2011 data presented by Nalla and Mamayek (2013), we noted that Hong Kong (HK) moved from being a hybrid regime to a flawed democracy in 2013, as noted in Table 7.1.

Effective Democracies vis-á-vis Police Oversight Mechanisms in Asian Democracies

Pyo (2008) identified four types of oversight mechanisms in his review of 16 Asian countries: HRCs, anticorruption agencies, ombudsmen, and specialized police complaints organizations. Barring some focused studies in Asia (e.g., South Korea—Kang & Nalla, 2011; and the Philippines—de Guzman, 2008a,b; HK—Wong, 2010; and China—Wu & Sun, 2009), scant attention has been paid to civilian oversight mechanisms in Asia. Whereas HRCs deal with issues related to discrimination, freedom of speech and assembly, fair trials, and integrity, anticorruption organizations exclusively examine charges of corruption against police officials as well as other public officials. Ombudsmen handle petitions and complaints from the public.

According to Pyo (2008), of the 16 countries he reviewed, 6 countries have an HRC, 10 have anticorruption agencies, and 11 have a national ombudsman. None of these mechanisms, however, were created exclusively for police oversight and accountability in any of these countries. HK is the only country that has a specialized police complaints organization. Taking Pyo's contribution as a framework, we have updated his table outlining various mechanisms of oversight in 25 countries in Asia and omitted three countries—Brunei, Maldives, and Macau—from the study as they were not ranked on the democracy scale.

Table 7.1 also lists all the countries included in the study with columns for democracy ranking and the existence of HRCs, anticorruption agencies,

Table 7.1 Rankings by Governance Indicators[a] and Police Oversight Mechanisms in Asia

	Rank[b]	Government Effectiveness[c]	Corruption Control[d]	Rule of Law[e]	Voice and Accountability[f]	Human Rights Commission[g]	Anticorruption Agency[g]	National Ombudsman[g]	Civilian Oversight[g]
Full Democracies									
South Korea	20	84	70	80	70	×	×	×	×
Japan	23	89	92	87	83			×	?
Flawed Democracies									
Taiwan	35	84	74	83	72			×	
India	38	47	35	53	58	×	×	×	?
Timor-Leste	43	12	17	10	52		×		
Indonesia	53	44	29	34	51	×	×	×	
Thailand	58	61	47	50	37	×	×	×	
Hong Kong	63	97	93	91	67		×	×	×
Malaysia	64	80	66	66	38	×	×	×	
Mongolia	65	31	38	45	51	×			
Philippines	69	58	33	36	48	×	×	×	×
Hybrid Regimes									
Singapore	81	100	97	96	54		×		
Bangladesh	84	22	21	19	34		×	×	
Sri Lanka	89	46	52	52	30	×		×	?
Cambodia	100	22	7	17	19	×	×	×	
Bhutan	107	67	78	59	39		×		
Pakistan	108	23	14	19	24	×	×	×	?
Nepal	111	17	23	27	28	×	×	×	

(Continued)

Table 7.1 (Continued) Rankings by Governance Indicators[a] and Police Oversight Mechanisms in Asia

	Rank[b]	Government Effectiveness[c]	Corruption Control[d]	Rule of Law[c]	Voice and Accountability[f]	Human Rights Commission[g]	Anticorruption Agency[g]	National Ombudsman[g]	Civilian Oversight[g]
					Authoritarian Regimes				
China	142	56	39	39	5		×	×	
Vietnam	144	44	35	38	9		×		
Afghanistan	152	7	2	0	11	×	×	×	
Laos	156	21	15	23	5				
Myanmar	155	4	11	6	4	×			
Iran	158	36	24	20	6				
North Korea	167	0	3	9	1				

a 2012 data from the World Governance Indicators, 2013 Update. Retrieved March 14, 2014, from http://www.govindicators.org.

b 167 nations were ranked, 1 = most democratic, 167 = least democratic. Source: EIU, Democracy Index, 2012. Retrieved March 14, 2014, from http://www.eiu.com/Handlers/WhitepaperHandler.ashx?fi=Democracy-Index-2012.pdf&mode=wp&campaignid=DemocracyIndex12.

c Perceptions of the quality of public services, the quality of the civil service and the degree of its independence from political pressures, the quality of policy formulation and implementation, and the credibility of the government's commitment to such policies. Percentile rankings among all countries range from 0 (lowest) to 100 (highest).

d Perceptions of the extent to which public power is exercised for private gain, including both petty and grand forms of corruption. Percentile rankings among all countries range from 0 (lowest) to 100 (highest).

e Reflects perceptions of the extent to which agents have confidence in and abide by the rules of society and, in particular, the quality of contract enforcement, property rights, the police, and the courts, as well as the likelihood of crime and violence. Percentile rankings among all countries range from 0 (lowest) to 100 (highest).

f Reflects perceptions of the extent to which a country's citizens are able to participate in selecting their government, as well as freedom of expression, freedom of association, and a free media. Percentile rankings among all countries range from 0 (lowest) to 100 (highest).

g Adapted from Nalla and Mamayek (2013).

ombudsmen, and CRBs. Wherever we were unable to confirm the existence of any of these agencies, we left the space blank. CRBs, which have the highest degree of citizen presence and responsibility in police oversight, are functioning in three Asian countries—South Korea, the Philippines, and HK, representing full democracy and flawed democracy. Efforts were made to introduce civilian oversight agencies in two flawed democracies, India and Sri Lanka, and in the hybrid regime of Pakistan. But either these were not fully instituted or are now defunct (CHRI, 2007). Except for Iran, Laos, and North Korea, every Asian country has an oversight agency in one form or another.

From Table 7.1 we see that the Philippines is the only country with all four types of police oversight mechanisms: HRC, anticorruption agency, ombudsman, and specialized police complaints organization. Although Japan, Singapore, and Vietnam have only a single government agency or department that deals with citizen complaints against any kind of government officials, Pyo (2008) speculates that such mechanisms without a civilian presence may be indicative of well-structured and functioning internal oversight procedures, as well as effective civil liberty and nongovernmental organization (NGO) watchdog groups. For countries such as India (flawed democracy) and Sri Lanka and Pakistan (hybrid regimes), there is evidence of efforts to establish civilian oversight instruments but information is lacking (Nalla & Mamayek, 2013).

Further analysis was done in South Korea (full democracy), the Philippines (flawed democracy), and HK (hybrid regime) to compare civilian oversight mechanisms. Among these, South Korea and the Philippines have had a close relationship with the United States, which has played a key role in shaping defense policies and in internal security matters, including law enforcement. In addition, we chose India, Thailand, Indonesia, Malaysia, from flawed democracies, and one country, China, from the authoritarian regimes to see how they differ in their oversight agencies. In the category of flawed democracies, we chose a range of countries that were colonized by different European colonizers, such as the United Kingdom (India, Malaysia), Holland (Indonesia), and Spain (the Philippines). We also chose one country from the list of flawed democracies, Thailand, which was never colonized and remains a constitutional monarchy.

Citizen Review Boards

South Korea

Korea, a former colony of Japan, became independent in 1945. The U.S. and U.N. forces helped the Republic of Korea (South) in defending itself from the Democratic People's Republic of Korea (North) between 1950 and 1953.

Today, South Korea is considered a modern democracy. It is committed to democratic policing, rule of law, and human rights protection (Kang & Nalla, 2011). It has instituted several supervisory mechanisms, including an HRC (National Human Rights Commission [NHRC]) and the Anti-Corruption and Civil Rights Commission (ACRC), which serves as both an anticorruption agency and the national ombudsman. It is also considering creating a specialized police complaints organization.

To enhance police accountability and transparency, Korea instituted a series of reforms in the early 1990s to ensure greater citizens' participation (Kang & Nalla, 2011). The NHRC and ACRC work on a larger scale, mitigating human rights abuses and dealing with corruption issues and complaints against public officials. However, the ACRC is without statutory investigative power (Pyo, 2008).

In 1999, the Korean National Police Agency established the Office of Hearing & Inspection at three levels—national, state, and local—to investigate complaints against police (Kang & Nalla, 2011). The Office of Hearing & Inspection failed to gain public trust largely because the chief of the state police appointed the members and the majority of the members were police officers (Kang & Nalla, 2011). In 2005, the Korean National Police Agency established the Civilian Review Committee, a committee comprising nine civilians with 2-year terms, to review the internal investigations of the police department (Kang & Nalla, 2011). Another step toward improving Korean oversight was taken in 2010, when the South Korean president ordered the creation of civilian programs for police misconduct and corruption (Choo, 2010). One month later, the Korean police introduced guidelines for formal civilian review boards that include academics, nonacademics, and legal professionals as members (Kang & Nalla, 2011; Park, 2010). Civilian Review Boards (CRBs), with 91 members, were formally launched on August 21, 2012, to cover the offices at police headquarters and state police departments (Min, 2012). However, no CRB offices were established at the local level (Cheon, 2012). This was done on a recommendation of the Police Reform Committee to the Commissioner General in May 2012 (Kim, 2012). The main aim of CRBs is to investigate corruption and misconduct charges and to make recommendations to the Chief of State Police or the Commissioner General. They have no power to determine disciplinary action.

The Philippines

The islands of the Philippines faced colonial subjugation at the hands of Spain and the United States in the 16th century and in 1898. It became a self-governing commonwealth in 1935 and attained freedom in 1946. The Philippine National Police's (PNP's) structure and organizational culture were influenced heavily by its former colonial rulers, Spain and the United

States. The United States primarily used the Philippine Constabulary, which became the PNP in 1990, as a means of "colonisation and subjugation of the Filipinos" (Varona, 2010, p. 103). The Philippine revolution in 1986 paved the way for various reforms in the law enforcement organization, including demilitarizing the police to make it a civilian organization. The People's Law Enforcement Board (PLEB), a civilian review board, was created in 1991 (de Guzman, 2008a). Still, the PNP structure strongly reflects military tradition, with sworn personnel, a central administration, and significant operational and strategic policies coming directly from national headquarters (de Guzman, 2008b).

According to Pyo (2008), there are four types of oversight mechanisms in the Philippines: an HRC (Commission on Human Rights of the Philippines), an anticorruption agency (Presidential Anti-Graft Commission), a national ombudsman (Office of the Ombudsman), and, most notably, a specialized police complaints organization, the PLEB. Considering that a majority of Asian nations do not have a specialized police complaints authority, PLEB is a "novel" piece of legislation (de Guzman, 2008a). PLEB was created through a collaboration of the National Police Commission and the PNP (Joshi, 2003). Each PLEB has five members with 2-year terms. Of the five members, two are nominated by local bodies (one from his/her respective *sangguniang* and one from the association of *barangay* captains). Of the three members, one must be a member of the Bar, a college graduate, or a central elementary school principal in the locality. They are selected by the Peace and Order Council based on their "probity and integrity" (R.A. No. 6975). The law also governs the dispersion of PLEB, mandating one board for every municipality and/or legislative district in a city, and a minimum of one PLEB per 500 city/municipal law enforcement personnel (R.A. 6975, Section 43). The PLEB has jurisdiction to hear and determine citizen complaints against the police using due process. The case must be decided within 60 days. The law allows the officers of the National Police Commission of the Philippines to consult, assist, and advise PLEB members. The law terms PLEB's decisions as "final and executory" (R.A. 6975).

Hong Kong

After 156 years of British colonial rule, HK became a Special Administrative Region of the People's Republic of China (PRC) in 1997. China's "one country, two systems" formula allows HK autonomy in all affairs other than foreign and defense for 50 years. In terms of police supervisory mechanisms, HK is a role model for Asian countries as it has an anticorruption agency (Independent Commission Against Corruption), an ombudsman, an HRC (NGO), and a specialized police complaints organization (Independent Police Complaints Commission [IPCC]; Pyo, 2008).

High levels of police abuse and contradictory low levels of citizen complaints were common in the 1960s (Wong, 2010). Any complaints against law enforcement were investigated and reviewed internally by the chief inspectors and district commanders (Wong, 2010). This changed in 1974, when the HK police created the "independent" Complaints Against Police Office (CAPO). Although scores of complaints were filed each year (about 3,000 to 4,000), a miniscule percentage was substantiated by the Independent Police Complaints Commission (IPCCom; Wong, 2010). This led to the creation of the Human Rights Committee in 1995. Experimentation with specialized police complaints civilian review boards comprising nonstatutory Unofficial Members of the Executive and Legislative Councils began in 1977 in HK. This was followed by the Police Complaints Council, which replaced the Unofficial Members of the Executive and Legislative Councils in 1986 and was later renamed the IPCCom in 1994 (Wong, 2010). In 1996, the IPCCom was empowered as a commission to refer complaints back to CAPO for reinvestigation. It permitted selected public members to sit in on CAPO investigation proceedings. It established special panels to monitor serious cases and submitted its reports to the governor on an annual basis. It laid its annual report before the Legislative Council for scrutiny (Wong, 2010, pp. 11–12). It does not handle investigation and discipline of police or receive initial complaints itself (Wong, 2010). It consists of 1 chairperson, 3 vice-chairpersons, 14 council members, and a 29-members-strong secretariat (Pyo, 2008).

Theoretically, CAPO appears structurally independent. But it is neither independent nor objective, as its members are police officers who return to their original postings after serving their terms (Wong, 2010). The current system of CAPO investigations that forwards reports to the IPCCom is recognized as "well-established" and "function[ing] adequately" (Wong, 2010, p. 20). People prefer to file a complaint with CAPO (police investigation system) rather than with the independent oversight mechanism, the IPCC (Wong, 2010). In a nutshell, HK's supervisory system is far more transparent, independent, sufficient at holding police accountable, and more democratic than its counterparts in China and the majority of Asian nations.

Other Forms of Police Oversight

India

With about 1.2 billion citizens, 2 million of whom are police officers, India is the world's most populous democratic country (Nalla & Madan, 2012). India gained independence from Great Britain in 1947 and is now a nation made up of 28 states and seven union territories, each with its own police force (Pyo, 2008). India continues to witness significant influences of British colonization in terms of both its legal system and its government (Wu et al., 2012). Typically strained by corruption, malpractice, and low levels of accountability, the relationship between the police and public at times is weak, and public sentiments typically suggest that the police role is to protect the government rather than to serve the citizens (Das & Verma, 1998; Joshi, 2003; Nalla & Madan, 2012; Wu et al., 2012).

Oversight mechanisms available in India are the NHRC, an anticorruption agency (the Central Vigilance Commission [CVC]), and a national ombudsman (Pyo, 2008). Although there are no specific oversight mechanisms for police, nor any provisions for civilian participation, the NHRC was established in 1993 to investigate human rights violations committed by government personnel. Adopted in 17 states, NHRC is a fact-finding organization with no enforcement powers, and police officers are rarely prosecuted or convicted (Perez, n.d.). A Director General of Police in each state heads each office of the NHRC, although any officer of an investigative agency or government agency can head the organization. The NHRC has its own staff and works alongside NGOs to investigate complaints against human rights (Pyo, 2008). The NHRC has persuaded state governments to set up "human rights cells" in police headquarters to help with processing complaints against the police, training, putting together workshops, and generally increasing human rights awareness (Joshi, 2003). However, Joshi (2003) noted that Indians are not supportive of filing complaints against the police and speculates that a lack of faith in the process and fear of police contribute to this reluctance.

The CVC was established by the Indian government in 1964 to combat issues of corruption and gained statutory status in 1998; the Central Vigilance Commission Act took effect in 2003 (CVC, 2012; Pyo, 2008). The powers and functions of the CVC as provided by the Central Vigilance Commission Act give it legal sanction to exercise superintendence over corruption in governmental departments (Joshi, 2003), a sanction not limited to police corruption. While in principle, the goals for CVCs are lofty, with the "political culture of impunity prevailing in government institutions, including the Police, it would take much more than such initiatives" to handle the problem of corruption (Joshi, 2003, p. 16).

The ombudsman, as an oversight mechanism, was originally suggested by the First Administrative Reforms Commission in 1966, which recommended a two-tier system with *Lokpal* at the central level and *Lokayukts* at the state level (Pyo, 2008). Legislation for *Lokpal* has been fruitlessly tabled by Parliament (at least eight times), and there are 17 states in which *Lokayukta* has been nonuniformly instituted (Pyo, 2008).

The India Supreme Court has mandated that national and state governments establish a dedicated civilian complaints agency at state and district levels; however, governments are choosing not to comply (Mehta, 2007). In instances where the agencies have been implemented, the model as conceived by the Supreme Court was ineffective, as the agencies were "watered down, with less independence and fewer powers, through problematic membership and appointment procedures, limited mandates and little power" (Mehta, 2007, p. 73).

Thailand

Thailand is included in this article for two unique reasons: It is the only Southeast Asian nation never to have been taken over by a European power, and it is a constitutional monarchy. Historically, Thailand has made three transitions to democracy: in 1973 and again in 1991–1992, through large demonstrations that forced generals out of their political offices, and in 1977, through a military-initiated transition that did not involve applied pressure from civil society (Lowry, 2008). The 1977 transition created a ruling regime that was considerably less democratic than those created by the transitions of 1973 and 1991–1992, arguably because the strength of civil society before a transition can influence the degree of democratization achieved (Lowry, 2008). Thailand continues to see violence in the deep south of the country, which increased rapidly in 2004 (National Human Rights Commission of Thailand [NHRCT], 2011). This violence is rooted in the excessive power used by administrative authorities, which is attributed to violent attacks by insurgents that result in violent retaliation by the government. Inequality in the distribution of justice, a weak local economy, and religious identities are also contributing factors (NHRCT, 2011).

With respect to police oversight mechanisms, Thailand has an NHRC, the Office of the National Anti-Corruption Commission, and a national ombudsman, all of which were created in the 1997 Constitution. Often called the "People's Constitution" because the people had full participation in the drafting process, the Constitution of Thailand of 2007 guarantees rights, freedoms, and equality but has been slow in implementation, causing the rights provided by the Constitution to be obstructed (NHRCT, 2011). Under the law, NHRCT is not permitted to disclose information obtained while carrying out its responsibilities, a restriction that severely deters its ability to function as an oversight body (NHRCT, 2011). In remarks made to the NHRCT (2011), the United Nations Human Rights Committee (Document CCPR/CO/84/THA, July 8, 2005) cited instances of police brutality that included extrajudicial killings and ill treatment of citizens by both the police and armed forces. The report also notes that in these instances, investigations did not lead to prosecutions and sentences corresponding to the severity of the crime. Ultimately, such instances contributed to a culture of impunity (NHRCT, 2011). The NHRCT recommends that the government reform the justice system by creation of a body to review laws and the administration of justice systems, such as the police, to ensure they abide by the Constitution.

The National Anti-Corruption Commission is in place to investigate corruption in the private sector, although the public still believes corrupt practices still occur (World Bank, 2012). In addition to anti-corruption efforts,
the Access to Information Law was created in 1997 and is considered to be
of great symbolic importance because it addresses the greater need for transparency and accountability within the public sector (World Bank, 2012).
Nonetheless, the Access to Information Law has many shortcomings, and the
number of citizens requesting information and placing complaints remains
low (World Bank, 2012).

Indonesia

Indonesia is the world's third most populous democracy and is currently the
home of the world's largest Muslim population (CIA, 2012). The Dutch began
Indonesian colonization as early as the 17th century. Indonesia declared independence from the Netherlands in 1945, after World War II, and was finally
recognized as independent in 1949. To address police oversight, Indonesia
has an NHRC (Komisi Nasional Hak Asasi Manusia [Komnas HAM]), an
anticorruption agency (Komisi Pemberantasan Korupsi), and a national
ombudsman (Komisi Ombudsman Nasional; Pyo, 2008). Indonesia does
not have any oversight mechanisms exclusively for police accountability, nor
does it afford citizens any role in these processes.

The Indonesian Police (Polri) is one of the largest police forces in the
world (Meliala, 2001). The Polri, a military wing of the armed forces, has
been a source of public loathing, cynicism, and complaints over human
rights issues due to its paramilitary policing style (Meliala, 2001). Meliala
(2001) further notes a value pattern that tends to follow militarism, in which
the police "rely on physical power, domination and the use of force where
torture, extrajudicial violence and killing become legitimate and indeed
required" (p. 421). It is no surprise that a paramilitary policing strategy, with
its propensity for the adoption of similar values, may face legitimacy concerns, let alone accountability.

Historically, the Indonesian police developed, following Indonesia's
independence in 1945, as the Body of State Police (BKN), with the sole
responsibility of fighting alongside the Army against Dutch and Japanese
occupation (Meliala, 2001). Following a series of shifting responsibilities,
periods of autonomy, and political influence, by 1968, Polri was a militaristic
police force fighting a "war against crime" that it carried out against the public, erasing any civilian orientation it once held (Meliala, 2001). Generally,
the loyalties of the Polri rest with the government rather than with the public
(Meliala, 2001).

Citizens are often extremely hesitant to express their cynicism about the
police because they are scared or because there are not sufficient oversight

mechanisms available (Meliala, 2001). Indonesia does not have an independent police complaints agency, and many people are afraid to go public through the media, although an increasing number of people have been filing complaints with the national commission of human rights (or Komnas HAM) or with NGOs (Meliala, 2001). When members of the public do speak out against or get in trouble with the law, it is wise of them to hire a higher-ranking military bodyguard if they do not have a family member who is a higher-ranking member (Meliala, 2001). One could also see this becoming an issue if the Indonesian police were acting legitimately in filing a case and a superior military officer asked it to be dismissed (Meliala, 2001).

Komnas HAM (*Hak Asasi Manusia* is the term for "human rights" in Bahasa Indonesian) was established by presidential decree in 1993 and consists of 25 members, originally appointed by the president and since appointed by commission-developed procedures (International Council on Human Rights Policy, 2004). The members claim that this allows for independence from the government, yet it also seems to decrease diversity of membership relative to Indonesia's regional and geographic diversity, and to make it more prone to human rights violations (International Council on Human Rights Policy, 2004). Komnas HAM generally is not only criticized for its failure to adequately investigate complaints but also for passing them to other relevant government departments. In addition, the fact that the chairperson is also the chairperson of the ruling party raises concerns about a potential conflict of interest. While the chairperson's individual integrity is widely respected, the dual roles exemplify how little political independence exists within the new system (International Council on Human Rights Policy, 2004).

Malaysia

Malaysia was a British colony, beginning in the late 18th century, until 1948, when each of the territories ruled by Britain on the Malay Peninsula, except Singapore, came together to create the Federation of Malaya, which gained independence in 1957 (CIA, 2012). In 1963, Malaysia was formed, with Singapore (until 1965), Sabah, and Sarawak into a federation (CIA, 2012). Malaysia's government, a constitutional elective monarchy, closely mirrors that of the Westminster parliamentary system, reflecting the nation's history of British colonial rule (Federation of International Trade Associations, 2012).

Malaysia has an HRC, an anticorruption agency, and a national ombudsman (Public Complaints Bureau) for oversight of government agencies. It also has an independent oversight body specifically targeting law enforcement agencies, the Enforcement Agency Integrity Commission, which was originally proposed by the Royal Commission of the Royal Malaysian Police. However, a proposed Independent Police Complaints and Misconduct Commission was never put in place for various reasons (Pyo, 2008; UNODC, 2011). An alternate Enforcement Agency Integrity Commission bill was drafted by the Minister of Interior and ultimately instituted in 2009. This independent oversight body oversees all law enforcement agencies (not specifically the police) and has the authority to receive and investigate complaints, as well as to visit detention facilities (UNODC, 2011). The commission makes recommendations to the appropriate bodies, including prosecutors and other disciplinary authorities. These authorities, in turn, review and make recommendations and report back to the commission within 2 weeks, at which point the commission releases the information to the public (UNODC, 2011). However, Malaysia does not have civilian oversight mechanisms.

Hybrid Regimes

Cambodia

Although Cambodia ranks higher relative to some other Asian countries such as Pakistan, Nepal, and Bhutan in this category, it ranks very low on government effectiveness, corruption control, rule of law, and other indicators. With limited financial resources, severe income inequality, a weak judicial system, only very basic legal services, and underdeveloped law enforcement, Cambodia is one of the most highly corrupt and ineffectively governed nations in Asia (Calavan, Briquets, & O'Brien, 2004).

Occasionally, political parties such as the Sam Rainsy Party, donors such as the World Trade Organization, NGOs, the private sector, or the media challenge the government on charges of corruption (Calavan et al., 2004).

Under pressure from donors, the first supreme audit institution, the National Audit Authority, was established in 2002 as a mechanism for civilian oversight of allocation of donor funds, although it lacked capacity (Calavan et al., 2004). However, on March 11, 2010, the National Assembly approved an anticorruption law under which the National Council Against Corruption was established. The Council is composed of 11 members, one of whom is appointed by each of the following: the King, the Senate, the National Assembly, the Royal Government, the National Audit Authority, the Ministry of National Assembly-Senate Relations and Inspection, the Council of Jurists, the Council for Legal and Judicial Reform, the Supreme Council of Magistracy, the Cambodia Human Rights Committee, and the Chair of the Anti-Corruption Unit. In addition, the National Council Against Corruption provided for the establishment of an anticorruption unit to independently investigate charges of corruption against the government. However, the membership of the unit consists of senior ministers who are appointed by royal decree at the request of the prime minister.

China

The PRC is the most populated country in the world. After World War II, the Communist Party developed an autocratic socialist system that largely controls the everyday life of its citizens. The mass-line model of policing, which refers to empowering the involvement of the masses in decision making as opposed to limiting it to a bureaucratic elite (Zhong, 2009), became the framework for enforcing the mandates of the Chinese Communist Party rather than the existing laws (Sun & Wu, 2010, p. 23). From 1949 to 1965, the mass-line style of policing, characterized by low levels of judicial oversight and high levels of police discretion, aimed primarily to protect the new government by minimizing any resistance (Sun & Wu, 2010).

China has continuously witnessed significant transitions in nearly every sector since the 1970s, including rapid economic growth and growing social inequality (Sun & Wu, 2010; Wu & Sun, 2009). China relies less on rule of law and more on "a strong emphasis on the role that connections and networking play in every aspect of social life, including the police-citizen relationship" (Wu & Sun, 2009, p. 173). The nation's goals of heightened economic development have fostered an atmosphere where police favor the interests of the wealthy business professionals who are seen as economically valuable and continuously disregard the interests of undervalued workers and residents who are seen to be making a lesser contribution to the PRC (Wu & Sun, 2009).

Wu and Sun (2009) propose that combining a Chinese culture that values and respects authority with a government policy that places priority on serving citizens may lead to high levels of community trust in the police. However, they acknowledge that the citizens' "respect" for authority may truthfully be fear and that the mistakes of the government may weaken its legitimacy (Wu & Sun, 2009). Evidence supports the argument that Chinese citizens have low levels of confidence in the legal and criminal justice system (Seymore & Finday, 1989; Wong, 2006). In contrast, Wu and Sun, in their research, found that 75% of respondents reported they trusted the police a lot or trusted the police to a degree, whereas Sun, Hu, and Wu (2012) similarly found that urban residents largely support local police. However, evidence suggests that younger Chinese and those who perceived themselves as having less political power appeared to have less trust in and more negative feelings toward the police (Wu & Sun, 2009).

The Chinese police possess various discretionary powers that Western police do not share, which potentially could be associated with the current corruption and misconduct witnessed in China (Wu & Sun, 2009). Although considered one of the most stable authoritarian regimes in the world, China has found itself in the middle of a "legitimacy crisis of its social control apparatus" (Sun et al., 2012, p. 88). Wu and Sun (2009; citing Yu & Ren, 2005) noted that within 2 months of its creation, the new telephone number 1-1-0, a complaints-against-police hotline, received a total of 26,065 citizen complaints, nearly 25% of which related to police corruption, nepotism, and unfair enforcement of laws.

China does not have in place an independent oversight mechanism for specialized complaints against the police that can effectively deter and punish misconduct (Sun & Wu, 2010; Wong, 2010). In a country where corruption and misconduct have been on the rise since the 1980s, governmental mechanisms attempting to curb the issue have been for the most part reactive, symbolic, and, ultimately, ineffective (Sun & Wu, 2010; Sun et al., 2012). Recent instances of misconduct have created an atmosphere in which citizens are pressuring the authorities for change (Sun & Wu, 2010). Citizens are able to file complaints against the police through the *xinfang* process, a rather informal all-purpose system for filing grievances in which citizens write letters to or meet in person with the nearest Party organ or governmental office (Wong, 2010).

Discussion and Conclusion

This chapter focused on countries that engage the public in police oversight in Asia. The countries that include citizens in a supervisory role represent a higher degree of democratic governance. There is a wide variation of oversight mechanisms for government agencies in Asia. Some nations have established external agencies with the sole responsibility to investigate and oversee complaints filed against the police, whereas other nations have allocated monitoring responsibility to existing agencies such as ombudsmen or national human rights institutions. Nearly all 25 Asian democracies have supervisory mechanisms in the form of HRCs, ombudsmen, or anticorruption bureaus, but only three of them have civilian monitoring. Of the two full democracies—South Korea and Japan—only South Korea has civilian monitoring of police, which was only recently established, in August 2012. This parallels the fact that 11 out of the top 20 ranked democracies in the world have CRBs (Nalla & Mamayek, 2013).

This chapter also suggests that not all flawed democracies are the same insofar as the existence of oversight mechanisms is concerned. Some are more progressive than others. For instance, why do countries like India, Pakistan, and Malaysia, all having similar colonial experiences, not have civilian oversight, but HK, another former British colony, does? Does the mere existence of civilian oversight truly reflect the effectiveness of police accountability? How effective are such mechanisms? Another interesting finding from this analysis is that HK (63rd rank) and the Philippines (75th rank) have CRBs, unlike India (39th rank), another flawed democracy. Interestingly, however, the Supreme Court of India has directed central and state governments to establish civilian oversight agencies at both the state and local levels, in response to which local state governments have exhibited strong opposition (CHRI, 2007). Where state governments have adopted the Supreme Court's mandate, the oversight mechanisms have been diluted with limited powers, making them toothless and ineffective (CHRI, 2007). Sri Lanka, another flawed democracy, is the best example. Although Sri Lanka has civilian oversight mechanisms for police agencies, as of 2007, these agencies "existed merely on paper and the members have not had any meetings, with many not even clear about their role and mandate" (CHRI, 2007, p. 73).

From the examples of India (flawed democracy), Sri Lanka, and Pakistan (hybrid regimes), it is clear that initiatives to create citizen oversight agencies are merely a token gesture by governments to appease the public, rather than a genuine effort to progress from a paramilitaristic police culture reflective of their colonial heritage.

References

Calavan, M. M., Briquets, S. D., & O'Brien, J. (2004). *Cambodian corruption assessment.* Cambodia: United States Agency for International Development (USAID).

Central Vigilance Commission (CVC). (2012). New Delhi, India. Retrieved October 31, 2012, from http://cvc.nic.in/.

Cheon, S. (2012). Citizen Review Board at police headquarters. *Newsis,* p. 2A.

Choo, S. (2010). The president indicated the importance of police reform. *Yonhap-News.*

CHRI. (2007). *Police Reform: An exchange of experiences from South Asia: Roundtable Report.* Retrieved July 8, 2015, from http://www.humanrightsinitiative.org/pro grams/aj/police/exchange/police_reform_an_exchange_of_experiences_from _south_asia_roundtable_report.pdf.

Das, D., & Verma, A. (1998). The armed police in the British colonial tradition: The Indian perspective. *Policing: An International Journal of Police Strategies and Management, 21,* 354–367.

de Guzman, M. C. (2008a). Complainants' views about civilian review of the police: A study of the Philippines. *Asian Journal of Criminology, 3*(2), 117–138.

de Guzman, M. C. (2008b). Perceptions of civilian review: Exploring the differences in reviewed and non-reviewed officers. *Justice Research and Policy, 10*(1), 61–85.

Economist Intelligence Unit (EIU). (2011). *Democracy Index 2011: Democracy under stress.* Retrieved October 31, 2012, from http://www.sida.se/Global/About%20 Sida/Så%20arbetar%20vi/EIU_Democracy_Index_Dec2011.pdf.

EIU, Democracy Index. (2012). Retrieved March 14, 2014, from http://www.eiu.com /Handlers/WhitepaperHandler.ashx?fi=Democracy-Index-2012.pdf&mode =wp&campaignid=DemocracyIndex12.

Federation of International Trade Associations (FITA). (2012). *Malaysia general information.* Retrieved October 31, 2012, from http://www.fita.org/countries/malaysia .html?ma_rubrique=cadre.

International Council on Human Rights Policy. (2004). *Performance & Legitimacy: National human rights institutions*. Retrieved October 31, 2012, from http://www.ichrp.org/files/reports/17/102_report_en.pdf.

Joshi, G. P. (2003). *Police practices: Obstructions to poor people's access to justice*. New Delhi, India: Commonwealth Human Rights Initiative. Retrieved October 1, 2012, from http://www.humanrightsinitiative.org/publications/police/police_practices_obstruction_to_poor_people.pdf.

Kang, W., & Nalla, M. K. (2011). Perceived citizen cooperation, police operational philosophy, and job satisfaction on support for civilian oversight of the police in South Korea. *Asian Journal of Criminology, 6*(2), 177–189.

Kim, H. (2012). Establishment of Police Reform Committee. *Yonhap News*, p. 3A.

Lowry, C. (2008). *Civil society engagement in Asia: Six country profiles (Japan, South Korea, The Philippines, Indonesia, India, Thailand)*. Asia Pacific Governance and Democracy Initiative (AGDI). Honolulu: East-West Center.

Lu, H., & Liang, B. (2011). Introduction: Public participation and involvement in the criminal justice system in Asia. *Asian Journal of Criminology, 6*(2), 125–130.

Mehta, S. (2007). *Feudal forces: Democratic nations, police accountability in Commonwealth South Asia*. Commonwealth Human Rights Initiative. Retrieved October 31, 2012, from http://www.humanrightsinitiative.org/publications/police/feudal_forces_democratic_nations_police_acctability_in_cw_south_asia.pdf.

Meliala, A. (2001). Police as military: Indonesia's experience. *Policing, 24*(3), 420–431.

Min, K. (2012). Establishment of Citizen Review Board. *Yonhap News*, p.2A.

Nalla, M. K., & Madan, M. (2012). Determinants of citizens' perceptions of police–community cooperation in India: Implications for community policing. *Asian Journal of Criminology* Online first. doi:10.1007/s11417-011-9110-2.

Nalla, M. K., & Mamayek, C. (2013). Democratic policing, police accountability, and citizen oversight in Asia: An exploratory study. *Police Practice and Research, 14*(2):117–129.

National Human Rights Commission of Thailand (NHRCT). (2011). Retrieved October 31, 2012, from http://www.nhrc.or.th/2012/wb/en/index.php.

Park, J. (2010). Police establish Civilian Review Board. *Donga-Daily*.

Perez, T. A. (n.d.) *External governmental mechanisms of police accountability: Three investigative structures*. Retrieved October 28, 2012, from http://www.vera.org/download?file=571/perez.pdf.

Pyo, C. (2008). *Background report: Examining existing police oversight mechanisms in Asia*. Paper presented at Improving the Role of the Police in Asian and Europe, Delhi, India.

Rahman, H. Z., & Robinson, M. (2006). Governance and state effectiveness in Asia. *IDS Bulletin, 37*(3), 130–149.

Seymore, J., & Finday, M. (1989). Show trials in China: After Tiananmen Square. *Journal of Law and Society, 16*, 352–359.

Sun, I., Hu, R., & Wu, Y. (2012). Social capital, political participation, and trust in the police in urban china. *Australian and New Zealand Journal of Criminology, 45*(1), 87–105.

Sun, I., & Wu, Y. (2010). Chinese policing in a time of transition, 1978–2008. *Journal of Contemporary Criminal Justice, 26*, 20–35.

Varona, G. (2010). Politics and policing in the Philippines: Challenges to police reform. *Flinders Journal of History and Politics, 26*, 101–125.

Walker, S. (2005). *The new world of police accountability.* Thousand Oaks, CA: Sage.

Wong, K. C. (2006). Legalism and constitutionalism in the People's Republic of China. *International Journal of Criminal Justice Sciences, 1*(2), 1–26.

Wong, K. C. (2010). Police powers and control in Hong Kong. *International Journal of Comparative and Applied Criminal Justice, 34*(1), 1–24.

World Bank. (2012). *Thailand: Experts share lessons for countering corruption.* Retrieved October 1, 2012, from http://go.worldbank.org/F8AJHMC8E0.

World Governance Indicators. (2013). *Update.* Retrieved March 14, 2014, from http://www.govindicators.org.

Wu, Y., Lambert, E. G., Smith, B. W., Pasupuleti, S., Jaishankar, K., & Bhimarasetty, J. V. (2012). An exploratory comparison of policing views between Indian and U.S. college students. *International Criminal Justice Review, 22*(1), 68.

Wu, Y., & Sun, I. (2009). Citizen trust in police: The case of China. *Police Quarterly, 12*(2), 170–191.

Zhong, L. (2009). Community policing in China: Old wine in new bottles. *Police Practice and Research, 4*, 157–169.

The Interface between Human Rights and Police Complaints in Europe

8

GRAHAM SMITH

Contents

In 2009, the Council of Europe published the *Opinion of the Commissioner for Human Rights Concerning Independent and Effective Determination of Complaints against the Police* (Commissioner for Human Rights, 2009a; Smith, 2010). The *Opinion* set out five effective investigation principles developed in the case law of the European Convention on Human Rights (ECHR) and recommended that compliance with human rights standards could most effectively be achieved by creation of an independent police complaints body (IPCB).

The police play a pivotal role in the human rights arena, and during the course of the last quarter of a century, the influence of human rights law has spread to touch many aspects of operational policing (Bayley, 2014; Das & Palmiotto, 2002; Murdoch & Roche, 2013). When performing their duties to prevent and detect crime, and maintain public order, the police serve to protect individual human rights. Operational law enforcement, which permits police to resort to coercive powers, *inter alia*, to arrest and engage in surveillance operations, intrinsically interferes with the human rights of suspects (this extends to the Public Prosecutor in jurisdictions where prosecuting authorities rather than the police have responsibility for criminal investigation). The police are vulnerable to complaints on two counts: that they violated individual human rights as a result of their acts or omissions (in breach of a negative obligation), on the one hand, or that they failed to protect human rights (in breach of a positive obligation), on the other. Focusing on developments in Europe, this chapter explores the interface between international human rights and police complaints. The chapter is separated into two sections. The first examines the standards laid down in the jurisprudence of the European Court of Human Rights for the investigation of complaints against the police, with references to other international instruments. The second section examines the promotion and monitoring of state compliance with the ECHR standards, with particular reference to a joint Council of Europe and European Union program to combat ill-treatment and impunity in five former Soviet bloc states.

The ECHR and Effective Investigation of Complaints against the Police

Since the adoption of the Universal Declaration on Human Rights by the United Nations (UN) General Assembly in 1948, international treaties have been introduced around the globe for the practical purpose of protecting human rights. The Council of Europe led the way with adoption of the ECHR in 1950; after many years discussion, the UN adopted the International Covenant on Civil and Political Rights in 1966; the Organisation of American States followed suit with the American Convention on Human Rights (ACHR) in 1969; and the Organisation of African Unity adopted the African Charter on Human and Peoples' Rights in 1981. A similar treaty does not currently exist in the Asia Pacific region.

International treaties protect human rights by laying down minimum standards that contracting state parties are obliged to comply with, as decided by regional human rights courts. In Europe, the European Court of Human Rights, which sits in the Council of Europe's home in Strasbourg, France, determines whether or not a state is liable for violation of the ECHR (Rainey, Wicks, & Ovey, 2014). Substantive rights that are of particular importance to a human-rights-based approach to police complaints are the right to life, under Article 2 of the ECHR, and prohibition of torture or inhuman or degrading treatment or punishment, under Article 3. In addition, the Court has relied on the obligation on states to secure to everyone within their jurisdiction the rights set out in the ECHR (Article 1) and the right to an effective remedy (Article 13). Alongside negative obligations not to violate a Convention right, states are subject to positive obligations that require them to take measures to protect human rights (Mowbray, 2004). Among the first of the positive obligations introduced by the Strasbourg Court was the requirement that prosecutors bring criminal proceedings for the purpose of protecting the right to privacy (under Article 8 of the ECHR), in *X & Y v. The Netherlands* (1985) 8 EHRR 235, and that police take operational measures to protect the rights of protesters to demonstrate under Article 11 (*Platform "Artze fur das Leben" v. Austria*, 1991, 13 EHRR 204). Included in the doctrine of positive obligations, the procedural obligation to effectively investigate arguable violations of substantive ECHR rights have been developed in the jurisprudence of the European Court of Human Rights (Mowbray, 2002; Smith, 2004). Difficulties associated with evidencing a negative violation of a right, because information may be restricted to state officials who also have responsibility for investigation, are prominent in this area of human rights law.

An early example of this type of procedural obligation was introduced by the Inter-American Court of Human Rights in the seminal forced disappearance case of *Velásquez Rodriguez v. Honduras* (1989), 28 ILM 291. Acknowledging that it was difficult to obtain direct evidence in cases where officials sought to conceal state involvement in the disappearance of an individual, the Inter-American Court ruled that violation was imputable on the basis of circumstantial evidence or logical inference that was consistent with the known facts. In regard to the obligation on a state to respect human rights (Article 1 of the ACHR), the Court observed that the authorities were required to effectively investigate alleged violations.

> The State is obligated to investigate every situation involving a violation of the rights protected by the Convention. If the State apparatus acts in such a way that the violation goes unpunished and the victim's full enjoyment of such rights is not restored as soon as possible, the State has failed to comply with its duty to ensure the free and full exercise of those rights to the persons within its jurisdiction. The same is true when the State allows private persons or groups to act freely and with impunity to the detriment of the rights recognized by the Convention. (*Velásquez Rodriguez v. Honduras*, para. 176)

The Inter-American Court of Human Rights took the failure of the Honduran authorities to investigate the reported disappearance of Manfredo Velásquez into consideration when ruling that the right to life (under Article 4 of the ACHR), right to humane treatment (under Article 5), and right to liberty (Article 7) had been violated. A few years later, the UN Human Rights Committee was to follow a similar line of reasoning in the case of *Mojica v. Dominican Republic* (Communication No. 449/1991, UN Doc. CCPR/C/51/D/449/1991, 1994).

Development of the obligation to conduct an effective investigation in the jurisprudence of the European Court of Human Rights can be traced back to a complaint of ill-treatment in police custody. In *Tomasi v. France* (1992), 15 EHRR 1, the Court relied on similar logic to the Inter-American Court of Human Rights in *Velásquez Rodriguez* when ruling that the applicant had been subjected to degrading and inhuman treatment in contravention of Article 3 of the ECHR. Several reasons were given for this decision. First, no one claimed that marks noted by medical examiners on Tomasi's body predated his period in detention, were self-inflicted, or occurred during an attempt to escape. Second, at his first appearance before the investigating judge, the complainant drew attention to the marks on his body and an expert was appointed to examine him. Third, four different doctors examined Tomasi and concurred on the timing of his injuries, which corresponded with the hours when he was in police custody. Although reference was not made to the rigor of the investigation into Tomasi's complaint that he had been assaulted by police officers, the Court was satisfied that the State's failure to offer an alternative explanation for his injuries was sufficient to establish a causal connection. In the similar case of *Ribitsch v. Austria* (1996), 21 EHRR 573, the Court expressly referred to the obligation of the government to provide a "plausible explanation" for injuries that had been recorded separately by two medical examiners, which the applicant complained were as a result of assaults committed by police officers when he was in custody.

Whereas ineffective investigation of the two previous complaints of police ill-treatment was inferred, in *McCann v. the United Kingdom* (1996), 21 EHRR 97, the implication that an effective official investigation must be conducted into an allegation that a state official violated the right to life was spelt out.

> The obligation to protect the right to life under this provision (Art. 2), read in conjunction with the State's general duty under Article 1 (Art. 2+1) of the Convention to 'secure to everyone within their jurisdiction the rights and freedoms defined in [the] Convention', requires by implication that there should be some form of effective official investigation when individuals have been killed as a result of the use of force by, *inter alios*, agents of the State. (*McCann v. the United Kingdom*, para. 161)

In making this observation the European Court of Human Rights referred to the UN (1989a) *Principles on the Effective Prevention and Investigation of Extra-Judicial, Arbitrary and Summary Executions* and UN (1990) *Basic Principles on the Use of Force and Firearms by Law Enforcement Officials*. Importance is attached to these international instruments because they require that an effective and prompt investigation must be carried out into the use of force by law enforcement officers that results in death or serious injury, and victims or bereaved relatives must have access to the investigative process. The European Court of Human Rights did not find it necessary to rule on the effectiveness of the investigation in *McCann*, where a coroner's inquest was held to establish the cause of death of three members of an Irish Republican Army Active Service Unit killed by members of the British Army's Special Air Service in Gibraltar.

Having asserted that killings by state officials, including police officers, must be officially and effectively investigated, that is regardless of whether or not a formal complaint had been made, a little more than a year later, the

Court considered the duty to investigate an allegation of torture. In *Aksoy v. Turkey* (1997) 23 EHRR 553, the Court followed the same approach adopted in *Tomasi* and *Ribitsch* and found that the suspension of the victim by his arms, which were tied behind his back (known as "Palestinian hanging"), was in violation of the prohibition of torture. The effectiveness of the investigation into the complaint of torture by the Turkish authorities was dealt with separately under Article 13 of the ECHR, the right to an effective remedy (again, the Court referred to an international human rights instrument in support of the judgment).

> ...where an individual has an arguable claim that he has been tortured by agents of the State, the notion of an "effective remedy" entails,... a thorough and effective investigation capable of leading to the identification and punishment of those responsible and including effective access for the complainant to the investigatory procedure. It is true that no express provision exists in the Convention such as can be found in Article 12 of the 1984 United Nations Convention against Torture and Other Cruel, Inhuman or Degrading Treatment or Punishment, which imposes a duty to proceed to a "prompt and impartial" investigation whenever there is a reasonable ground to believe that an act of torture has been committed. However, in the Court's view, such a requirement is implicit in the notion of an "effective remedy" under Article 13. (*Aksoy v. Turkey*, para. 98)

McCann was not referred to in *Aksoy* or when the Court delivered a similar judgment in *Aydin v. Turkey* (1997), 25 EHRR 251, another torture case, in September 1997.

At this stage in the emerging nexus between human rights law and police complaints, the European Court of Human Rights had followed separate pathways in concluding that there was a duty to effectively investigate alleged breaches by law enforcement officers of the right to life and prohibition of torture. For alleged violations of the right to life, the procedural obligation to investigate was for the purpose of giving practical effect to the protections afforded under Article 2 of the ECHR. For allegations of torture or ill-treatment, in contrast, the obligation was an element of the right to an effective remedy under Article 13, and not under Article 3. The Court demonstrated a willingness to extend the duty to investigate other substantive rights when finding that there had been a violation of Article 13 for failure to effectively investigate the alleged destruction of homes and property purposely by agents of the state (in breach of the right to privacy under Article 8) in *Mentes v. Turkey* (1997), 26 EHRR 595.

The Strasbourg jurisprudence on effective investigations developed rapidly in the next few years in a series of applications involving allegations of unlawful killing, torture, and enforced disappearance. In *Kaya v. Turkey*

(1998), 28 EHRR 1, the absence of an effective investigation was material to the finding that there had been violations of both the right to life and to an effective remedy. After concluding that there was insufficient evidence to find beyond reasonable doubt that the victim had been unlawfully killed by security forces, the Court went on to rule that violation of Article 2 was as a result of the failure of the Turkish authorities to conduct an effective investigation.

> ...the procedural protection of the right to life inherent in Article 2 of the Convention secures the accountability of agents of the State for their use of lethal force by subjecting their actions to some form of independent and public scrutiny capable of leading to a determination of whether the force used was or was not justified in a particular set of circumstances. (*Kaya v. Turkey*, para. 87)

The Court clarified the difference between the investigative obligations in the two articles in *Kaya* by explaining that the duties on the state under Article 13 were broader than implied in Article 2. Whereas the obligation under Article 2 served to establish whether the use of fatal force was justified, the purpose of the investigative duty under Article 13 was to remedy the harm suffered by bereaved relatives, which entitled a complainant or bereaved relatives to have effective access to the investigation process. Some years later, the Court was to expand on the purpose of the Article 2 obligation in *Jordan v. the United Kingdom* (2003), 37 EHRR 52 (see further):

> The essential purpose of such investigation [under Article 2] is to secure the effective implementation of the domestic laws which protect the right to life and, in those cases involving State agents or bodies, to ensure their accountability for deaths occurring under their responsibility. (*Jordan v. the United Kingdom*, para. 105)

In the forced disappearance case of *Kurt v. Turkey* (1998), 27 EHRR 373, the European Court of Human Rights was not persuaded that the beyond reasonable doubt evidential burden should be relaxed when asked to determine that the right to life and prohibition of torture had been breached. The applicant made reference to the decision of the Inter-American Court of Human Rights in *Velásquez Rodriguez* (see discussion on p. 161), and unsuccessfully sought to establish that the European Court's reasoning in *Tomasi* should also be applied in circumstances where the State had failed to satisfactorily account for the disappearance of a person. The Court explained that it was unable to find a violation of Article 2 for failure to conduct an effective investigation in the absence of concrete evidence: of the fatal shooting, for example, by state agents that was present in the *McCann* and *Kaya* judgments. The same reasoning was applied to the applicant's Article 3 claim. There was sufficient evidence, however, for the Court to conclude that the victim had been taken into custody by members of the security forces and that there had been a "particularly grave" violation of the substantive and procedural limbs of Article 5, the right to liberty (*Kurt v. Turkey*, para. 129), and Article 13.

In regard to the duty to investigate alleged violations of the right to life by private persons (which the Inter-American Court of Human Rights established in *Velásquez Rodriguez*), the Article 2 obligation was extended to include killings by nonstate agents, which the state had knowledge of, in *Ergi v. Turkey* (1998), 32 EHRR 388.

> …this [investigative] obligation is not confined to cases where it has been established that the killing was caused by an agent of the State. Nor is it decisive whether members of the deceased's family or others have lodged a formal complaint about the killing with the relevant investigatory authority. In the case under consideration, the mere knowledge of the killing on the part of the authorities gave rise *ipso facto* to an obligation under Article 2 of the Convention to carry out an effective investigation into the circumstances surrounding the death. (*Ergi v. Turkey*, para. 82)

The threshold for investigation of an alleged violation of Article 2 of the ECHR involving the acts of a private person was further explained in *Osman v. the United Kingdom* (2000), 29 EHRR 245, when the European Court ruled that there would be a duty on the police to take operational measures to protect the right to life in cases where the police *ought* to have known about a real and immediate risk to life (para. 116).

In the torture case of *Assenov v. Bulgaria* (1999), 28 EHRR 652, the Strasbourg Article 2 jurisprudence on the obligation to conduct an effective investigation was applied to Article 3.

> …where an individual raises an arguable claim that he has been seriously illtreated by the police or other such agents of the State unlawfully and in breach of Article 3, that provision, read in conjunction with the State's general duty under Article 1 of the Convention to "secure to everyone within their jurisdiction the rights and freedoms defined in…[the] Convention," requires by implication that there should be an effective official investigation. This investigation, as with that under Article 2, should be capable of leading to the identification and punishment of those responsible… If this were not the case, the general legal prohibition of torture and inhuman and degrading treatment and punishment, despite its fundamental importance,… would be ineffective in practice and it would be possible in some cases for agents of the State to abuse the rights of those within their control with virtual impunity. (*Assenov v. Bulgaria*, para. 102)

The Court's insistence that a high evidential standard was required for it to find that the right to life had been violated in forced disappearance cases was relaxed in *Timurtas v. Turkey* (2001), 33 EHRR 6, which was distinguished from *Kurt* on the facts. Referring to the absence of a "plausible explanation," introduced in *Ribitsch*, circumstantial evidence was relied on and the Court ruled that there had been multiple violations of the ECHR, including substantive violation of Article 2 and breach of the procedural obligation to conduct an effective investigation. Furthermore, the Court was satisfied beyond reasonable doubt that the victim had been subjected to torture and found that there had been a substantive violation of Article 3. As in the *Aksoy* and *Aydin* torture cases, the failure to effectively investigate the alleged breach was dealt with under Article 13. Despite the European Court's recalibration of its forced disappearance jurisprudence, in closer alignment with that developed by the Inter-American Court, questions have been asked of the principles underpinning the decisions of the Strasbourg Court and its conservatism when considering allegations that states attempted to evade censure for serious human rights violations (Antkowiak, 2002; Claude, 2010; Sethi, 2001).

In *Jordan v. the United Kingdom*, the European Court of Human Rights, referring extensively to international instruments and ECHR case law, summarized the developments of the preceding years to explain the nature of the obligation on a state to act on its own motion and conduct an effective investigation into an alleged killing by an agent of the state, which, in light of the *Assenov* judgment, also applies to torture, inhuman or degrading treatment, or punishment allegations.

> ...to be effective, it may generally be regarded as necessary for the persons responsible for and carrying out the investigation to be independent from those implicated in the events... This means not only a lack of hierarchical or institutional connection but also a practical independence. (para. 106)
>
> The investigation must also be effective in the sense that it is capable of leading to a determination of whether the force used in such cases was or was not justified in the circumstances...and to the identification and punishment of those responsible... The authorities must have taken the reasonable steps available to them to secure the evidence concerning the incident, including *inter alia* eye witness testimony, forensic evidence and, where appropriate, an autopsy which provides a complete and accurate record of injury and an objective analysis of clinical findings, including the cause of death... Any deficiency in the investigation which undermines its ability to establish the cause of death or the person or persons responsible will risk falling foul of this standard. (para. 107)
>
> A requirement of promptness and reasonable expedition is implicit... It must be accepted that there may be obstacles or difficulties which prevent progress in an investigation in a particular situation. However, a prompt response by the authorities in investigating a use of lethal force may generally

be regarded as essential in maintaining public confidence in their adherence to the rule of law and in preventing any appearance of collusion in or tolerance of unlawful acts. (para. 108)

...there must be a sufficient element of public scrutiny of the investigation or its results to secure accountability in practice as well as in theory. The degree of public scrutiny required may well vary from case to case. In all cases, however, the next-of-kin of the victim must be involved in the procedure to the extent necessary to safeguard his or her legitimate interests. (para. 109)

In similar fashion to the way in which the European Court of Human Rights aligned the effective investigative obligation that was first read into Article 2, in *McCann*, into Article 3, in *Assenov*, the investigative duty that was first introduced to allegations against private persons in regard to Article 2, in *Ergi*, was later applied to private persons alleged to have breached Articles 3 and 8 in *MC v. Bulgaria* (2005), 40 EHRR 20, a rape case: "the Court considers that States have a positive obligation inherent in Articles 3 and 8 of the Convention to enact criminal-law provisions effectively punishing rape and to apply them in practice through effective investigation and prosecution" (para. 153).

Shortly after this expansion of the effective investigation obligation, in recognition of the difficulty with evidencing whether discrimination played a part in breaches of the ECHR, the Court was to impose an additional duty on states to thoroughly examine the evidence to determine whether or not there may have been discriminatory motives for an alleged violation of the right to life in *Nachova v. Bulgaria* (2005), 42 EHRR 43.

To summarize, during the space of less than 12 years, between 1992 and 2004, the Strasbourg jurisprudence laid down standards for the investigation of alleged human rights violations. The interface between human rights and police complaints in Europe currently rests on the duties laid down by the European Court of Human Rights on a state to conduct an effective investigation into death or injury alleged to have been caused by a police officer that is independent, adequate, prompt, open to public scrutiny, and involves the complainant in the investigation process. The standards discussed previously, succinctly laid down in *Jordan*, were reaffirmed in *Ramsahai v. The Netherlands* (2008), 46 EHRR 43, when the Court found that a delay of 15 hours before police handed over the investigation of a fatal shooting by a colleague to independent investigators was in breach of Article 2. On the issue of independent investigation the Court observed: "What is at stake here is nothing less than public confidence in the State's monopoly on the use of force" (para. 325). In regard to Article 3, the threshold is not necessarily high. In *Stefan Iliev v. Bulgaria* (Application No. 53121/99, Judgment of May 10, 2007), the Court ruled that an independent and effective investigation was required into a complaint by a 72-year-old man who alleged that he was left with minor injuries after an assault by police officers. Although the injuries sustained were insufficient to amount to inhuman or degrading treatment, the allegation that they were caused by police when acting unlawfully warranted an investigation that was capable of establishing the criminal liability of the officers whom were responsible. Failure of the police (or prosecuting authorities in states where the Public Prosecutor has responsibility for criminal investigations) to effectively investigate to the same standard analogous allegations against private persons will leave the investigative authority liable to a complaint of having failed to protect human rights.

In addition to the international instruments cited by the European Court of Human Rights mentioned previously, the Court has also referred to guidance on the investigation of violations of the right to life and prohibition of torture provided in the Minnesota Protocol (UN, 1989b) and the Istanbul Protocol (UN, 2004), respectively.

Promoting and Monitoring State Compliance with ECHR Investigation Standards

The European Court of Human Rights sits at the hub of a network of Council of Europe institutions that has evolved to regulate compliance with the ECHR (de Beco, 2012; Directorate General Human Rights and the Rule of Law, 2014). Accession of former Soviet bloc states to the Council in the 1990s, following which there was an unprecedented increase in the caseload of the Court, prompted a far-reaching reorganization of the Strasbourg institutions in the 2000s (Helfer, 2008).

Execution of the judgments of the Court by national governments found to be in breach of human rights is supervised by the Committee of Ministers (2014). The Committee ensures compliance with individual measures ruled necessary by the Court as a consequence of violation, for example, payment of compensation to a victim. In addition, the Committee oversees any general measures required to protect against similar violations occurring in the future, for example, improvement to the efficacy of investigation mechanisms.

Created in 1990, by Article 1 of the European Convention for the Prevention of Torture and Inhuman or Degrading Treatment or Punishment (Council of Europe, 1987), the European Committee for the Prevention of Torture (CPT) organizes country visits and inspects how people are treated when held in detention facilities, including police custody (Kicker, 2012; Murdoch, 2006). The CPT serves a preventative function, and recommendations on how human rights protections may be improved are included in reports to national governments after country visits (CPT, 2006). In countries where the CPT has identified systemic failure to protect human rights, it is not unusual for the European Court of Human Rights to cite reports (see, e.g., reference to the CPT, 2000, report of a visit to the United Kingdom regarding deficiencies in arrangements to investigate complaints against the police in *Jordan v. the United Kingdom*, para. 93).

Established in 1999, by Resolution 99/50 of the Committee of Ministers (1999), the primary function of the Commissioner for Human Rights is to promote awareness and respect for human rights. For this purpose, the Commissioner also arranges country visits, liaises with civil society, and undertakes thematic inquiries (Sivonen, 2012). Other Strasbourg institutions especially interested in police complaints include the European Commission against Racism and Intolerance (2007) and the Group of States against Corruption (Dzhekova, Gounev, & Bezlov, 2013): civil society and human rights defenders (Amnesty International, 2014; Human Rights Watch, 2014) also make meaningful contributions.

The number of violations of Articles 2 and 3 of the ECHR due to the lack of an effective investigation increased dramatically in the 2000s. After the European Court of Human Rights commenced publishing statistics on violations, the annual total increased more than 10-fold in the space of 5 years, from 10 in 2003 to 118 in 2008 (see Figure 8.1). As a percentage of the total violations annually, lack of effective investigation increased from 1.3% in 2003 to 9.4% ($n = 179$) in 2011 and fell back to 8.6% in 2013 ($n = 118$). The Russian Federation ($n = 372$) and Turkey ($n = 305$) account for 65.6% of the total of 1,032 lack of effective investigation violations between 2003 and 2013. Ukraine ($n = 75$), Romania ($n = 68$), Bulgaria ($n = 50$), and the Republic of Moldova ($n = 40$) have also been regularly called to account before the Court for their failure to investigate allegations of serious abuse.

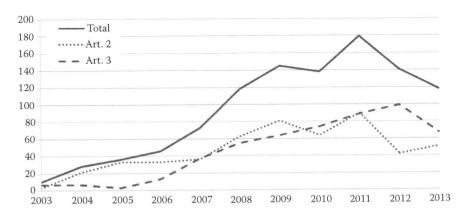

Figure 8.1 Violations of Articles 2 and 3 of the ECHR due to lack of an effective investigation: 2003–2013. (From European Court of Human Rights annual reports, 2003–2013, retrieved from http://www.echr.coe.int/Pages/home.aspx?p =echrpublications&c=.)

With concern mounting, a number of Council of Europe initiatives were launched, including a thematic inquiry on police complaints by the Commissioner for Human Rights (2007); a Committee of Experts (Steering Committee for Human Rights, 2010) was established for the purpose of issuing guidance on eradicating impunity for serious breaches of human rights (Committee of Ministers, 2011); and a joint Council of Europe and European Union program to combat impunity for ill-treatment in the five former Soviet bloc states of Armenia, Azerbaijan, Georgia, Moldova, and Ukraine was also established (Council of Europe/European Union, 2011, 2014; Svanidze, 2009).

In the summer of 2008, the Commissioner for Human Rights (2008), Thomas Hammarberg, organized an expert workshop that was attended by senior representatives of IPCBs. Published the following year, the *Opinion of the Commissioner for Human Rights concerning Independent and Effective Determination of Complaints Against the Police* (Commissioner for Human Rights, 2009a) outlines the five investigation standards developed in the case law of the ECHR and proposes how they may be effectively implemented. Recommending that the creation of an IPCB with powers to investigate complaints represents an ideal way of ensuring compliance with ECHR investigation standards, the *Opinion* currently serves as a core policy document on police complaints (Commissioner for Human Rights, 2009b). In the five years since publication, however, there has been limited success in achieving reform. Since 2009, two new IPCBs with powers of investigation have been established in Europe, in countries that had not been singled out for criticism. In 2012, the Independent Police Complaints Authority of Denmark was created (Commissioner for Human Rights, 2014b; Johansen, 2014), and the Police Investigations and Review Commissioner replaced the Police Complaints Commissioner in Scotland the following year (Scott, 2013). The government of Norway has not acted to date on a recommendation to set up an IPCB by an independent commission of inquiry (Norges Offentlige Utredninger, 2009).

In 2013, the Commissioner for Human Rights (2013b, 2014a), Nils Muižnieks, found it necessary to revisit the theme of police misconduct and highlighted concern with death and ill-treatment in custody, disproportionate use of force when policing demonstrations and/or arresting suspects, violence targeted against minorities and migrants, and abusive stops and searches targeted against minorities and migrants. Reiterating the importance of independent mechanisms for investigating complaints against the police, the Commissioner pointed to allegations of torture and ill-treatment in police custody in Greece (Commissioner for Human Rights, 2013a: see also CPT, 2012; UN Special Rapporteur on Torture, 2011) and the Republic of Moldova (Commissioner for Human Rights, 2013c: see also UN Special Rapporteur on Torture, 2009; and see further discussion on p. 171) and excessive use of force when policing protests in Spain (Commissioner for Human Rights, 2013c: see also CPT, 2013), Turkey (Commissioner for Human Rights, 2013d), and Ukraine (Commissioner for Human Rights, 2014c; see also CPT, 2013; and see following discussion).

The joint Council of Europe/European Union project to combat ill-treatment and impunity in five former Soviet bloc states, which commenced in 2009 and was extended in 2011 until 2014, illustrates how Strasbourg resources may be harnessed to promote human rights compliant police complaints systems. Ukraine became the 37th member of the Council of Europe in November 1995 and was joined by neighboring South Caucuses states Armenia, Azerbaijan, Georgia, and the Republic of Moldova by January 2001. In Table 8.1, violations of the right to life and prohibition of torture recorded against these five states are presented. Since accession, there have been a total of 232 substantive violations of Articles 2 and 3 and 133 for lack of an effective investigation.

Further indication of the problems faced by these states is given in the annual reports of the Committee of Ministers on the supervision of the execution of judgments and decisions of the European Court of Human Rights. The 2013 Annual Report (Committee of Ministers, 2014) records that the execution of 11 lack of effective investigation judgments that involve the five states (Murdoch & Svanidze, 2015), some of which date back to 2005, was under enhanced supervision. These are procedures reserved for judgments that have been determined to require urgent individual measures, pilot judgments, or disclose major structural and/or complex problems (Committee of Ministers, 2014, para. 24).

With the overarching objective of strengthening capacity to effectively investigate allegations of ill-treatment, the purpose of the program was to support the national authorities to develop complaints systems that comply

Table 8.1 Violations of Articles 1 and 2 of the ECHR by South Caucuses States, Republic of Moldova, and Ukraine: Until 2013

| | Article 2 | | Article 3 | | |
	Deprivation of Life	Ineffective Investigation	Torture	Inhuman/ Degrading Treatment	Ineffective Investigation
Armenia	–	–	1	7	1
Azerbaijan	–	1	1	9	5
Georgia	1	3	–	16	8
Republic of Moldova	2	6	8	61	34
Ukraine	9	27	12	105	48

Source: European Court of Human Rights (2014, pp. 202–203).

with international standards, giving particular attention to the training of judges, prosecutors, police officers, penitentiary officials, and lawyers. In pursuit of these objectives, the program drew on the expertise of Strasbourg institutions, practitioners, and scholars to organize a series of international events, including seminars, training courses, and exchange visits.

Although the criminal justice systems that operate in each country are jurisdictionally distinct, there were clearly identifiable commonalities in the administration of police complaints in the baseline assessments conducted at the beginning of the program. Three institutions have primary responsibility for handling complaints: the Ministry of Internal Affairs (renamed the Police Department in Armenia in 2002), the Office of the Prosecutor-General (Office of the Chief Prosecutor in Georgia), and the Office of the Ombudsman (known as the Human Rights Defender in Armenia, the Human Rights Commissioner in Azerbaijan, the Office of the Public Defender in Georgia, the Parliamentary Advocate in Moldova, and the Parliamentary Human Rights Commissioner in Ukraine).

In each country, the Ministry of Internal Affairs is responsible for policing, and a separate department in the Ministry (Directorate of Internal Security in Armenia, Department of Internal Investigations in Azerbaijan, General Inspectorate in Georgia, Internal Security Service in Moldova, and Internal Security Service in Ukraine) handles and investigates complaints of misconduct, which may be referred to the local police department. The Office of the Prosecutor-General is responsible for prosecuting crime, including the direction and control of criminal investigations. In Armenia, an independent body, the Special Investigation Service, was set up in 2007 to investigate allegations against public officials; and in Moldova, prosecutions of police may be delegated to military prosecutors. The Office of the Ombudsman may record a complaint against the police and recommend that it is investigated by the appropriate authority, but it does not have powers to investigate, and neither the Ministry of Internal Affairs nor the Office of the Prosecutor-General has a duty to keep the Ombudsman informed of the progress or outcome of a complaint.

With three institutions sharing responsibility for complaints against the police, and in the absence of a central authority with specific duties to record, track, and analyze complaints, the systems in each of these five states are haphazardly organized, and there is the potential for complaints to be processed in duplicate or get lost in the system. When measured against the ECHR investigation standards, procedures have been found wanting, and recommendations that each country should "establish a genuinely independent and effective system for the investigation of cases involving alleged human rights violations by law enforcement officials" (Council of Europe and European Union, 2013) have been an enduring feature of the program. Although reforms have been introduced—to criminal procedure codes, creation of a police disciplinary committee, and human rights legislation in Azerbaijan (Smith, 2013), for example—that are consistent with the objectives of the program, there have been significant barriers to reform in the region (Hammarberg, 2013), not least of which are difficulties attributable to lack of political will and acknowledgement by senior policy makers and practitioners that police complaints reform is not a national priority in their countries.

Conclusion

In this chapter, the insinuation of human rights law into police complaints practice as developed and promoted in Europe has been explored. The first section tracked the development of five investigation standards in the case law of the ECHR—independence, adequacy, promptness, public scrutiny, and victim involvement. In the second section, Council of Europe mechanisms for regulating compliance with human rights standards have been outlined, and particular attention has been paid to a program combating ill-treatment and impunity in five former Soviet bloc states—Armenia, Azerbaijan, Georgia, Moldova, and Ukraine. The difficulties encountered with the implementation of reform in the region reinforce the view that accountable policing is a work in process that harnesses the resources and efforts of a broad range of local, national, and international actors.

Acknowledgments

The author is grateful to Jim Murdoch, Mahir Mushteidzada, and Eric Svanidze for their assistance with the section on the Council of Europe and European Union's South Caucuses, Moldova, and Ukraine program combating ill-treatment and impunity. The usual caveat applies.

References

Amnesty International. (2014). *Amnesty International Report 2013: The state of the world's human rights.* London: Amnesty International.

Antkowiak, T. M. (2002). Truth as right and remedy in international human rights experience. *Michigan Journal of International Law, 23*(4), 977–1013.

Bayley, D. (2014, March 17). Human rights in policing: A global assessment. *Policing and Society*, advanced online publication.

Claude, O. (2010). A comparative approach to enforced disappearances in the inter-American Court of Human Rights and the European Court of Human Rights Jurisprudence. *Intercultural Human Rights Law Review, 5*, 407–462.

Commissioner for Human Rights. (2007, December 3). *There must be no impunity for police violence,* Viewpoint. Strasbourg: Council of Europe.

Commissioner for Human Rights. (2008). *Police complaints mechanisms: Ensuring independence and effectiveness expert workshop, Strasbourg 26–27 May 2008 expert workshop report*, CommDH(2008)16. Strasbourg: Council of Europe.

Commissioner for Human Rights. (2009a). *Opinion of the Commissioner for Human Rights concerning independent and effective determination of complaints against the police*, CommDH(2009)4. Strasbourg: Council of Europe.

Commissioner for Human Rights. (2009b). *Contribution of the Commissioner for Human Rights to the work of the Committee of Experts on Impunity (DH-I)*, CommDH(2009)32. Strasbourg: Council of Europe.

Commissioner for Human Rights. (2013a). *Report by Nils Muižnieks, Commissioner for Human Rights of the Council of Europe, following his visit to Greece from 28 January to 1 February 2013*, CommDH(2013)6. Strasbourg: Council of Europe.

Commissioner for Human Rights. (2013b). *2nd quarterly activity report 2013 by Nils Muižnieks, Council of Europe Commissioner for Human Rights*, CommDH(2013)16. Strasbourg: Council of Europe.

Commissioner for Human Rights. (2013c). *Report by Nils Muižnieks, Commissioner for Human Rights of the Council of Europe, following his visit to Spain from 3 to 7 June 2013*, CommDH(2013)18. Strasbourg: Council of Europe.

Commissioner for Human Rights. (2013d). *Report by Nils Muižnieks, Commissioner for Human Rights of the Council of Europe, following his visit to Turkey from 1 to 5 July 2013*, CommDH(2013)24. Strasbourg: Council of Europe.

Commissioner for Human Rights. (2014a, February 25). *Police abuse—A serious threat to the rule of law*, Human Rights comment. Strasbourg: Council of Europe.

Commissioner for Human Rights. (2014b). *Report by Nils Muižnieks, Commissioner for Human Rights of the Council of Europe, following his visit to Denmark from 19 to 21 November 2013*, CommDH(2014)4. Strasbourg: Council of Europe.

Commissioner for Human Rights. (2014c). *Report by Nils Muižnieks, Commissioner for Human Rights of the Council of Europe, following his visit to Ukraine from 4 to 10 February 2014*, CommDH(2014)7. Strasbourg: Council of Europe.

Committee for the Prevention of Torture (CPT). (2000). *Report to the United Kingdom Government on the visit to the United Kingdom and the Isle of Man carried out by the European Committee for the Prevention of Torture and Inhuman or Degrading Treatment or Punishment from 8 to 17 September 1997*. Strasbourg: Council of Europe.

Committee for the Prevention of Torture (CPT). (2013). *Report to the Spanish Government on the visit to Spain carried out by the European Committee for the Prevention of Torture and Inhuman or Degrading Treatment or Punishment (CPT) from 31 May to 13 June 2011*, CPT/Inf (2013) 6. Strasbourg: Council of Europe.

Committee for the Prevention of Torture or Inhuman and Degrading Treatment or Punishment (CPT). (2006). *The CPT standards: Substantive sections of the CPT's General Reports*. Strasbourg: Council of Europe.

Committee for the Prevention of Torture or Inhuman and Degrading Treatment or Punishment (CPT). (2012). *Report to the Government of Greece on the visit to Greece carried out by the European Committee for the Prevention of Torture and Inhuman or Degrading Treatment or Punishment (CPT) from 19 to 27 January 2011*, CPT/Inf (2012) 1. Strasbourg: Council of Europe.

Committee of Ministers of the Council of Europe. (1999). *Resolution (99) 50 on the Council of Europe Commissioner for Human Rights, adopted by the Committee of Ministers on 7 May 1999*. Strasbourg: Council of Europe.

Committee of Ministers of the Council of Europe. (2011, March 30). *Guidelines of the Committee of Ministers of the Council of Europe on eradicating impunity for serious human rights violations*. Strasbourg: Council of Europe.

Committee of Ministers of the Council of Europe. (2014). *Supervision of the execution of judgments and decisions of the European Court of Human Rights: 7th annual report of the Committee of Ministers*. Strasbourg: Council of Europe.

Council of Europe. (1987). *European Convention for the Prevention of Torture and Inhuman or Degrading Treatment or Punishment*. European Treaties ETS No. 126 Strasbourg, 26XI.1987. Strasbourg: Council of Europe.

Council of Europe/European Union. (2011). *Ill-treatment: Combating ill-treatment and impunity in South Caucasus, Moldova and Ukraine*. Retrieved from http://www.jp.coe.int/cead/jp/default.asp?TransID=151.

Council of Europe/European Union. (2013). *Reinforcing the fight against ill-treatment and impunity, Regional Stocktaking Conference: Investigation of serious human rights violations by law enforcement officials, Strasbourg 24 September 2013*. Strasbourg: Council of Europe.

Council of Europe/European Union. (2014). *Ill-treatment II: Reinforcing the fight against ill-treatment and impunity*. Retrieved from http://www.jp.coe.int/cead/jp/default.asp?TransID=212.

Das, D., & Palmiotto, M. J. (2002). International human rights standards: Guidelines for the world's police officers. *Police Quarterly, 5*(2), 206–221.

De Beco, G. (2012). Introduction: The role of European human rights monitoring mechanisms. In G. de Beco (Ed.), *Human rights monitoring mechanisms of the Council of Europe* (pp. 1–16). Abingdon: Routledge.

Directorate General Human Rights and the Rule of Law. (2014). *Practical impact of the Council of Europe monitoring mechanisms in improving respect for human rights and the rule of law in member states*. Strasbourg: Council of Europe.

Dzhekova, R., Gounev, P., & Bezlov, T. (2013). *Countering police corruption: European perspectives*. Sofia: Center for the Study of Democracy.

European Commission against Racism and Intolerance. (2007). *General Policy Recommendation No. 11: On combating racism and racial discrimination in policing*. Strasbourg: Council of Europe.

European Court of Human Rights. (2014). *Annual Report 2013*. Strasbourg: Registry of the European Court of Human Rights.

Hammarberg, T. (2013). *Georgia in transition. Report on the human rights dimension: Background, steps taken and remaining challenges*, addressed to High Representative and Vice-President Catherine Ashton and Commissioner for Enlargement and European Neighbourhood Policy Stefan Füle. Brussels: European Union.

Helfer, L. R. (2008). Redesigning the European Court of Human Rights: Embeddedness as a deep structural principle of the European human rights regime. *European Journal of International Law, 19*(1), 125–159.

Human Rights Watch. (2014). *World report 2014: Events of 2013*. New York: Seven Stories Press.

Johansen, A. (2014). The rise and rise of independent police complaints bodies. In J. Fleming (Ed.), *The future of policing* (pp. 446–462). Abingdon: Routledge.

Kicker, R. (2012). The European Committee for the Prevention of Torture and Inhuman or Degrading Treatment or Punishment (the CPT). In G. de Beco (Ed.), *Human rights monitoring mechanisms of the Council of Europe* (pp. 43–70). Abingdon: Routledge.

Mowbray, A. (2002). Duties of investigation under the European Convention on Human Rights. *International and Comparative Law Quarterly, 51*(2), 437–448.

Mowbray, A. (2004). *The development of positive obligations under the European Convention on Human Rights by the European Court of Human Rights.* Hart Publishing: Oxford.

Murdoch, J. (2006). Tackling ill-treatment in places of detention: The work of the Council of Europe's 'Torture Committee'. *European Journal on Criminal Policy and Research, 12*(2), 121–142.

Murdoch, J. & Roche, R. (2013). *The European Convention on Human Rights and Policing: A handbook for police officers and other law enforcement officials.* Strasbourg: European Union/Council of Europe.

Norges Offentlige Utredninger. (2009). *Et ansvarlig politi. Åpenhet, kontroll og læring. Evalueringsrapport fra utvalget oppnevnt av Justis-og politidepartementet* (Transl. Responsible law enforcement: Transparency, control and learning). Government Administration Services.

Rainey, B., Wicks, E., & Ovey, C. (2014). *Jacobs, White and Ovey: The European Convention on Human Rights.* Oxford: Oxford University Press.

Scott, K. B. (2013). A single police force for Scotland: The legislative framework (2). *Policing, 7*(2), 142–147.

Sethi, G. S. (2001). The European Court of Human Rights' jurisprudence on issues of forced disappearances. *Human Rights Brief, 8*(3), 11.

Sivonen, L. (2012). The Commissioner for Human Rights. In G. de Beco (Ed.), *Human rights monitoring mechanisms of the Council of Europe* (pp. 17–42). Abingdon: Routledge.

Smith, G. (2004). Rethinking police complaints. *British Journal of Criminology, 44*(1), 15–33.

Smith, G. (2010). Every complaint matters: Human Rights Commissioner's opinion concerning independent and effective determination of complaints against the police. *International Journal of Law, Crime and Justice, 38*(2), 59–74.

Smith, G. (2013). Roundtable discussion on the 'State of implementation of the Law of the Republic of Azerbaijan on ensuring the rights and freedoms of individuals held in detention facilities and enhancing the complaint review procedures.' Retrieved from https://www.escholar.manchester.ac.uk/api/datastream?publicationPid=uk-ac-man-scw:225138&datastreamId=FULL-TEXT.PDF.

Steering Committee for Human Rights. (2010). *Terms of reference of the Committee of Experts on Impunity(DH-I)*, DH-I(2010)03. Strasbourg: Council of Europe.

Svanidze, E. (2009). *Effective investigation of ill-treatment: Guidelines on European standards.* Strasbourg: Council of Europe/European Union.

United Nations (UN). (1989a). *Principles on the effective prevention and investigation of extra-judicial, arbitrary and summary executions.* Geneva: UN Office of the High Commissioner for Human Rights.

United Nations (UN). (1989b). *Minnesota protocol: Manual on the effective prevention and investigation of extra-legal, arbitrary and summary executions*. Geneva: UN Office of the High Commissioner for Human Rights.

United Nations (UN). (1990). *Basic principles on the use of force and firearms by law enforcement officials*. Adopted by the Eighth United Nations Congress on the Prevention of Crime and the Treatment of Offenders, Havana, Cuba, 27 August to 7 September 1990. Geneva: UN Office of the High Commissioner for Human Rights.

United Nations (UN). (2004). *Istanbul protocol: Manual on the effective investigation and documentation of torture and other cruel, inhuman or degrading treatment or punishment*. Geneva: UN Office of the High Commissioner for Human Rights.

United Nations (UN) Special Rapporteur on Torture. (2009). *Report of the Special Rapporteur on torture and other cruel, inhuman or degrading treatment or punishment, Manfred Nowak: Mission to the Republic of Moldova*, A/HRC/10/44/Add.3. Geneva: UN Office of the High Commissioner for Human Rights.

United Nations (UN) Special Rapporteur on Torture. (2011). *Report of the Special Rapporteur on torture and other cruel, inhuman or degrading treatment or punishment, Manfred Nowak: Mission to Greece*, A/HRC/16/52/Add.4. Geneva: UN Office of the High Commissioner for Human Rights.

Citizen Oversight in the United States and Canada

Applying Outcome Measures and Evidence-Based Concepts

9

GEOFFREY P. ALPERT
TYLER CAWTHRAY
JEFF ROJEK
FRANK FERDIK

Contents

Democratic governments empower the police to regulate the conduct of citizens and to protect their rights. Citizens also expect officers to respond to their needs in a skilled and professional manner. When allegations of excessive force, racism, and other forms of misconduct and corruption surface, citizens question the foundation on which the police authority is based and departments' abilities to control the actions of their own officers. For many, even the courts and politicians have failed at deterring officers from engaging in proscriptive behaviors, especially those that violate the welfare and safety of the public (Punch, 2009). To address these shortcomings, stakeholders have called for citizen oversight agencies to investigate and adjudicate claims of police misconduct and corruption. The philosophical justification for civilian oversight is twofold: (1) compensate for governmental failures to combat police deviance and (2) equalize the balance of power between public officials and citizens. As Terrill (1988a) notes, citizen oversight:

> ...is based on the premise that although the public has relinquished to the police the authority to enforce the law, the public retains the right to control the police bureaucracy externally, if the need arises. (p. 239)

Walker and Archbold (2014) state that the environment of new police accountability present within the United States now "recognises the value of regular input to a police department from outside experts" (p. 15). Whether termed *external*, *citizen*, or *civilian* oversight, the existence of citizen accountability initiatives has become common practice in democratic nations (Prenzler, 2011), with each agency varying in relation to the degree of citizen involvement in the mechanisms of complaint review. The purpose of this chapter is to provide an overview of this form of police accountability in the United States and Canada. First, attention is given to the evolution of citizen oversight in both countries. Second, an examination and explanation of several specific examples of these contemporary models and their practices are provided. Third, we argue the importance of citizen oversight as a viable option for reducing the occurrence of unlawful police behavior and satisfying citizen demands for increased police accountability. Fourth, the chapter concludes with a discussion of the utility of using a range of robust outcome measures and adopting the framework of evidence-based policing (EBP) to strengthen the case for continued citizen oversight.

Evolution of Citizen Oversight

United States

Policing scholars have commented extensively on the existence of officer misconduct and corruption within American police departments (Goldsmith, 1969;

Petterson, 1978; Punch, 2009; Walker, 2000). Many agencies during the early history of the United States were inefficient organizations with pervasive corruption and abuse as they were staffed with poorly qualified and untrained officers (Haller, 1976; Walker, 1977). Special commissions reviewing police behavior in the early part of the 20th century repeatedly cited the observation of such problematic behavior, particularly in the form of brutality. As the President's Commission on Law Enforcement and Administration of Justice (1967) reports:

> The National Commission on Law Observance and Enforcement (the Wickersham Commission), which reported to President Hoover in 1931, found considerable evidence of police brutality. The President's Commission on Civil Rights, appointed by President Truman, made a similar finding in 1947. And, in 1961, the U.S. Civil Rights Commission concluded that "police brutality is still a serious problem throughout the United States." (p. 3)

These concerns prompted periodic waves of police reform directed at professionalizing the conduct of officers by establishing minimal qualifications that included a law-abiding background, formalized and regular officer training, and adoption of standard operating procedures, among other improvements. However, Walker and Archbold (2014) note that "despite its achievements, the professionalization movement left many problems unaddressed, the most important being control of police officer on-the-street behavior" (p. 10).

The continuing pattern of police abuse, misconduct, and corruption, coupled with the failure of government to address these problems in a transparent way, led to a movement of citizen involvement in the police accountability process (Lewis, 2000). Although volunteer attorneys in the Los Angeles area during the 1920s proposed the idea of having private citizens evaluate complaints against police officers, it was the 1931 Wickersham Commission that recommended the creation of "some disinterested agency" in each city to assist people with their complaints (Walker, 2000). Similar recommendations were proposed over the years, but it often took a race riot, other type of civil unrest, or catastrophic event to spark reform. Unfortunately, politicians disinterested in the issue of police corruption and, more specifically, police brutality blocked attempts to create these types of agencies. Nonetheless, continuing racial tensions and riots that erupted in cities such as New York, Detroit, Washington, DC, and Los Angeles in the 1940s spearheaded the creation of the first citizen oversight agency in the United States (Walker, 2000). Formally instituted in 1948, the Complaint Review Board for the Metropolitan Police in the District of Columbia was the first oversight agency developed in the United States (Walker, 2000).

This oversight agency was composed of three citizens, who reviewed complaints referred by the police chief and offered suggestions on the proper disposition of each case. However, an informal coalition of politicians and law enforcement representatives was successful in impeding its development and capabilities. Although the agency would remain in existence until the mid-1990s, the political challenges, funding constraints, and a chronic inability to handle a large and growing caseload led to its demise. Although reformers saw this failure as a setback, other oversight agencies throughout the country were able to develop and gain traction.

Philadelphia created the next noteworthy oversight agency in 1958, called the Philadelphia Police Advisory Board. Directors and members of the American Civil Liberties Union and the mayor, Richardson Dilworth, were serious in their efforts to reform the police. An executive order created the agency, which consisted of a board of citizens who would receive complaints, refer them to the police department for investigation, and after reviewing the department's reports, make recommendations for action (see Terrill, 1988b). Similar to the Washington experience, this board suffered from a lack of public and private support, financial stability, and an overwhelming number of cases that collectively led to its downfall in 1969 (Walker, 2000).

The backlash against citizen oversight by police unions, police officials and associations, including the International Association of Chiefs of Police, continued to limit the viability of citizen review boards. Arguments against oversight included the belief that the police could discipline their own, that corruption was not as rampant as the media led the public to believe, and that oversight would undermine police autonomy and ability to perform its job effectively (Walker, 2000). For example, opponents of citizen oversight, most notably powerful police unions, were successful in their efforts to diminish any momentum on the part of oversight advocates in New York City, leading the New York City Civilian Complaint Review Board to suffer the same fate as that of the Washington and Philadelphia boards. Teamed with the Policeman's Benevolent Association, police unions staged a successful campaign in New York to influence citizens to vote in favor of a referendum to abolish the New York City Civilian Complaint Review Board in 1966 (Walker, 2000).

Another wave of civil unrest in major cities in the United States during the late 1960s and early 1970s reversed this trend and reinstated a serious call for citizen accountability of the police. As public confidence and trust in government agencies waned, the notion of increased police accountability was resurrected. As an example, Kansas City established a citizen review system in 1969 that survives today. Walker (2000) acknowledges that the Kansas City initiative survived because it was created by an ordinance, which cannot be repealed with the same ease as an executive order, and because police officials began to accept the idea of citizen oversight. Police endorsement simultaneously increased public support, which thereby led to a renewed growth in this accountability mechanism across the country. In fact, cities such as Berkeley, Detroit, and San Francisco, among others, have developed and maintained citizen oversight agencies since the 1970s and 1980s. New York has also reconstituted an all-civilian review board. Moreover, as of 2014, more than 120 citizen oversight agencies operate across the United States (National Association of Citizen Oversight of Law Enforcement [NACOLE], 2014).

Canada

Although police misconduct and corruption in Canada have not received the same level of public and scholarly attention as in the United States, the problem exists in many of the same ways. As Campbell, Mahaffy, Stewart, and Trepanier (2004, p. 1) note:

> Corruption within Canada's law enforcement services is not a new phenomenon. The Caron inquiry of the early 1950s looked into corruption among Montreal officers involved in prostitution and gambling. The provincial Keable inquiry in Quebec and the related MacDonald Commission of the late 1970s examined police wrongdoing following the October crisis. More recent incidents of police corruption and police misconduct in Canada include assaults committed by Vancouver police officers, police involvement in the freezing deaths of aboriginal men in Saskatchewan, and a litany of corruption-related charges facing members of Toronto's police force.

Driving the need for change in the handling of complaints against Canadian law enforcement were strained police-minority relations, lack of transparency and consistency in the complaints process, and ineffective measures to control police misbehavior (Landau, 2000).

The more progressive political climate of the 1980s and a demand for increased responsibility and professionalism of the police by members of the public eventually led to the introduction of citizen oversight in Canada. According to Landau (2000), the Metropolitan Toronto Police Force Complaints Project Act 1981, which formally established Canada's first review board, was contingent upon

> ...at least a decade of hostile, even volatile, police-community relations. These issues were compounded by findings of procedural irregularities and criminal wrongdoing within a number of Canadian police forces, including the Royal Canadian Mounted Police and the Metropolitan Toronto Police Force. In each instance, the completely internal handling of complaints against police, and the lack of transparency in the process were identified as significant barriers to police accountability and legitimacy to the public. (pp. 65–66)

Landau (2000) further states that the Toronto model

> Was one in which the responsibility for management and discipline within the force rested with the police, but which established a civilian authority—the Public Complaints Commissioner—who could intervene when that responsibility was breached. (p. 66)

Initially, the review board was severely limited in both its investigative and adjudicative power(s), as well as the range of departments it was permitted to oversee. Only the Toronto police force was subjected to this oversight, and the legal powers of the commissioner were restricted simply to monitoring the investigation, monitoring the decision(s) of the chief of police, and initiating a review of the claim if either the officer-defendant or citizen-complainant requested it (Landau, 2000, p. 67). Contrary to the American police response to citizen oversight, the Toronto police force was originally supportive of the idea, mostly because of the heightened level of involvement of the chief in disposing of and resolving cases, as it was he who initiated most investigations and rendered the final decision concerning responsibility and discipline (Lewis, 2000).

Citizen review of the Toronto police complaint process was seen by many as a watershed moment in Canadian police accountability. Passage of the Metropolitan Toronto Police Force Complaints Act 1984 made the civilian review board permanent, and the Police Services Act 1990 expanded its coverage to include all police services in Ontario (Landau, 2000, p. 68). According to complainants, positive aspects of the Ontario complaint process were that citizens could lodge them with an agency that was separate from the police force, which limited the "intimidation factor" associated with filing complaints directly with the police (Landau, 2000, p. 68). Also, all complaints had to be officially recorded with copies sent to the complainant, chief, and officer(s) in question. Chiefs were required to update complainants every 30 days regarding the status of the complaint and what actions had been taken to resolve it (Landau, 2000, p. 68). This behavior though prompted the police to voice concerns over the operation of these review boards.

The Ontario Provincial Police Association and various chiefs within the province responded unenthusiastically to the increased autonomy and powers invested in citizen oversight based on this legislative action (Landau, 2000). This response led to legislative proposals to decrease substantially the powers of review boards and change the dynamics of citizen oversight in Ontario. Passed in November 1997, Bill 105 increased the discretionary powers of the chief in dealing with complaints. For example, the chief could dismiss claims if she/he perceived them to be "frivolous, vexatious or made in bad faith" and had the authority to take no action on a claim that did not directly involve police policies or practices (Landau, 2000, p. 74). The requirement that the chief inform citizens and the new office of complaints (The Ontario Civilian Commission on Police Services [OCCOPS]) of the claim's status was also eliminated under the provisions of Bill 105.

Nonetheless, in keeping with the demand for citizen oversight, other Canadian provinces began instituting civilian review boards. The Royal Canadian Mounted Police, for instance, created the Public Complaints Commission, which grants the civilian agency "an active monitoring and inquiry role, while maintaining the major investigative and disciplinary decision-making within the police structure" (Lewis, 2000, p. 169). Quebec, Manitoba, British Columbia, and other provinces have all passed legislation creating civilian review boards that are very similar, if not equal to, the Toronto model (Lewis, 2000). Currently, there are 21 municipal, provincial, and federal citizen oversight agencies operating throughout Canada (Canadian Association for Civilian Oversight of Law Enforcement [CACOLE], 2014). As with the American experience, most officers have been resistant to the idea of citizen oversight, with even the public expressing notable ambivalence towards some agencies (Landau, 2000, p. 68).

Contemporary Models of Citizen Oversight in the United States and Canada

As civilian review boards have been created over the years, there exists distinct variability in their structure and procedure. Some differ in terms of where and how complaints can be filed, the exact nature of citizen and police department input, investigative and adjudicative powers of each side, agency independence from the police department, and, as a result of these differences, the outcome measures that may be used. To understand better the structure and function of these boards, Walker (2000) created a classification schema distinguishing four models of oversight, which is presented in Table 9.1. His models are best described on a continuum, where Class I systems represent the greatest involvement of citizens and Class IV reflect the least involvement.

Class I systems, or what Walker (2000) refers to as Citizen Review Boards, represent review bodies composed of nonpolice personnel that are autonomous from law enforcement agencies. These boards have complete investigative responsibility (investigates complaints and makes recommendations for

Table 9.1 Models of Oversight Agency Responsibilities[a]

Responsibilities	Class I Systems	Class II Systems	Class III Systems	Class IV Systems
Complete investigative responsibility	×			
Autonomous agency	×			
Nonpolice members	×			
Mixed police–citizen investigations		×		
Appellate-review only			×	
Auditor system				×
Policy recommendation ability	×	×		×

[a] Models based on Walker's (2000) classification of citizen oversight approaches.

disciplinary action) of complaints, as well as responsibility for making policy recommendations. Class II systems, Police Review/Citizen Oversight, include agencies where investigation of the complaint and disciplinary recommendations are conducted by the police department, but the citizen board has input into the review and analysis of reports. Class III systems, Police Review/ Citizen–Police Appeal Board, represent a model where police departments maintain responsibility over the investigation, review, and disposition of the case, but complainants can appeal the outcome to a board composed of officers and citizens. Class IV systems reflect an independent auditor approach where the investigation, review, and disposition of cases are handled internally by the agency, but a citizen-based body (individual auditor or group) reviews the complaint process as a means of transparency and regulation, with the ability to make policy recommendations on the review process. This final class of agency was originally developed in the United States as a political compromise to satisfy community demands for police oversight without the more intrusive features of other oversight models that police unions vocally opposed (Walker & Archbold, 2014). However, Walker and Archbold (2014) suggest that this police auditor system can be a more effective form of oversight in the long-term, as its standing audit functions have the ability to create police organizational change via the agency's ability to extract internal information and continually follow up on policy recommendations.

The following examples illustrate how these systems work. The oversight bodies we selected come from one Canadian province and three cities in the United States, including Ontario, Canada; St. Paul, Minnesota; Portland, Oregon; and San Jose, California. The discussion of each oversight body provides a review of the elements that classify it within Walker's (2000) framework, along with additional insight into the functioning of each body.

In addition to the classification schema provided previously, Walker and Archbold (2014) have provided the most comprehensive method to evaluate citizen oversight agencies. In summary form, the model includes the following:

- Open and accessible information available to the public about complaint procedures
- Whether non-English-speaking individuals have access to information regarding complaint procedures, including complaint forms, in all relevant languages
- Independence of the agency from the police department
- Timely investigations of complaints
- Reduction in number of officer misconduct cases
- Ability of the agency to consistently and fairly investigate and adjudicate claims
- The reception the complainant receives by the agency and police department when filing a complaint

- How the complaint is categorized and recorded
- Resources and staffing of the oversight agency
- Cost-effectiveness to taxpayers
- Whether the agency influences police
- Whether the oversight agency helps bridge any divide between police and community

Walker and Archbold's (2014) work demonstrates the importance and difficulties of evaluating citizen oversight agencies using a variety of measures. He suggests using EBP concepts and robust outcome measures to evaluate citizen oversight. Ideally, a discussion of each oversight agency would clarify whether these characteristics are present and would incorporate comparative measures. Unfortunately, we are limited to the annual reports produced by these oversight bodies and other public materials, which often do not provide the detailed measurements Walker suggests.

Class I System

Ontario Province

As noted in the previous section, civil unrest, lack of transparency, and ineffective anticorruption measures prompted a demand for external accountability of Toronto's police force. Passage of the Metropolitan Toronto Police Force Complaint Project Act 1981 created the first citizen oversight agency in Canada. Despite public concern over perceived illegitimacy of the review board, government officials agreed to make it permanent and to expand its powers by overseeing all Ontario police services with the passage of the Metropolitan Toronto Police Force Complaint Act 1984 and the Police Services Act of 1990 (Landau, 2000). These legislative changes created the Office of the Public Complaints Commissioner and the Special Investigations Unit (SIU).

These two organizations were the high point in the development of citizen oversight in Ontario until the late 1990s. A change in government in Ontario in 1995 resulted in the Public Complaints Commissioner being disestablished and responsibility for complaint investigation as well as adjudication largely being handed back to police services (LeSage, 2005). The passage of Bill 105 in 1997 invested some oversight powers in the OCCOPS, but complainants and officer-defendants expressed dissatisfaction with the new process (Landau, 2000). Citizens perceived the system to be "biased, in-favor of the police, and ineffective at minimizing officer misconduct" (Landau, 2000, p. 67), a sentiment that was likely due to the lack of complete autonomy the OCCOPS had from the police departments throughout Ontario province.

The oversight landscape changed again in 2009 when the Office of the Independent Police Review Director (OIPRD) opened. The office was established based on recommendations given to the Ontario government by former Chief Justice of the Superior Court, Mr. Patrick LeSage, after a review of the police complaints system conducted in 2004 and 2005 (OIPRD, 2010, pp. 5–6). It has been given more extensive powers than its predecessor. The OIPRD has a director who cannot be a serving or former police officer, and its staff cannot be serving police officers (OIPRD, 2014a). When the OIPRD was established, it was given responsibility for managing the intake of formal complaints, monitoring the complaint investigation process, auditing police complaints to identify systemic or ongoing issues, recommending policy changes based on these reviews, as well as conducting its own investigations into police conduct complaints at the discretion of the director (OIPRD, 2014a,b).

At complaint intake, the OIPRD makes a decision on whether the complaint should be investigated or dismissed or whether it is better dealt with under a different law or act. Once this determination is made, the complaint is classified as either a conduct, policy, or service issue. Both policy and service issues are automatically referred onto the relevant police chief to investigate, and the investigation is monitored by the OIPRD. Conduct complaints are screened to decide whether the complaint should be investigated by the police service, the OIPRD, or another police service. The outcome of the complaint is decided upon by the police chief in the case of a police investigation or by the OIPRD director after an OIPRD investigation. In a police-managed investigation, the investigative report is reviewed by the OIPRD, and the director may confirm the decision, give directions to the chief of police for further action, take over the investigation, or assign it to another police service. If a complaint is substantiated, the chief of police is responsible for resolving the complaint, by either informal resolution if it is a less serious complaint or a disciplinary hearing if it is deemed serious.

Given the OIPRD's ability to initiate independent investigations, its independence from the police, auditing, systemic review, and policy recommendation powers, it can be characterized as both a Class I and IV system. However, unlike a Class I system, the final decision on the penalty or type of police discipline imposed still resides with the police, and the OIPRD does not have the power to make disciplinary recommendations. It is best described as a civilian investigative auditor agency rather than a citizen review board.

The OIPRD has been in operation for a shorter time frame than the other agencies examined in this chapter. In addition, it provides oversight for a larger number of police officers, roughly 24,000 across Ontario province (OIPRD, 2014b). From April 2010 until March 2014, an average of 3,500 complaints was filed annually by citizens in Ontario province to the

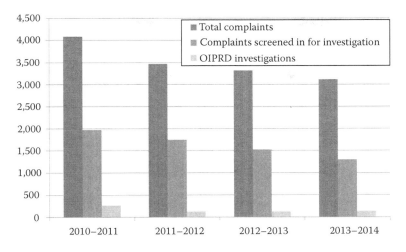

Figure 9.1 OIPRD complaints against Ontario police officers. (From OIPRD, 2011, pp. 13 and 19; 2012, pp. 55 and 57; 2013, pp. 46 and 49; 2014, pp. 52 and 56.)

OIPRD. Figure 9.1 shows a steady decline in the total number of complaints filed over the last 4 years. In its first full year of operation (2010–2011), the OIPRD received 4,083 complaints; this has since fallen to 3,114 in 2013–2014. Similarly, the number of complaints screened in for investigation has decreased from 1,927 in 2010–2011 to 1,297 in 2013–2014. Figure 9.1 indicates that after an initial high of 259 in 2010–2011, the number of investigations undertaken by the OIPRD has reduced to the low 100s over the past 3 years.

Requests for review of investigative decisions have also decreased from 126 in 2010–2011 to 72 in 2013–2014 (OIPRD, 2011, p. 26; 2014b, p. 58). Despite the OIPRD being in operation for a relatively short period, these numbers indicate that the agency may be experiencing some early success. The history of citizen oversight in Ontario provides an indication of the importance of agencies developing robust outcome measures to justify their continued work and existence when faced with external pressures.

The OIPRD is not the only civilian oversight agency that operates in Ontario; it works alongside the SIU and the Ontario Civilian Police Commission (OCPC). The SIU, established in 1990, has a limited mandate focused on investigating potentially criminal conduct of police officers that result in serious injury, death, or allegations of sexual assault (SIU, 2014), whereas the OCPC is the successor to the OCCOPS and is now responsible for hearing appeals against disciplinary decisions on matters of alleged police officer misconduct (OCPC, 2014). Although both of these agencies play important roles in the overall framework of civilian oversight in Ontario, they are not examined here as they fall outside the scope of this chapter.

Class II System

St. Paul

Created in 1993, the Police–Civilian Internal Affairs Review Commission (PCIARC) began overseeing investigations into the inappropriate conduct of St. Paul police officers. Then police chief William Finney urged city council members to adopt a procedure that would permit civilians the opportunity not only to make recommendations regarding case disposition but also to aid in the investigative process (Finn, 2001). According to Finn (2001), hearings into police wrongdoing are typically closed, there is no appeals process regarding final decisions, neither the Internal Affairs Unit (IAU) nor the PCIARC makes public their disciplinary recommendations, no party to these investigations acts as a mediator, and although the commission maintains the power to subpoena witnesses, it infrequently uses it.

Similar to both the Class I and IV systems, the PCIARC has the ability to make policy recommendations to the police department, and it is open to hearing cases involving excessive use of force, discrimination, poor public relations, improper procedure, and firearm discharges that do not follow proper police training. However, unlike a Class I system review board, the PCIARC does not have the authority to initiate its own investigations, and it does not operate independently of the police department. Most investigations are conducted in tandem with the police department's IAU, and although the PCIARC may make recommendations regarding punishment, it is the chief who makes all such final decisions (Finn, 2001). In fact, the chief is not obliged to follow any PCIARC disciplinary recommendations, but he/she must acknowledge the findings and make any determinations according to them. These procedural criteria coincide with Walker's (2000) Class II system classification scheme. The limited purview of the PCIARC's operations means the outcome measures that can be used by the commission are similarly restricted.

The 2009 and 2012 PCIARC annual reports offer additional insight into the inner workings of this oversight model, as well as any successes it has had in working both with its respective police department and community members. Throughout 2012, PCIARC and IAU members convened 10 times and reviewed 90 cases, which resulted in 193 separate charges of improper action by members of the department. Of those charges heard, 12 were sustained, 89 were not sustained, 58 were exonerated, and 34 were unfounded (PCIARC, 2012). Until 2009, the PCIARC had never invoked its power to subpoena, but it utilized this ability in 2009 on two separate occasions—both of which involved PCIARC "fact-finding" efforts that required interviews with two separate witnesses. Finally, St. Paul's civilian review board appears to have had some success in getting the police department to adopt various policy recommendations. According to the PCIARC's annual reports, not only has the commission managed to make both its representative body more diverse and reflective of community demographics, but it also managed to get the St. Paul police department to diversify its personnel. Even more, as of 2009, increased training of both IAU and PCIARC members is required regarding case handling and disposition, and each year, both departments are now required to publish their annual findings, thereby making them accessible to the public (PCIARC, 2010).

Class III System

Portland

The Portland, Oregon, Internal Investigations Auditing Committee (PIIAC) was established in 1982 by a majority vote from city residents. Following reports of racial bias and prejudice on behalf of Portland police officers in the 1970s and 1980s, city council and community members agreed to respond to many of the concerns. However, city council members were successful in minimizing the powers of the PIIAC and ensuring it did not have any investigative authority. During the late 1980s and early 1990s, reports of officer misconduct subsided and the simultaneous resignation of various PIIAC members prompted the city council to pass legislation that effectively abolished the agency (Independent Police Review [IPR], 2011). Episodes of police corruption, including a controversial shooting, revitalized discussions about police accountability shortly thereafter though. As a result, in 2001, the contemporary version of Portland's citizen auditor agency, the IPR, was instituted and continues to the present day (IPR, 2011).

The IPR is composed of a director and nine civilian volunteers who form the Citizen Review Committee (CRC). When the IPR was constituted in 2001, it was given the authority to manage the intake of complaints, monitor the complaint investigation process conducted by the Police Bureau's Internal Affairs Division (IAD) and the discipline recommended, as well as manage officer and citizen appeals of complaint review outcomes. During the intake process, the IPR collects initial information from the complainant and witnesses and makes a recommendation on whether the complaint should be dismissed, sent to a mediation program managed by the IPR, or forwarded to the Police Bureau's IAD for investigation. In addition to monitoring the investigations, the IPR director was given the authority to initiate an investigation of a specific complaint or class of complaints where they believe IAD has not conducted an adequate investigation, representing at some level a board-determined appellate function. In addition, if an officer or citizen appeals a complaint outcome, the CRC is then responsible for conducting this review.

These functions do not provide a clear-cut classification in Walker's (2000) four-class schema but are more of a hybrid. The IPR is not an autonomous body with complete investigative authority, nor does it conduct complaint investigations jointly with police internal affairs investigators. It does have responsibility for appellate review of cases, leading to its classification here as a Class III system under Walker's schema. The IPR also has monitoring responsibility for the investigative process that represents an audit function discussed in the following section. In 2010, however, the city council voted to expand the IPR's oversight authority and increase the transparency of the Portland Police Bureau's (PPBs) investigative procedures (IPR, 2012). These changes included the following:

(1) Increased investigative authority for independent investigations by granting the IPR subpoena authority to compel civilian witness testimony and the production of evidence, and authorizing the IPR to initiate investigations in cases of community concern even when no actual complaint was filed.
(2) Increased IPR's role in investigations conducted by the Police Bureau: requiring IPR approval before an administrative investigation is closed, authority for IPR to challenge post investigatory findings recommended by the Police Bureau, and authority to challenge discipline recommendations.
(3) Restructured the Police Bureau's disciplinary review board to make the IPR a voting member and thereby increasing civilian influence in discipline recommendations. (IPR, 2012, p. 2)

These changes suggest the IPR has maintained political support. It also makes the classification of the IPR into Walker's (2000) schema less clear-cut, possibly existing between a Class III and Class II system.

Since the IPR was established, there has been an overall general decline in the total number of community allegations made against PPB officers. Figure 9.2 demonstrates the fall in allegations from a high of 2,827 in 2003 to only 937 in 2013. The most significant decreases occurred from 2004 to 2005, when allegations reduced by 317, and 2007 to 2008, when they declined by 610. Over the 10-year period of 2003 to 2013, there was a drop in total allegations of 67.8%. Figure 9.2 shows a similar trend with community use of force allegations with some fluctuation. In 2004, the public made 225 allegations of improper or excessive use of force by PPB officers. However, by 2010, this number had dropped to only 62. The years 2011 and 2010 saw an increase in use of force allegations to above 100, but 2013 saw another drop down to 73, representing a reduction of 67.5% over a 9-year period.

In 2013, the IPR handled the intake and initial review of 409 citizen complaints. The IPR dismissed 256 (76%) of these complaints, 75 (22%) complaints were referred to IAD, and 7 (2%) were sent to mediation (IPR, 2014). The majority of dismissed cases were the result of the IPR finding in their initial review that there was no misconduct in 127 or 50% of cases and not

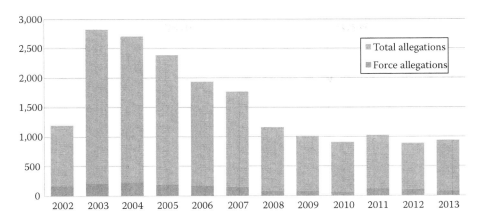

Figure 9.2 IPR community allegations against PPB officers. (From Independent Police Review Division, 2004, pp. 20 and 24; 2007, p. 9; 2010, p. 37; 2012, p. 29; 2014, p. 27.)

being able to prove misconduct in 43 cases (17%). In addition to these intake processing efforts, the IPR also engaged in a variety of community outreach efforts that included meeting with community members and organizations to discuss the IPR, as well as arranging public forums for Police Bureau leaders to engage the public on various issues.

The CRC heard five formal appeals in 2013 and one in January 2014, which included two allegations of excessive force, one allegation of improper search, two allegations of rudeness, and two allegations of unprofessional off-duty conduct (IPR, 2014). The committee voted to support the original PPB decision of "unproven" regarding one of the excessive force allegations, while recommending that one of the decisions be changed from "exonerate" to "unproven." The allegation of improper search and one of the rudeness allegations were initially challenged by the CRC, who voted to change the finding from "unproven" to "sustained." This was declined by the police chief, and at a subsequent meeting, the CRC was unable to reach a majority to appeal the case to the City Council, so it was closed. The CRC requested that the other allegation of rudeness be investigated further by the IPR or IAD and, after this occurred, voted to change the original finding from "exonerate" to "unproven." In one of the allegations of unprofessional off-duty conduct, the committee voted to change the original finding from "unproven" to "exonerate," whereas in the case of the other allegation, the CRC voted initially to change the finding from "unproven with debriefing" to "sustained." The chief initially declined this decision, and before the committee could meet a second time, the officer resigned. The range of expanded powers the IPR has received illustrates the importance of agencies adopting wide-ranging outcome measures to gauge the performance of oversight agencies in all areas of operation.

Class IV System

San Jose

Created by a city ordinance in 1993, San Jose's Independent Police Auditor (IPA) system is responsible for providing independent oversight of the complaint process through the objective review of police misconduct investigations (IPA, 2012). Similar to the other oversight agencies, it was started because there existed a public perception that the internal investigations unit of the San Jose Police Department (SJPD) failed to effectively address complaints of officer misconduct. Board members include a director, two senior analysts, a general analyst, and a specialist. Their duties include responding to citizen requests to review departmental decisions on misconduct cases, identifying potential witnesses to determine if claims can be corroborated, working within a 65-day timeline to complete reviews, making recommendations to the SJPD to improve their practices, and engaging in community activities to improve relations between the police and public. Collectively, these functions classify the San Jose IPA as a Class IV system or "police auditor" under Walker's (2000) and Walker and Archbold's (2014) framework.

From 2010 to 2013, the IPA made a combined 74 policy recommendations to the SJPD (IPA, 2012, 2013b). For example, while the department required officers to track the race/ethnicity of individuals stopped for automobile searches, there was no such requirement when pedestrians were stopped. Because the IPA does not distinguish between these types of stops and considers identifying and addressing potential discriminatory practices important, the department now requires officers to collect the same information for traffic and pedestrian stops. Also, the SJPD used to issue citations to homeless people sleeping in their cars. However, the IPA conducted an investigation and uncovered no city ordinance that prohibits this behavior; therefore, the SJPD is no longer permitted to engage in such practices. Another policy recommendation accepted by the SJPD was a requirement that IA and IPA officials be trained jointly regarding the investigation of officer misconduct. Taught by Stanford University professors, training on investigation focuses primarily on bias-based policing practices that have a harmful effect on community morale. The IPA is extremely active within the community, engaging in a wide range of community outreach programs (IPA, 2012, 2013a). It organizes events, meetings, and presentations that bring together members of both the community and law enforcement. Concerns that both sides have regarding police practices and other related issues are raised and attempts

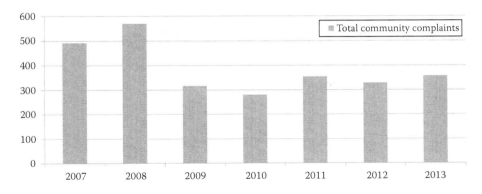

Figure 9.3 IPA and SJPD community complaints 2007–2013. (From: IPA, 2009, p. 29; 2010, p. 24; 2011, p. 70; 2012, p. 88; 2013, p. 14; 2014, p. 28.)

are made by IPA representatives to mediate any disputes. Despite these positive activities, the agency warns that failure on behalf of IA to close all investigations within a 300-day time period may undermine the IPA's oversight role. The IPA requires at least 65 days to complete all reviews and must stay within that time period to maintain its promise of expediting its review procedures (IPA, 2012).

The IPA helped reduce the number of community complaints filed against police officers from 2007 to 2013. Figure 9.3 shows a reduction in the number of community complaints received by IPA and the SJPD during this period. From highs of 491 complaints filed in 2007 and 569 filed in 2008, they have declined to their lowest point of 281 in 2010. This was followed by a slight increase in 2011 to 355, with the intake stabilizing in the low to mid 300s for the past 2 years. Both the IPA's policy recommendations and its extensive community outreach program appear to have had a notable effect on the total number of complaints lodged against SJPD officers.

Future Challenges

Regardless of the police force or country, repeated accounts of officer misconduct voiced by the public can seriously undermine their level of trust, confidence, and support in law enforcement officials. Governmental responses to police corruption include court hearings, legislative mandates, internal investigations, and coroner's inquests. Unfortunately, not only have these measures failed to resolve police accountability problems, but also some have failed to earn credibility among citizens. In response, oversight committees composed of citizens who look into and/or oversee the investigative procedures of police departments have gained considerable support in recent decades. Our review provides an illustration of different models of citizens' oversight that have emerged to improve transparency and accountability of law enforcement agencies.

As noted previously, it is important to emphasize that most of our data are taken from reports produced by police agencies or their related oversight bodies, which introduces potential bias in how these models are presented. This dependence on agency reports is largely the product of a limited body of independent empirical literature evaluating these citizen-based systems. Future research should focus on mixed-methods studies whereby outcome variables can be supplemented with qualitative interviews with citizen-complainants and officer-defendants about their perceptions of the processes and outcomes. Surveys can also be administered to involved parties to obtain more generalizable findings. Collectively, these data would provide the potential for developing comparative performance measures that could be used to evaluate oversight bodies that reflect similar forms of review.

Setting the research issues aside, it is important to recognize that citizen oversight is an evolving framework. The traditional intent of citizen oversight has been to develop a transparent complaint system that creates a perception of fairness on the part of the complainant and subject officer. In addition, and perhaps more importantly, such oversight is meant to provide a more effective and objective review process that will address current misconduct and provide a general deterrent to future officer misconduct. Livingston (2004) observes that such efforts have generally focused on the reactive investigation of individual complaints.

Livingston notes, however, that even in the best circumstances, this reactive approach will face limitations in creating change that will reduce future misconduct. For example, many individuals who feel they have been a party to misconduct do not file complaints, even in the most hospitable citizen systems. She also notes how many complaints reviewed by citizen boards are "one-on-one confrontations," where there is little additional evidence to determine whether the officer or a complainant is telling the truth, resulting in a large number of unsubstantiated complaints. Combined, these issues will prevent the identification of misconduct or failure to discipline it, assuming some portion of unsubstantiated complaints reflects misconduct. As a result, Livingston calls for a more proactive form of citizen review that involves evaluating factors that create opportunities or circumstances for misconduct as a means to develop policies that better regulate officer behavior. Her argument is not meant to discredit traditional approaches to citizen review but instead to enhance the role of these oversight bodies. This view is supported by Walker and Archbold (2014), who claimed that the auditor functions of external oversight through policy recommendations and consistent follow-up can create police organizational change.

Livingston's suggestion reflects a comprehensive form of Walker's (2000) Class I system, or what Harris (2012) and others (Lewis, 2000) call "holistic" approaches to citizen review. Although such a model provides perhaps the maturation to the ideal in transparency and oversight, Harris (2012) observes that it will continue to face the same challenges in development and sustainability with regard to a lack of political will, limited authority, and an inability to counter police opposition. In fact, it can be argued that holistic models will face much stronger opposition in the United States and Canada, given the inclusion of a preventative policy recommendation that intrudes on an activity that police managers have generally viewed as their domain. As indicated in our analysis, police managers may sometimes be reluctant to accept recommendations, let alone afford authority to mandate policy changes from individuals who they view as having little experience or expertise in managing police organizations. This highlights the argument that success in citizen oversight, in whatever form, will hinge on police leadership that is open to cooperating with such citizen bodies (Harris, 2012; Livingston, 2004).

It is also important to acknowledge that the future expansion of citizen oversight in the United States and Canada faces additional and unique challenges due to the more fractured nature of police services relative to countries such as Australia and England, where citizen oversight has a strong presence. There are approximately 18,000 state and local law enforcement agencies in the United States (Reaves, 2011) and nearly 400 provincial and municipal police services in Canada (Swol, 1999). In light of these agency figures, there are just over 120 citizen oversight agencies in the United States (NACOLE, 2014) and 21 in Canada at the municipal, provincial, and federal levels (CACOLE, 2014). This gap in oversight is partially misleading in Canada given that many municipal police services fall under the authority of legislatively adopted citizen oversight bodies at the provincial level, such as the OIPRD discussed earlier. However, the political autonomy of municipal and county governments in the United States does not provide such provincial authority to regulate the respective police services at the state level. Thus, a very small percentage of agencies in the United States are covered by some form of citizen oversight, and any growth will only come through individual community decisions across these numerous jurisdictions. This means battling the issues of political will, autonomy, police resistance, and funding across hundreds of diverse jurisdictions.

The Role of Outcome Measures

Illustrating the successes of existing citizen oversight agencies can provide the means to battle the obstacles of lack of political will, police resistance, and funding issues across the fragmented jurisdictions of the United States and Canada. If existing agencies focus on measuring the outcomes of their work, they can both help justify their continued existence in the face of external pressures, while generating evidence that can support the expansion of citizen oversight to other jurisdictions. The range of different oversight bodies in existence within the United States and Canada offers an opportunity to demonstrate the merits of differing models of oversight.

Advocates of citizen review argue that independent oversight can impact on police and the community in a range of ways, including sustaining higher numbers of complaints, disciplining more police for misconduct, improving community relations, as well as deterring police deviance (Walker, 2000). Clear indications of these successes have the potential to counter both lack of political will for and police resistance to independent oversight. Robust outcome measures across the full range of activities undertaken by citizen oversight agencies can provide this (Prenzler, 2000; Lewis & Prenzler, 2008). All of the agencies examined in this chapter have developed some performance measures, yet some of their responsibilities extend beyond the measures they report. If agencies do not measure the activities they undertake, it makes justifying the continued existence of such initiatives that much harder if they are challenged by outside pressures.

Oversight agencies face significant challenges when seeking to measure their impact. The diversity of variables, conflicts in data interpretation, as well as disparities between agencies' designated power and actual resources all present challenges to developing accurate performance indicators (Walker, 2000). If agencies focus chiefly on a small number of quantitative indicators, such as overall complaint numbers, complaints investigated, or the sustain rate of complaints, they present only a limited picture of their work (Walker, 2000; Walker & Archbold, 2014). Lewis and Prenzler (2008) suggest that only through the adoption of a "diverse set of indicators" can oversight agencies measure their real achievements rather than just counting activity. They discuss four broad groups of possible performance indicators that could assist citizen oversight organizations in developing performance measures.

The first group concerns "procedural integrity." This category focuses on measuring appropriate compliance with proper procedures during the complaint investigation process (Lewis & Prenzler, 2008). A key element of these procedures is ensuring that investigations are fair to complainants, police, and oversight staff (Filstad & Gottschalk, 2011; Walker & Archbold, 2014). It is primarily aimed at ensuring that the rights of complainants and the accused are protected, as well as ensuring their safety from intimidation or discrimination (Lewis & Prenzler, 2008). The authors identify as possible performance measures surveys of stakeholders involved in the complaint investigation process, as well as the outcome of the evidence briefs and subsequent comments from judicial officials (Lewis & Prenzler, 2008).

The second category is "procedural rigor," which is concerned with how well the investigation is carried out, including whether interviews are thorough and leads are fully investigated (Lewis & Prenzler, 2008; Walker & Archbold, 2014). A common criticism leveled at police internal affairs investigations during misconduct inquiries has been that complaints against police were poorly investigated (Miller, 2010; Walker & Archbold, 2014). Therefore, measuring rigor is important as a means of demonstrating the strength of complaint investigations that are independent of police. The outcome measures proposed for procedural integrity can also be used to measure rigor and supplemented with other indicators, such as independent case audits and reviews of failed prosecutions (Lewis & Prenzler, 2008). The third area covered is timeliness, meaning the speed at which complaints are resolved, which can be measured by tracking the progress of a complaint (Lewis & Prenzler, 2008). This category is important to all parties involved. Complainants want to know the result of their complaint within a reasonable timeframe and police officers want investigations into their conduct concluded as quickly as possible (De Angelis & Kupchik, 2007; Prenzler & Ronken, 2001). This is also a significant problem within the United States (Walker & Archbold, 2014). However, measuring timeliness is complicated by other factors like making sure an agency has adequate resources, as well as ensuring that investigations are thorough yet carried out within reasonable timeframes (Lewis & Prenzler, 2008).

The final area discussed by Lewis and Prenzler (2008) is "contribution to police integrity." This category addresses the contribution made by oversight agencies to deterring police misconduct and maintaining the overall integrity of law enforcement (Lewis & Prenzler, 2008). Measuring the deterrence capacity of citizen oversight agencies can be difficult if oversight agencies rely on basic quantitative indicators (Brereton, 2000). Changes in these indicators are difficult to attribute to just one cause, rather there is more utility in measuring whether agencies have been successful in building conditions that support deterrence (Brereton, 2000). This may be done through a wide range of measures such as surveys of complainant satisfaction, perceptions of the public about corruption, their confidence in the police as well as their awareness of the oversight agency (Lewis & Prenzler, 2008). Similarly, ethical climate surveys of policing organizations may provide insight into how officers view misconduct, the likelihood of being caught, and the fairness of complaint outcomes (Lewis & Prenzler, 2008). The procedural integrity indicators mentioned previously may also be used (Lewis & Prenzler, 2008). Complaints data can be used to complement these indicators by monitoring changes in complaint volume and type, through disaggregating data to identify problem areas as a means of conducting targeted studies (Lewis & Prenzler, 2008).

Instituting the suggested outcome measures across these areas offers its own challenges to oversight agencies. Moving away from the core business of agencies toward evaluation requires additional funds, resources, and time (Lewis & Prenzler, 2008; Walker & Archbold, 2014). Nonetheless, wide-ranging indicators can provide agencies with substantial evidence to support their continued operation as well as adapt their own strategies and processes where necessary. Outsourcing evaluation operations may offer agencies an opportunity to reduce their own costs (Lewis & Prenzler, 2008). Larger studies can be conducted over longer timeframes, allowing agencies to benefit but still balance potential costs (Lewis & Prenzler, 2008). The importance of independent oversight agencies developing measures like those discussed in the preceding paragraphs cannot be understated. Governments are increasingly insisting that agencies show appropriate returns for money invested (Greene, 2013). This desire has been strengthened by the events of the 2008 economic recession and the resulting shrinking budgets of many local governments (Walker & Archbold, 2014). Many of the possible positive outcomes of the work done by oversight agencies examined in this chapter may be going unmeasured and therefore unnoticed by police, government officials, and the wider community. If agencies further develop their own body of evidence to support their role in maintaining law enforcement integrity in the United States and Canada, they will strengthen the case for their continued existence and perhaps future expansion.

A Place for Evidence-Based Oversight

The development of comprehensive outcome measures is perhaps only the first step that oversight agencies can take to strengthen their position in the United States and Canada. The data yielded from new performance measures offer agencies the opportunity to evaluate and further develop their methods. Utilizing the paradigm of EBP may help citizen oversight agencies take advantage of this opportunity. Evidence-based practice is not unique to policing but was inspired by similar strategies used first in medicine and then within other social sciences (Welsh, 2006). Proponents of this approach describe it as using empirical research to prove "what works" in policing to inform agency decision making (Greene, 2013; Sherman, 2013).

Sherman (2013) explains that the approach can be divided into three stages of practice; these include "targeting, testing, and tracking." Targeting involves conducting and applying research as a means of directing resources to where they are most needed. Once this has been done, the testing phase should take place to evaluate available methods as a means of finding the optimal way to address the identified problem. This is finally followed by tracking: internally monitoring the implemented practices and the impact they are having on the problem and the public. The institutional proximity of law enforcement and independent oversight suggest that these principles are just as relevant and applicable to citizen oversight as they are to policing.

The framework of EBP has the potential to maximize the value of the wide-ranging data set gathered from expanded performance indicators. Using these data as part of a feedback loop offers significant opportunities for program innovation and development (Sherman, 1998). Adoption of this strategy may increase both the efficacy and legitimacy of citizen oversight agencies (Greene, 2013; Sherman, 2013). This is particularly important in an environment where governments are continually searching for cost-effective solutions to societal problems (Greene, 2013). The use of a police-developed strategy has the potential to improve the perceptions of independent oversight among an essential stakeholder group that can be resistant to its existence (Wells & Schafer, 2007). The principles of EBP may even assist agencies through innovation to move beyond their current predominantly reactive response to police misconduct.

Conclusion

This discussion of the challenges to holistic approaches to citizen oversight and the expansion of agencies under some form of oversight, particularly in the United States, is not intended to present a pessimistic view or deride the relevance of these efforts. Instead, it is meant to take stock on the current practices of citizen oversight and some of the real challenges ahead if this is going to become a common practice in North American law enforcement. At the same time, it is important to not overlook the progress that has been made. A number of citizen oversight models, including some of the ones discussed in this chapter like the San Francisco, San Jose, and Portland models, appear to be accepted by their respective publics as viable approaches to police officer monitoring. These advances provide an increased level of legitimacy to citizen oversight and successful agencies worthy of emulation.

References

Brereton, D. (2000). Evaluating the performance of external oversight bodies. In A. Goldsmith & C. Lewis (Eds.), *Civilian oversight of policing* (pp. 105–124). Portland, OR: Oxford Publishing.

Campbell, E., Mahaffy, N., Stewart, D., & Trepanier, M. (2004). *Canada's approach to battling police corruption*. 18th International Conference of the International Society for the Reform of Criminal Law. Miller Thomson, LLP.

Canadian Association for Civilian Oversight of Law Enforcement (CACOLE). (2014). *Civilian oversight in Canada*. Retrieved http://www.cacole.ca/resources/links /civilLin-lien-eng.shtml.

De Angelis, J., & Kupchik, A. (2007). Citizen oversight, procedural justice, and officer perceptions of the complaint investigation process. *Policing, 30*, 651–671.

Filstad, C., & Gottschalk, P. (2011). Performance evaluation of police oversight agencies. *Policing & Society, 21*, 96–109.

Finn, P. (2001). *Citizen review of police: Approaches and implementation*. Washington, DC: National Institute of Justice.

Goldsmith, A. (1969). External review and self-regulation: Police accountability and the dialectic of complaints procedures. In A. Goldsmith (Ed.), *Complaints against the police: The trend to external review* (pp. 13–63). Oxford: Clarendon Press.

Greene, J. (2013). New direction in policing: Balancing prediction and meaning in police research. *Justice Quarterly, 31*, 193–228.

Haller, M. (1976). Historical roots of police behavior: Chicago, 1890–1925. *Law and Society Review, 10*, 303–323.

Harris, F. (2012). Holding police accountability theory to account. *Policing, 6*, 240–249.

Independent Police Auditor (IPA). (2009). *IPA year end report—2008*. Retrieved from http://www.sanjoseca.gov/DocumentCenter/View/3149.

Independent Police Auditor (IPA). (2010). *IPA year end report—2009*. Retrieved from http://www.sanjoseca.gov/DocumentCenter/View/3150.

Independent Police Auditor (IPA). (2011). *IPA year end report—2010*. Retrieved from http://www.sanjoseca.gov/ArchiveCenter/ViewFile/Item/145.

Independent Police Auditor (IPA). (2012). *IPA year end report—2011*. Retrieved from http://www.sanjoseca.gov/ipa/reports/11ye.pdf.

Independent Police Auditor (IPA). (2013). *IPA year end report—2012*. Retrieved from http://www.sanjoseca.gov/DocumentCenter/View/29599.

Independent Police Auditor (IPA). (2014). *IPA year end report—2013*. Retrieved from http://www.sanjoseca.gov/DocumentCenter/View/29599.

Independent Police Review (IPR). (2004). *Annual report—2003*. Retrieved from http://www.portlandonline.com/auditor/index.cfm?c=54264&a=54001.

Independent Police Review (IPR). (2007). *Annual report—2005-2006*. Retrieved from http://www.portlandonline.com/auditor/index.cfm?c=54264&a=186307.

Independent Police Review (IPR). (2010). *Annual report—2009*. Retrieved from http://www.portlandonline.com/auditor/index.cfm?c=54264&a=302553.

Independent Police Review (IPR). (2011). *Annual report—2010*. Retrieved from http://www.portlandonline.com/auditor/index.cfm?c=27727&a=350057.

Independent Police Review (IPR). (2012). *Annual report—2011*. Retrieved from http://www.portlandonline.com/auditor/index.cfm?c=27727&a=402840.

Independent Police Review (IPR). (2014). *Annual report—2013*. Retrieved from http://www.portlandonline. com/auditor/index.cfm?c=27727&a=507332.

Landau, T. (2000). Back to the future: The death of civilian review of public complaints against the police in Ontario, Canada. In A. Goldsmith & C. Lewis (Eds.), *Civilian oversight of policing* (pp. 63–83). Portland, OR: Oxford Publishing.

LeSage, P. (2005). *Report on the police complaints system in Ontario*. Retrieved from http://www.attorneygeneral.jus.gov.on.ca/english/about/pubs/LeSage/en-fullreport .pdf.

Lewis, C. (2000). Police complaints in metropolitan Toronto: Perspectives of the public complaints commissioner. In A. Goldsmith (Ed.), *Complaints against the police: The trend to external review* (pp. 153–177). Oxford: Clarendon Press.

Lewis, C., & Prenzler, T. (2008). Police oversight agencies: Measuring effectiveness. In B. Head, A. J. Brown & C. Connors (Eds.), *Promoting integrity: Evaluating and improving public institutions* (pp. 199–219). Surrey: Ashgate Publishing.

Livingston, D. (2004). The unfulfilled promise of citizen review. *Ohio State Journal of Criminal Law, 1,* 653–669.

Miller, S. (2010). What makes a good internal affairs investigation. *Criminal Justice Ethics, 29,* 29–40.

National Association of Citizen Oversight of Law Enforcement (NACOLE). (2014). Retrieved from http://nacole.org/nacole-resources/oversight-agencies/links -to-oversight-agencies-u-s/.

Office of the Independent Police Review Director (OIPRD). (2010). *Statement of operations—October 19, 2009–March 31, 2010.* Retrieved from http://www .oiprd.on.ca/EN/PDFs/Annual-Report-2009-2010_E.pdf.

Office of the Independent Police Review Director (OIPRD). (2011). *Annual report—2010–2011.* Retrieved from http://www.oiprd.on.ca/EN/PDFs/Annual -Report-2010-2011_E.pdf.

Office of the Independent Police Review Director (OIPRD). (2012). *Annual report—2011–2012.* Retrieved from http://www.oiprd.on.ca/EN/PDFs/Annual -Report-2011-2012_E.pdf.

Office of the Independent Police Review Director (OIPRD). (2013). *Annual report—2012–2013.* Retrieved from http://www.oiprd.on.ca/EN/PDFs/Annual -Report-2012-2013_E.pdf.

Office of the Independent Police Review Director (OIPRD). (2014a). Retrieved from http://www.oiprd.on.ca/EN/AboutUs/Pages/Legislation.aspx.

Office of the Independent Police Review Director (OIPRD). (2014b). *Annual report—2013–2014.* Retrieved from http://www.oiprd.on.ca/EN/PDFs/Annual -Report-2013-2014_A_E.pdf.

Ontario Civilian Police Commission (OCPC). (2014). Retrieved from http://www .ocpc.ca/english/aboutocpc/aboutus.html.

Petterson, W. (1978). Police accountability and civilian oversight of policing: An American perspective. In A. Goldsmith (Ed.), *Complaints against the police: The trend to external review* (pp. 259–291). Oxford: Clarendon Press.

Police–Civilian Internal Affairs Review Commission (PCIARC). (2010). *City of Saint Paul: Annual report—2009.* Retrieved from http://www.stpaul.gov/Document Center/Home/View/13234.

Police–Civilian Internal Affairs Review Commission (PCIARC). (2012). *City of Saint Paul: Annual report—2012.* Retrieved from http://www.stpaul.gov/Document Center/View/70374.

Prenzler, T. (2000). Civilian oversight of police. *The British Journal of Criminology, 40,* 659–674.

Prenzler, T. (2011). The evolution of police oversight in Australia. *Policing & Society, 21,* 284–303.

Prenzler, T., & Ronken, C. (2001). Models of police oversight: A critique. *Policing & Society, 11,* 151–180.

President's Commission on Law Enforcement and Administration of Justice. (1967). *Task force report: The police.* Washington, DC: US Government Printing Office.

Punch, M. (2009). *Police corruption: Deviance, accountability and reform in policing.* Portland, OR: Willan Publishing.

Reaves, B. A. (2011). *Census of state and local law enforcement agencies, 2008.* Washington, DC: Department of Justice, Bureau of Justice Statistics.

Sherman, L. (1998). *Evidence-based policing.* Washington, DC: Police Foundation.

Sherman, L. (2013). The rise of evidence-based policing: Targeting, testing, and tracking. *Crime and Justice, 42,* 377–451.

Special Investigations Unit (SIU). (2014). Retrieved from http://www.siu.on.ca/en /investigate_what.php.

Swol, K. (1999). *Police personnel and expenditures in Canada—1997 and 1998.* Ottawa: Statistics Canada.

Terrill, R. (1988a). Civilian oversight of the police complaints process in the United States: Concerns, developments and more concerns. In A. Goldsmith (Ed.), *Complaints against the police: The trend to external review* (pp. 291–323). Oxford: Clarendon Press.

Terrill, R. (1988b). Police accountability in Philadelphia: Retrospect and prospects. *American Journal of Police, 7,* 79–99.

Walker, S. (1977). *Critical history of police reform.* Lexington, MA: Lexington Books.

Walker, S. (2000). *Police accountability: The role of citizen oversight.* Los Angeles, CA: Wadsworth Publishing.

Walker, S., & Archbold, C. (2014). *The new world of police accountability* (2nd ed.). Thousand Oaks, CA: SAGE Publications.

Wells, W., & Schafer, J. (2007). Police scepticism of citizen oversight: Officers' attitudes toward specific functions, processes, and outcomes. *Journal of Crime and Justice, 30,* 1–25.

Welsh, B. (2006). Advocate: Evidence-based policing for crime prevention. In D. Weisburd & A. Braga (Eds.), *Police innovation contrasting perspectives* (pp. 305–321). Cambridge, UK: Cambridge University Press.

Police Independent Oversight in Australia and New Zealand

10

GARTH DEN HEYER
ALAN BECKLEY

Contents

Independent and objective oversight of police organizations in Australia and New Zealand is essential to ensure the accountability and the effectiveness of police activities and safeguards the rights of members of the public against overreaction, use of excessive force, or misconduct committed by individual or collective police officers. The public's opinion and trust in the police are at stake when the accountability of the police is questioned to the extent that the situation moves away from the ideal "policing by consent" paradigm in western liberal democracies.

This chapter examines the history of independent oversight of police forces in Australia and New Zealand and comments on their scope, powers, and effectiveness in their objective of ensuring the integrity of police organizations. The definition and description of the differing independent oversight bodies are listed through examination of official discourse, websites, and documented material. Analysis of the investigation revealed a wide range of approaches, constitutions, and powers within this ever-changing arena; whereas each state and territory has some form of independent oversight, none of the bodies examined are exactly the same as another. Some good practice is recognized by many, but the only observed trend is toward cross-public sector integrity commissions, which subsume the role of police independent oversight into a body that scrutinizes the integrity of the whole public sector. Whether this is the most effective approach remains to be seen.

Background

The British model of policing (Emsley, 2012) has been adopted by a number of liberal democracies, including Australia and New Zealand. This model gives police officers wide-ranging statutory powers of arrest, search, and seizure and enables them to use coercive force to resolve or remedy policing incidents which are in addition to the common law powers of citizens to "keep the peace" (Ross, 2007, p. 151). Owing to the use of these powers having been exceeded by police officers, it became necessary to establish independent oversight bodies to keep abuse of coercive powers under check. The role of an independent oversight body is to scrutinize the actions of police officers independently and objectively. The principles link to the trust that the public hold of the police and to police effectively fulfilling their role while safeguarding the rights of individual citizens, especially vulnerable members of society (Bartkowiak-Theron & Asquith, 2012, p. 4). This chapter will examine the stages in the development of oversight bodies in Australia and New Zealand within the context of international research and current practice.

History of Policing in New Zealand

During early colonization, New Zealand did not have an organized national police force. Law and order were managed by local magistrates and then by provincial authorities. In 1846, the centralized Armed Constabulary was formed, but provincial growth placed too many demands upon it, leading to provincial councils forming their own police forces in 1853 (Hill, 1986). This fragmented law enforcement system changed in 1867 when the national Armed Constabulary force was formed (Hill, 1986). In 1877, this Armed

Constabulary amalgamated with the provincial police forces to become the New Zealand Constabulary force. The rules and regulations of 1852 laid down the requirements to join Governor Grey's Armed Constabulary Force: A man had to be of good character, sober, and able to read and write. Training placed an emphasis on foot and mounted drill (Hill, 1989).

In 1886, Parliament passed the Police Force Act, giving New Zealand its first national civil police force (Hill, 1989). This force was separate from the military and was to be unarmed except in grave emergencies and was to be based on the principles of policing devised by Rowan and Mayne, the first commissioners of the London Metropolitan Police (Hill, 1989).

History of Policing in Australia

The first record of an officially appointed police officer in Australia was a free settler named John Smith who was appointed to the post of constable by Governor Arthur Phillip in 1788, the year of colonization, after being formally claimed by Great Britain in 1770. The structure and style of policing introduced in New South Wales (NSW), which has been described as a "colonial" model (Emsley, 2012), were based on a format that was introduced in Ireland in the 19th century. The constituents of this are a paramilitary style of centralized "command and control" management organization. Owing to Australia's "convict population" roots, the police kept aloof from mainstream society and lived in military-style barracks. Evidence suggests that policing in most of Australia has not developed significantly from this style of policing (Finnane, 1994, p. 7). Although policing in Australia is primarily state based, the Australian Federal Police (AFP) is based on a different policing style and responsible for law enforcement at the national level with additional international responsibilities.

History of Independent Oversight Bodies in Australia and New Zealand

Before 1963, there was no independent oversight of policing in Australia (United Nations, 1963). The need for an ombudsman was recognized later owing to the many (61) Royal Commissions and Commissions of Inquiry into policing activities (Beckley, 2013). Over the following 50 years, many of the inquiries into policing recommended that independent oversight bodies be introduced to ensure police accountability (Lewis, 2007). In this regard, specific recommendations were made in Queensland (Fitzgerald, 1989), NSW (Wood, 1997), and Western Australia (Kennedy, 2004). Several research studies have investigated the progression of independent oversight bodies in

Table 10.1   Comparison of Integrity Institutions in Place in Australian and New Zealand Jurisdictions

	Auditor-General	Ombudsman	Police Oversight Body	Anticorruption Commission	Crime Commission	Police
New Zealand	✓	✓	✓ Independent Police Conduct Authority (IPCA)			✓
Commonwealth	✓	✓ Ombudsman oversees complaints against police (Cat 3—serious)	✓ Australian Commission for Law Enforcement Integrity (Cat 4—corruption)		✓ Australian Crime Commission—covers all states and territories	✓
New South Wales (NSW)	✓	✓ Ombudsman oversees complaints against police—less serious nature	✓ Police Integrity Commission	✓ Independent Commission Against Corruption	✓ New South Wales Crime Commission	✓
Northern Territory	✓	✓				✓
Queensland	✓	✓		✓ Crime and Corruption Commission		✓
South Australia	✓	✓	✓ Independent Commissioner Against Corruption—Office for Public Integrity			✓
Tasmania	✓	✓ Remit: government departments; local councils; water, sewerage Corps; prisons; state-owned companies; Government Business Enterprises	✓ Integrity Commission			✓
Victoria	✓	✓	✓ Independent Broad-based Anti-corruption Commission (IBAC)			✓
Western Australia	✓	✓	✓ Corruption and Crime Commission			✓

Source: Adapted and updated January 2015 from Proust (2010, p. 57, Appendix F).

Australia (den Heyer & Beckley, 2013; Office for Public Integrity [OPI], 2007; Prenzler, 2011). The current independent oversight body arrangements are summarized and discussed in the following sections.

Information regarding independent oversight arrangements in Australia and New Zealand was sourced from research published by the authors (den Heyer & Beckley, 2013) and is presented in Table 10.1.

Overview of Independent Oversight Body Powers

As most of the independent oversight bodies within this study have common powers, this section will summarize the current situation as identified from the authors' previous research. All of the organizations that perform oversight of the Australian and New Zealand police have their "own motion" powers, which means that they can investigate any matter that comes to their attention, whether it has been officially reported to them or not. Police oversight bodies have the discretion to determine whether they will investigate or not. Several police oversight bodies have police officers seconded to their staff to carry out investigations, whereas others do not. The Police Integrity Commission (PIC) of NSW is expressly forbidden to employ police officers or ex-police officers from NSW Police (den Heyer & Beckley, 2013).

All independent oversight bodies in the study have the power to conduct investigations, and most have royal commission-like coercive investigative powers except for the Independent Police Complaints Authority (IPCA), the Commonwealth Ombudsman, and the NSW Ombudsman. Suspects identified by the oversight bodies are not compelled to answer incriminating questions, although this is a power in the remaining state oversight organizations. All organizations except IPCA have powers of entry, and many have powers to obtain listening devices to aid their investigations. Although none of the bodies have the power to impose disciplinary sanctions on police officers, this remains in the domain of the chief police officers; all have the power to make recommendations on procedural issues (den Heyer & Beckley, 2013).

Reporting/Scrutiny of External Oversight
Bodies in Australia and New Zealand

Each report released by independent police oversight bodies is scrutinized by democratically elected bodies as in Table 10.2.

This chapter will now discuss independent oversight bodies in greater detail, commencing with New Zealand and followed by the states and territories of Australia.

Table 10.2   Current Reporting/Scrutiny of External Oversight Bodies in Australia and New Zealand

Jurisdiction	External Body	Date Established	Reports to
New Zealand	Independent Police Conduct Authority	1989	Parliament
Commonwealth	Commonwealth Law Enforcement Integrity Commissioner	2006	Commonwealth Attorney-General
New South Wales	Police Integrity Commission	1996	Parliamentary Committee
Northern Territory	Ombudsman	1976	Parliament
Queensland	Crime and Corruption Commission	2014	Parliamentary Committee
South Australia	Independent Commissioner Against Corruption, Office for Public Integrity, Police Ombudsman	2013	Parliamentary Committee
Tasmania	Integrity Commission	2011	Parliament
Victoria	Independent Broad-based Anti-corruption Commission (IBAC)	2012	Parliamentary Integrity Commissioner
Western Australia	Corruption and Crime Commission	2004	Parliamentary Committee and Parliamentary Inspector

Source: Adapted from Broadhurst R. & Davies, S. E. (Eds), *Policing in context: An introduction to police work in Australia*, Oxford University Press, Sydney, Australia, p. 97, 2009.

Developments in Independent Oversight of Police—New Zealand and Australia

New Zealand

The New Zealand Independent Police Conduct Authority (IPCA) is an independent Crown Entity under the Crown Entities Act 2004 and was created by the Independent Police Conduct Authority Act 1988. The IPCA, established in 1989, was initially known as the Independent Complaints Authority and is composed of a single person with a small number of staff.

The IPCA Act 1988 defined the Authority's function as to receive complaints alleging misconduct or neglect of duty, or concerning police practice, policy, or procedure, and to investigate incidents where a member of police causes or appears to have caused death or serious bodily harm (IPCA, 2011a, p. 4). The Authority's primary role was to maintain public confidence in the police and to increase the general effectiveness of the police

(IPCA, 2011a, p. 4). Owing to the Independent Complaints Authority's reliance on police conducting investigations that have arisen from complaints, the Authority was perceived as lacking independence and, in 2007, implemented a number of structural and procedural changes. The changes were designed to ensure that the new IPCA had the responsibility for the independent oversight of the police and was "seen to be independent of the functions and influence of the Police" (IPCA, 2011a, p. 5).

Since November 2007, the institution has undergone continual transformation, including the change of name to the IPCA, the appointment of additional investigators (which included former and retired U.K. and New Zealand police officers and qualified solicitors), and changes to the Authority's legislation, structure, and operations (IPCA, 2012a). The changes included the establishment of an Authority Board, which may be composed of up to five members, and for the Authority to conduct its own investigations of serious matters, report on them, and actively monitor less serious complaints that have been referred to the police (IPCA, 2011a). The new framework provides independence for the Authority and ensures that it makes its investigative findings based on the facts and on the law. The Authority has the same powers as a Commission of Inquiry, to summon witnesses and gather evidence (IPCA, 2012b).

Further legislative, procedure, and policy change has been proposed that "would complete the process of transforming the Authority from a reviewing body into a fully independent investigative body" (IPCA, 2012a). The Authority's independence is achieved through three separate but interrelated critical factors: (1) legislative or statutory independence, (2) operational independence, and (3) impartiality.

The IPCA Act empowers the Authority when it receives a complaint to investigate the complaint, or refer it to the police for investigation under the Authority's oversight ability, or to defer action, or to not take any action (IPCA, 2011b). The current practice is for the majority of complaints to be referred to the police for investigation, especially those complaints pertaining to breaches of the Police Code of Conduct. The most serious complaints or those that involve public interest are undertaken by the Authority (IPCA, 2011b). The Authority, upon the completion of a Police or Authority investigation, determines "whether there was any breach of practice, policy or procedure, and whether any police act or omission was contrary to law, unreasonable, unjustified, unfair, or undesirable" (IPCA, 2011b, p. 5), and the Authority must inform the police of its findings. If the Authority is not satisfied with the police response to its recommendations, the Authority must inform Minister of Police and the Attorney-General, who, in turn, must inform Parliament (IPCA, 2012a).

The legislation identifies the Authority as an independent entity, and although the IPCA Act requires the Authority to maintain secrecy in respect of complaints and investigations, it does have the discretion to publish public reports (IPCA, 2012a). The Authority is required to make four monthly reports to the Minister of Justice (IPCA, 2012a) and to present an Annual Report to Parliament, which demonstrates how the Authority has performed against its budget and performance measures. During 2012–2013, IPCA received 1997 complaints, out of which no further action was taken in 952 cases.

Australia: Commonwealth—AFP and Australian Capital Territory

The history of federal policing (the AFP) dates back to 1978, when Sir Robert Mark, the former commissioner of the London Metropolitan Police, was appointed to inquire into and report on the needs and requirements of a police force with national and international coverage (Mark, 1978). The Harrison (1997) inquiry investigated allegations of corrupt police practices in the AFP, and the main recommendations of the inquiry, which was never published, focused on the investigation of complaints against police. Later, the Fisher (2003) review recommended further changes to the internal investigation of complaints and discipline. This was followed by the introduction of the Law Enforcement Integrity Commissioners Act 2006 and the Australian Commission for Law Enforcement Integrity (ACLEI), which is an independent oversight agency tasked with, among other things, investigating police corruption in the AFP. A Parliamentary Joint Committee (PJC) interim report reviewing ACLEI (PJC on ACLEI, 2009, p. vii) recommended the addition of a corruption "prevention and education unit," and the final report (PJC on ACLEI, 2011) recommended widening the scope of ACLEI to include investigations into corruption in a large number of public sector organizations and amending certain parts of the founding legislation.

In summary, the oversight body for the Commonwealth of Australia consists of an ombudsman who oversees or investigates serious complaints against police (Category 3) and ACLEI, which investigates allegations of police corruption (Category 4). Less serious incidents of police misconduct (Category 1 and 2) are investigated by the police and overseen by the ombudsman. In 2012, the AFP was criticized by the Commonwealth Ombudsman for taking too long to investigate serious complaints against police and the low substantiation rate, especially in cases of use of force. The acting ombudsman was quoted as saying: "…to date the measures the AFP has taken to address the issue have not proved to be effective" (Peatling, 2012). ACLEI (2013, p. 51) stated that there were a total of 78 allegations of corruption reported in 2012–2013, out of which 56 were notified by law enforcement agency heads, although that number was significantly down from 73 in 2011–2012.

New South Wales

In NSW, an ombudsman was appointed in 1979 to oversee matters of police integrity, and in 1988, the Independent Commission Against Corruption (ICAC) was formed to examine misconduct across the entire public sector. The Wood Royal Commission (1997) was a major driver of change after its wide-ranging investigation into police corruption; subsequently, the findings of the inquiry have been endorsed by a 10-year review (Parliament of NSW, 2006). The Wood Commission recommended a standing body for investigating serious police misconduct and corruption (PIC, 2012; Ross, 2007, p. 153; Section 8A Police Act 1990), which resulted in the formation of the PIC and has robust royal commission powers of investigation (Police Integrity Commission Act, 1996). The NSW Ombudsman oversees and investigates complaints of a less serious nature.

The operating procedures of the PIC have been updated to include modern investigation standards in that the gathering of intelligence and a "tasking and coordination group" (Kleiven, 2007, p. 259) have been introduced with a developing expertise in investigation (PIC, 2012). The PIC's function is also to prevent, detect, and investigate serious police misconduct, including the investigation of misconduct of nonsworn support staff in the NSW Police Force and Crime Commission. In terms of the research, education, and prevention function, the PIC has a research team, which has produced many authoritative reports on police misconduct and suggested solutions.

In 2012–2013, there were only eight (0.675% of all complaints) full PIC investigations arising from complaints, whereas the total of all complaints assessed was 1145 against police officers and 40 against unsworn police staff (PIC, 2013, p. 18). An academic study (Goodman-Delahunty, Beckley, & Hanckel, 2012) criticized the way that NSW Police Force dealt with complaints, and the PIC recently investigated the complaints system (Dinning & Barnett, 2014, p. 27). After the death of Roberto Laudisio-Curti, who, although unarmed, was Tasered by NSW police several times, a review of investigations into police critical incidents was inaugurated under Robert McClelland, a former federal attorney-general. Among many other things, the review suggested a merger between the PIC and ICAC, but this was strongly resisted by PIC Commissioner Bruce James (Patty, 2014).

Northern Territory

The Northern Territory (NT) has an ombudsman in place who oversees all complaints against public officials. This arrangement has been unchanged, with only minor amendments since 1976, although the Ombudsman Act 2009 provided new "own motion" powers and allowed police officers to make complaints against their colleagues. The NT ombudsman also has a scrutiny function over the NT police regarding the use of surveillance devices.

An NT inquiry into the investigation of an alleged child homicide (Morling, 1987) spanned almost 32 years before being concluded in 2013. Alice (Lindy) and Michael Chamberlain were convicted of the 1980 murder of their young baby daughter, Azaria, at Ayers Rock. The Chamberlains maintained that a dingo had abducted their daughter, but that story was said, during the Morling (1987, Chapter 5) inquiry, to be "preposterous and incapable of belief"; there was criticism of police actions to protect the crime scene of the incident and subsequent forensic examination. There were four coronial inquests on the case, a criminal trial and a royal commission (Brown, 2012); the final inquest produced a death certificate that read: "[t]he cause of her [Azaria] death was the result of being attacked by a dingo" (Puddy, 2012).

The 2013 Annual report by the Ombudsman NT listed that out of 2,243 "approaches" (either complaints or requests for information), 418 (18.64%) were related to the police, fire, and emergency services (Ombudsman NT, 2013). The approach of the ombudsman is to allocate the approach or complaint back to the relevant public service to resolve in the first instance if it is not too serious. Last year, there were no incidents relating to the police that were regarded as "major inquiries" by the ombudsman. The NT ombudsman recorded 49% of approaches finalized within 7 days and 70% within 28 days. There is an informal resolution process (complaint resolution process) for complaints against police: category 2 complaints (less serious) and category 1 complaints (more serious). In 2013 substantiated complaints numbered 135 (Ombudsman NT, 2013).

Queensland

The first independent oversight body in Queensland, the Criminal Justice Commission, was set up after recommendations from a royal commission (Fitzgerald, 1989). Fitzgerald (1989) investigated the major issue of police corruption; the terms of reference for the commission were extended twice, which linked to incidents investigated by several other inquiries. The Criminal Justice Commission was introduced and had the responsibility of investigating cross-public sector misconduct but was superseded (Crime and Misconduct Act 2001) by the wider-based Crime and Misconduct Commission (CMC), which also had the remit for the investigation of serious and organized crime (CMC, 2011a). On July 1, 2014, the CMC was superseded by the Crime and Corruption Commission (CCC), although, as this is written, no reports have yet been published on the new organization. The CCC is understood to have "the same broad remit" (CMC, 2014, p. 1) but will deal only with "the most serious and systemic corrupt conduct" in public sector organizations. After a high-level review of the CMC, the serious crime investigation section was given additional statutory powers.

Although most police misconduct investigations are conducted internally by police officers, the CMC reviewed all misconduct allegations. CMC investigators only actually investigate approximately 1% (which numbered 58 in 2013) of all complaints against police by using the "devolution principle" (CMC, 2013c, p. 26); the total number of allegations against police in 2012–2013 was 5,240, which was down from 6,167 in 2011–2012 (CMC, 2013c, p. 27). The devolution principle has been gradually adopted over time, but the most serious allegations are retained for investigation by the CMC. Where cross-public sector integrity commissions such as CMC operate, statistics reveal that complaints against police make up a large percentage of their business; indeed, in 2013, 51% of all complaints received related to Queensland Police Service (QPS) personnel (CMC, 2013c, p. 25).

Following the Operation Tesco inquiry (CMC, 2011b) which reported on police misconduct in a variety of settings in the Gold Coast area, including the notorious "blue light taxis" (Prenzler, Beckley, & Bronitt, 2013, p. 298), the QPS compiled a detailed action plan to address the recommendations. Other CMC activities include a report into the use of electronic Taser weapons by the police by the research and training function (CMC, 2012b). The importance of prevention of corruption is emphasized by the CMC exemplified by the analysis of the QPS' gifts and gratuities policy (Prenzler, Beckley, & Bronitt, 2012) and research conducted into improving misconduct and enhancing the ethical culture in the police workforce (CMC, 2013a,b).

South Australia

South Australia experienced several serious incidents that were investigated by royal commissions. The Bright (1970) report investigated police actions at a public demonstration about the involvement of Australia in the Vietnam War. The tribunal was critical of police tactics and made several recommendations not only to better manage future events but to also uphold rights to lawful assembly and freedom of speech. Another incident that was investigated was the sacking of the South Australian police commissioner Harold Salisbury in 1978 by the state government on the grounds that he misled the government "as to the nature and extent of the activities of the Police Special Branch" (Mitchell, 1978). The royal commission agreed that the police commissioner had misled the government, and his sacking was justified, but that there was reason to amend sections of The Police Regulations Act, 1952–1973.

South Australia was the first state in Australia to have an independent oversight body specifically for the police. The Police Complaints Authority commenced business in 1985 following the findings of the Grieve Committee of Inquiry (1983). The Independent Commissioner Against Corruption

(Independent Commissioner Against Corruption Act 2012) was introduced in 2013, in South Australia, which is similar in operation to Victoria's Independent Broad-based Anti-corruption Commission (IBAC) and has the Office of Public Integrity for the oversight of all public officers. The main objective of ICAC is "...to identify and investigate serious and systemic corruption in public administration..." (Attorney General's Department, 2013, p. 1). Less serious matters than corruption are referred to the relevant body for investigation. There are three levels of seriousness of wrongdoing in public office: corruption, misconduct, and maladministration, which are each defined under the Act. Where it establishes transgressions, ICAC will refer actual or potential issues for prevention and reduction to the appropriate public body. It will also provide education and evaluate policies and procedures for compliance with good practice. No annual reports have yet been published to ascertain the number of inquiries the Office of Public Integrity has undertaken.

Tasmania

The only significant inquiry into police activity in Tasmania was the Commission of Inquiry (Mahoney, 2000), which related to the death of Joseph Gilewicz, who was shot dead during a police operation conducted by the Special Operations Group of the Tasmania Police in 1991 after a domestic incident (Tapp, n.d.). The Commission found that there had been a cover up by police over the shooting as Gilewicz had been unarmed and there were significant inconsistencies in the police evidence.

In terms of independent oversight of the police, an Ombudsman was appointed in Tasmania in 1978; subsequently, a cross public sector Integrity Commission has been established in 2010. Unusually, the Integrity Commission Tasmania (ICT) was introduced (Integrity Commission Act 2009) not as a consequence of police corruption but because of misconduct by politicians after the publication of the report by the Joint Select Committee on Ethical Conduct (2009). The primary role of the Integrity Commission is "to raise the standard of conduct, ethics and propriety in the public sector through prevention, education and advice" (ICT, 2010a). The report suggested an overhaul of oversight mechanisms to coordinate them and make them consistent. Training would also be required for all public officers.

According to the Act (Section 4) there are two levels of misconduct. "Serious misconduct" is defined as "conduct that, if proved, could constitute a crime or serious offence or provide reasonable grounds for terminating the employment or appointment of the public officer." Misconduct is defined as breaching a code of conduct, dishonest or improper performance, misuse of public resources, and interfering with the honest performance of another public officer. Misconduct does not include conduct by a public officer in connection with a proceeding in parliament (ICT, 2010b). The ICT has wide coercive powers of investigation, powers of search and entry, and the mandate to operate surveillance devices. According to the ICT 2012–2013 report (ICT, 2013, p. 33), it has completed an audit of all complaints against Tasmanian police officers and has reviewed the police internal complaint handling system. Of the 66 complaints received, 6 are "currently under consideration, assessment or investigation" (p. 29) and 24 (36.4%) are related to the police and emergency management category (p. 32).

Victoria

When the Beach (1976) inquiry investigated serious allegations against members of the Victoria Police, the recommendations from the report were not immediately accepted and implemented. A further inquiry, Norris (1980), reported and amended the list of proposed changes and they were then implemented. Independent oversight of police was carried out by the post of Deputy Ombudsman (Police Complaints). The post of Deputy Ombudsman was introduced in 1988 and was superseded by the Office of Police Integrity (OPI) in 2004. Subsequently, the Proust (2010) review produced a review of Victoria State Government integrity and anticorruption systems.

The resulting IBAC is a cross-public sector integrity commission that incorporated the role of police oversight from the OPI (2012) and extends its scrutiny to the judiciary, members of parliament, police, and support staff (Proust, 2010, pp. 11–14) by the Independent Broad-based Anti-corruption Commission Amendment (Investigative Functions) Act 2011.

When the 2013 IBAC Annual Report (IBAC, 2013, p. 16) was published, only 11 OPI matters "continued" to a full investigation out of a total of 638 "assessable disclosures/complaints" (1.7% of all complaints made to the IBAC). This is similar to the percentage experienced by other comparable Australian independent oversight bodies. One area that appeared to be functioning well was the training function of the body, which provided 72 education initiatives (IBAC, 2013, p. 13). There have been a number of inquiries into the actions of chief commissioners of police between 2009 and the present day. First, an inquiry was instigated by OPI into unauthorized hospitality received by Christine Nixon (Prenzler et al., 2013, p. 296). Later, there were concerns about the deputy commissioner and his relationship with a police officer who was a ministerial adviser (OPI, 2011), and the chief commissioner at that time, Simon Overland, resigned in 2012, having misled the public over crime statistics (Ferguson & Le Grand, 2012).

Western Australia

The state of Western Australia has had an ombudsman in post since 1971; subsequently, a Parliamentary Select Committee (Tomlinson, 1996, p. iii) has inquired into several matters, including the accountability of police and the Internal Affairs Unit of the Western Australia Police (WAPOL). An anticorruption commission was set up in 1996 and was superseded by the Corruption and Crime Commission (CCC), which was introduced as a result of the findings of the Kennedy royal commission (2004). The Kennedy inquiry established evidence of a wide range of corrupt and criminal conduct carried out by police officers in WAPOL. Although WAPOL had attempted to deal with "gender issues" within the force, these had not been satisfactorily addressed (Kennedy, 2004, p. 6). The report recommended that the Police Act 1892 be updated (Kennedy, 2004, p. 12), a number of changes to the human resource management systems, and the management and investigation of internal discipline and complaints against police be overhauled (Kennedy, 2004, p. 15).

The CCC has investigated police use of force, specifically in the use of electronic Taser weapons (WAPOL, 2010). After an investigation into the "management of misconduct" by the CCC, it was able to report that, overall, 96% of high-risk complaints cases were dealt with (by WAPOL) correctly, but some were inadequately investigated (mainly Taser incidents). All medium-risk cases were dealt with correctly and some low-risk cases were incorrectly categorized and as such dealt with. The CCC report made seven recommendations for improving the approach that WAPOL take in reviewing its procedures for investigating police misconduct (CCC, 2011, p. xxi). The number of "notifications of reviewable police action" (CCC, 2013, pp. 10–12) has decreased substantially by 645 (33%) in 2013, when compared with the number in 2011–2012. The 2013 notifications of reviewable police action represented 50% of all complaints against public officials; the CCC investigated the most serious incidents being approximately 1.5% of all allegations (CCC, 2013, p. xvii).

Critique and Emerging Issues

This chapter has listed and described the arrangements that are in place for independent oversight of the police in Australia and New Zealand along with a description of the roles, responsibilities, and functions of police oversight bodies. Aspects of police accountability in Australia and New Zealand appear to suffer from a perennial problem in that police organizations do not seem to learn from earlier mistakes, which appear to be evident from examining the findings and recommendations of royal commissions and inquiries over decades (den Heyer & Beckley, 2013). It has been explained that there is a myriad of approaches that are difficult to summarize, justify, and categorize despite the importance ascribed to public trust in the police and upon which public opinion, procedural justice, and accountability depends. The diversity of oversight bodies is exemplified in the common acceptance of strong coercive powers that override centuries-old human rights but define the basis of corruption in a number of different ways. The analysis of independent oversight bodies, working alongside their respective police forces in Australia and New Zealand, has also revealed a number of common findings. Practitioners from these bodies have unanimously stated that good working relationships exist between the parties despite the fact that the raison d'etre of independent oversight bodies is to hold the police accountable for their actions (den Heyer & Beckley, 2013).

Independent oversight bodies act on behalf of the community and can add to the level of trust and confidence held by the public in the police, while ensuring that police officers maintain high levels of integrity. Three procedures ensure that oversight bodies achieve this: (1) investigating complaints against police by an independent and objective process, either through the supervision of an investigation or from the use of nonpolice investigators (CMC, 2012a; OPI, 2012; PIC, 2012); (2) good communication that brings openness and transparency to the investigation of complaints against police, although it should be noted that there is a tendency in recently formed integrity commissions to hold hearings in camera (Fyfe & Millar, 2012); and (3) in serious cases, using independent highly skilled investigators along with the use of own motion powers to investigate cases that intelligence or inquiries have revealed but have not been reported to the oversight body. In respect of the independence and the objectivity of the investigation of complaints against police, an inquiry in 1970 noted that a chief commissioner of Victoria police "was unable to investigate satisfactorily the allegations" of corruption in his police force (Kaye, 1971, p. 8). However, the detailed information for each state and territory highlighted the low number of complaints investigated independently.

The long-standing oversight arrangements are prima facie rigorous and robust, but a recent study (Goodman-Delahunty et al., 2012) that surveyed legal practitioners and community advisers about complaints against NSW police found that investigations into police misconduct were criticized for being insufficiently independent and that complaint procedures administered by the police were not user-friendly. The PIC recently completed an investigation into "system problems and solutions" in the NSW Police Force complaints system, which made several recommendations but was advised by the police that "it does not have a corporate strategy for collecting and disseminating 'good ideas' derived from complaint investigations" (Dinning & Barnett, 2014, p. 27). This appears to be a major oversight as part of the value of analyzing complaints against police is to "identify opportunities to learn lessons and adopt good practice" (Her Majesty's Inspectorate of Constabulary, 2011, p. 4), and "...such learning is vital to assist police to develop really skilled practice" (Neyroud & Beckley, 2001, p. 155). The complaints against police systems in other jurisdictions have also been investigated and improved by independent oversight bodies.

When completing earlier research (den Heyer & Beckley, 2013), the authors interviewed a number of independent oversight body practitioners who believed that their organization was effective at achieving accountability of the police force they scrutinized, although independent research with legal practitioners and community advocates disclosed an opposing view (Goodman-Delahunty et al., 2012). The independent oversight practitioners consistently identified that their organizations were undergoing continual change, with a focus on the prevention of corruption rather than on its subsequent detection. Several comments were also made by practitioners in regard to the role of investigating police officers, which was difficult and onerous and was a specialist task that required specific focus. In comparison, they considered that a generalized approach would be a less effective method for investigating police corruption (den Heyer & Beckley, 2013). There appears to be a need to communicate the independent oversight bodies' confidence in the system to members of the public so that the accountability and legitimacy of the police is not in constant question. One way to do this might be to highlight the good work of the independent oversight bodies that use integrity testing methods and proactive investigative procedures.

It was not until 1976 that the first ombudsman was appointed, followed by the first independent oversight body in 1985. It is disappointing that police independent oversight bodies are not coordinated, consistent, and comprehensive across Australia and New Zealand with harmonized policies, practices, and procedures (Porter & Prenzler, 2011). Although the move toward cross-sector integrity commissions has been discussed, there are historical factors that have caused differences in the scope, constitutions, powers, and roles and responsibilities of independent oversight bodies. A guiding factor is the date that the oversight body was formed; in addition, several oversight bodies have undertaken significant change since their formation. Some bodies were created to investigate specific examples of misconduct, which were examined through a Commission of Inquiry, whereas other bodies were created after thematic examinations of the structure, scope, roles, and responsibilities of the police organization. Practitioners and external researchers have noted that major structural developments in police accountability were principally from internal investigation/oversight (pre-1980) but have moved toward external oversight (1980–2000) and, from 2000 to the present day, to cross-public sector integrity commissions (Prenzler & Faulkner, 2010).

As identified earlier, there have been recent moves in Victoria and South Australia to a cross-public sector model of independent oversight, which has been said to provide a "more comprehensive, coherent and coordinated integrity system" toward minimizing corruption in public office (Proust, 2010, p. xii). It seems self-evident that corruption does not exist within the police alone, and to effectively address police corruption, the police organization should exist alongside other public sector organizations that positively aspire toward integrity (Beckley, 2012). The move toward cross-public sector oversight organizations appears to be a logical conclusion to this assertion, but only time will tell if this approach achieves the desired outcome.

Conclusion

Taking a strategic view of the accountability of the police, much work remains to be done, especially when one considers the results of recent research that identified public dissatisfaction with the current oversight body arrangements (Goodman-Delahunty et al., 2012; Goodman-Delahunty, Beckley, & Martin, 2014). Taking into account the requirements of the public toward investigating complaints against police, investigations must not only be independent and objective, they must incontrovertibly be seen to be so. One development is that police forces around the world are experimenting with the use of body-worn video cameras (McDermott, 2013), but this, according to the United Kingdom, "is not a silver bullet" (Sommers, 2014, p. 1). This use of technology is not only beneficial for the complainant against police activity, it also protects the officer against spurious complaints. Trust in the police by the community and legitimacy in the policing function should be recognized in policing systems that rely on "policing by consent." Today's society is questioning and knowledgeable. It is the sophisticated and powerful independent oversight bodies that hold police accountable and investigate lapses in integrity, but in Australia and New Zealand, they come in many shapes, varieties, and forms. Although the independent oversight bodies are subject to scrutiny from powerful parliamentary committees, it is questionable whether they retain respect and credibility in the keen gaze of public opinion.

References

Attorney General's Department. (2013). *The Independent Commissioner Against Corruption (ICAC) and the Office for Public Integrity (OPI): Factsheet*. Adelaide: Government of South Australia.

Australian Commission for Law Enforcement Integrity. (2013). *Annual report of the Integrity Commissioner 2012–2013*. Canberra: Author.

Bartkowiak-Theron, I., & Asquith, N. L. (Eds.). (2012). *Policing vulnerability*. Sydney: The Federation Press.

Beach, B. (1976). *Board of inquiry into allegations against members of the Victoria police force, report*. Melbourne: Victoria Government Printer.

Beckley, A. (2012). Capacity building to foster anti-corruption in policing organizations. In P. Aepli (Ed.), *Toolkit on police integrity*. Geneva: DCAF.

Beckley, A. (2013). Royal commissions into policing—Australia. *Salus Journal, 1*(3), 33–52.

Bright, C. H. (1970). *Report on the September moratorium demonstration.* Adelaide: Government Printer.

Broadhurst, R., & Davies, S. E. (Eds.). (2009). *Policing in context: An introduction to police work in Australia.* Sydney: Oxford University Press.

Brown, M. (2012, June 9–10). Three decades to reach justice. *The Sydney Morning Herald,* News Review, p. 6.

Corruption and Crime Commission. (2011). *Report on the management of misconduct by Western Australia police.* Perth: Author.

Corruption and Crime Commission. (2013). *Annual report 2013.* Perth: Author.

Crime and Misconduct Commission. (2011a). *Crime and misconduct commission annual report 2010–11.* Brisbane: Author.

Crime and Misconduct Commission. (2011b). *Operation Tesco: Report of an investigation into allegations of police misconduct on the Gold Coast.* Brisbane: Author.

Crime and Misconduct Commission. (2012a). Personal communication.

Crime and Misconduct Commission. (2012b). *An update on Taser use in Queensland.* Brisbane: Author.

Crime and Misconduct Commission. (2013a). *Monitoring police ethics: A 2013 survey of Queensland recruits and first year constables.* Brisbane: Author.

Crime and Misconduct Commission. (2013b). *Improving misconduct reporting in the QPS: The importance of ethical culture.* Brisbane: Author.

Crime and Misconduct Commission. (2013c). *Annual report 2012–13.* Brisbane: Author.

Crime and Misconduct Commission. (2014). *Annual report 2013–14.* Brisbane: Author.

den Heyer, G., & Beckley, A. (2013). Police independent oversight in Australia and New Zealand. *Police Practice and Research: An International Journal, 14*(2), 130–143.

Dinning, B., & Barnett, P. (2014). *Project Cyril: Using the NSW police force complaints system to identify system problems and solutions.* Sydney: Police Integrity Commission.

Emsley, C. (2012). Marketing the brand: Exporting British police models 1829–1950. *Policing, 6*(1), 43–54.

Ferguson, J., & Le Grand, C. (2012). Simon Overland crisis prompts force to lose toxic culture. *The Australian.* Retrieved from http://www.theaustralian.com .au/national-affairs/state-politics/overland-crisis-prompts-force-to-lose-toxic -culture/story-e6frgczx-1226286706909 (accessed July 11, 2015).

Finnane, M. (1994). *Police and government: Histories of policing in Australia.* Melbourne: Oxford University Press.

Fisher, W. K. (2003). *A review of professional standards in the Australian Federal Police.* Canberra: Australian Federal Police.

Fitzgerald, T. (1989). *Commission of inquiry into possible illegal activities and associated police misconduct 1989.* Brisbane: Goprint.

Fyfe, M., & Millar, R. (2012). Corruption hearings to be secret. *The Age.* Retrieved from http://www.theage.com.au/victoria/corruption-hearings-to-be-secret-2012 0419-1xa5s.html (accessed July 11, 2015).

Goodman-Delahunty, J., Beckley, A., & Hanckel, B. (2012). *Complaints against police: Resolving disputes or escalating them? The NSW police force complaints process: Experiences of community advocates and legal practitioners.* Sydney: Community Legal Centres NSW.

Goodman-Delahunty, J., Beckley, A., & Martin, M. (2014). Complaints against the New South Wales Police Force: Analysis of risks and rights in reported police conduct. *Australian Journal of Human Rights, 20*(2), 81–105.

Grieve, I. C. (1983). *Report of the committee on complaints against the police: A committee established to examine and report to the chief secretary on the establishment of an independent authority to receive and investigate complaints from the public about police activities.* Adelaide: The Committee, 1983.

Harrison, I. (1997). *An inquiry into allegations of corruption within the Australian Federal Police.* Unpublished.

Her Majesty's Inspectorate of Constabulary. (2011). *Without fear or favour—A review of police relationships.* London: Author.

Hill, R. (1986). *The history of policing in New Zealand: Policing the colonial frontier* (Vol. 1, Pt. 1). Wellington, New Zealand: V. R. Ward.

Hill, R. (1989). *The history of policing in New Zealand: The colonial frontier tamed. New Zealand policing in transition, 1867–1886* (Vol. 2). Wellington, New Zealand: Wright and Carman Limited.

Independent Broad-Based Anti-corruption Commission. (2013). *Annual report 2012–13.* Melbourne: Author.

Independent Police Conduct Authority. (2011a). *Statement of intent 2011/12–2013/14.* Wellington: Author.

Independent Police Conduct Authority. (2011b). *Annual report 2010–2011.* Wellington: Author.

Independent Police Conduct Authority. (2012a). People and structure. *IPCA.* Retrieved January 20, 2012, from http://www.ipca.govt.nz.

Independent Police Conduct Authority. (2012b). Personal communication.

Integrity Commission Tasmania. (2010a). Raising the standard of public sector conduct, ethics and propriety. *Integrity Commission.* ICT. Retrieved from http://www.integrity.tas.gov.au.

Integrity Commission Tasmania. (2010b). *What is misconduct and who are public officers?* Hobart: Author.

Integrity Commission Tasmania. (2013). *Annual report 2012–2013: Essential to ensuring trust in government.* Hobart: Author.

Joint Select Committee on Ethical Conduct. (2009). *Final report: "Public office is public trust."* Hobart: Parliament of Tasmania.

Kaye, W. (1971). *Board of inquiry into allegations of corruption in the police force in connection with illegal abortion practices in the state of Victoria.* Melbourne: Government of Victoria.

Kennedy, G. A. (2004). *Royal commission into whether there has been corrupt or criminal conduct by any Western Australian police officer.* Perth: Western Australia Government.

Kleiven, M. E. (2007). Where's the intelligence in the national intelligence model? *International Journal of Police Science & Management, 9*(3), 257–273.

Lewis, C. (2007). Leading for integrity and effective accountability: A challenge from within. In M. Mitchell & J. Casey (Eds.), *Police leadership and management.* Sydney: The Federation Press.

Mahoney, D. (2000). *Commission of inquiry relating to the death of Joseph Gilewicz.* Hobart: Parliament of Tasmania.

Mark, R. (1978). *Report to the Minister for Administrative Services on the organisation of police resources in the Commonwealth area and other related matters.* Canberra: Australian Government Publishing Services.

McDermott, J. (2013). Body worn video: A case for modernising the police. *Police Oracle.* Retrieved from http://www.policeoracle.com/news/Crime/2013/Jul/18/Body-worn-video-A-case-for-modernising-policing_68152.html/features.

Mitchell, R. F. (1978). *Report on the dismissal of Harold Hubert Salisbury Royal Commission on the dismissal from Office of Commissioner of Police.* Adelaide: Government Printer, South Australia.

Morling, T. R. (1987). *Royal Commission into Chamberlain convictions.* Darwin: Northern Territory Government Printer.

Neyroud, P., & Beckley, A. (2001). *Policing, ethics and human rights.* Cullompton: Willan Publishing.

Norris, J. G. (1980). *Committee appointed to examine and advise in relation to the recommendations made in Chapter 8 of Volume 1 of the report of the Board of Inquiry appointed for the purpose of inquiring into and reporting upon certain allegations against Members of the Victoria police force.* Melbourne: Victorian Government Printer.

Office of Police Integrity. (2007). *Past patterns—Future directions: Victoria Police and the problem of corruption and serious misconduct.* Melbourne: Author.

Office of Police Integrity. (2011). *Crossing the line: Report of an investigation into the conduct of a member of Victoria police undertaking secondary employment as a Ministerial Adviser and his relationship with a Deputy Commissioner of Victoria police.* Melbourne: Author.

Office of Police Integrity. (2012). Personal communication.

Ombudsman Northern Territory. (2013). *Annual report 2012/13.* Darwin: Author.

Parliament of New South Wales. (2006). *Committee on the Office of the Ombudsman and the Police Integrity Commission. Ten year review of the police oversight system in New South Wales.* Sydney: Government of NSW.

Parliamentary Joint Committee on the Australian Commission for Law Enforcement Integrity. (2009). *Inquiry into law enforcement integrity models.* Canberra: Senate Printing Unit.

Parliamentary Joint Committee on the Australian Commission for Law Enforcement Integrity. (2011). *Inquiry into the operation of the Law Enforcement Integrity Commissioner ACT 2006, Final report.* Canberra: Australian Government.

Patty, A. (2014). Police integrity commission decries McClelland review of investigations into police. *The Sydney Morning Herald.* Retrieved from http://www.smh.com.au/nsw/police-integrity-commission-decries-mcclelland-review-of-investigations-into-police-20140223-33aez.html (accessed July 11, 2015).

Peatling, S. (2012). Federal police slow to deal with complaints. *The Sydney Morning Herald.* Retrieved from http://www.smh.com.au/national/federal-police-slow-to-deal-with-complaints-20120128-1qmxf.html#ixzz2V0y2VDAj (accessed July 11, 2015).

Police Integrity Commission. (2012). Personal communication.

Police Integrity Commission. (2013). *Annual report 2012–2013.* Sydney: Author.

Porter, L., & Prenzler, T. (2011). *A national stocktake of police integrity strategies.* Unpublished.

Prenzler, T. (2011). The evolution of police oversight in Australia. *Policing and Society, 21*(3), 284–303.

Prenzler, T., Beckley, A., & Bronitt, S. (2012). *Rethinking police gifts and benefits policies.* CEPS Briefing Paper 2012, July Issue 14. Brisbane: Australian Research Council Centre of Excellence for Policing and Security.

Prenzler, T., Beckley, A., & Bronitt, S. (2013). Police gifts and benefits scandals: Addressing deficits in policy, leadership and enforcement. *International Journal of Police Science and Management, 15*(4), 294–304.

Prenzler, T., & Faulkner, N. (2010). Towards a model public sector integrity commission. *Australian Journal of Public Administration, 69*(3), 251–262.

Proust, E. (2010). *Review of Victoria's integrity and anti-corruption system.* Melbourne: Public Sector Standards Commissioner.

Puddy, R. (2012). The dingo did it … here's the proof. *The Australian.* Retrieved from http://www.theaustralian.com.au/news/nation/the-dingo-did-it-heres-the -proof/story-e6frg6nf-1226393523986?utm.

Ross, G. (2007). Police oversight: Help or hindrance? In M. Mitchell & J. Casey (Eds.), *Police leadership and management.* Sydney: The Federation Press.

Sommers, J. (2014). Integrity: Body worn video "is not a silver bullet." *Police Oracle.* Retrieved from http://www.policeoracle.com/news/Police+IT+and +Technology/2014/Mar/24/Integrity-Body-worn-video-is-not-a-silver-bullet -_80033.html.

Tapp, P. A. (n.d.). *Disquiet, the police killing of Joe Gilewicz: The justifiable homicide of an Australian veteran.* E-book.

Tomlinson, D. (1996). *Interim report of the Select Committee on the Western Australia Police Service.* Perth: Parliament of Western Australia.

United Nations. (1963). *1963 Seminar on the role of the police in the protection of human rights.* New York: Author.

Western Australia Police. (2010). *Post implementation review of Taser Western Australia Police.* Perth: Author.

Wood, J. R. T. (1997). *Royal Commission into the New South Wales Police Service: Final report, Volume II: Reform.* Sydney: New South Wales Government.

Toward a Model System

IV

Police Professional Standards Units and External Oversight Agencies

Can There Be Productive Collaboration?

11

LOUISE PORTER

Contents

Expanding on Porter (2013), this chapter outlines the contributions that external oversight agencies can, and do, bring to police reform, with a focus on proactive activities. This chapter discusses how a problem-oriented approach can help to frame these efforts and promote the value of collaborative partnerships between oversight and police agencies to improve policing services to the community. The challenges of collaborations are discussed, but several case study examples present evidence that productive relationships have led to improvements in policing, at least at the jurisdictional level.

Introduction/Background

Historically, police reform efforts have typically been exclusively externally driven, with criticisms of police organizational culture being unwilling or unable to identify and respond to internal problems. External accountability was seen as necessary for change, as well as necessary for any possibility of public confidence that change was genuine. However, since their establishment, external oversight agencies have traditionally been reactive rather than proactive agents of reform. Indeed, their very creation is often a response to crisis (Prenzler & Ronken, 2001; Smith, 2009). With the evolution of police oversight and accountability frameworks, however, many oversight agencies have broadened their functions to offer advice/consultancy, education and training, and recommendations regarding policy and practice. Further, police are increasingly being handed back the responsibility for their own reform, with police departments striving for a reputation for professionalism, self-regulation, and learning. Indeed, what were once titled "internal affairs" departments, or "internal investigations" units are now more frequently named "professional standards" departments, reflecting a broadening of their role from responding to cases of suspected misconduct to more generally addressing and enhancing the professionalism of the organization. Thus, both oversight and police agencies have moved toward a more proactive reform-oriented position, away from the reactive and possibly reactionary. This presents new opportunities for the police–oversight relationship in terms of collaboration for shared goals.

Compliance versus Collaboration

When examining police reform efforts, or indeed any sort of organizational change attempts, it is clear that many initiatives lack traction; that is, they fail to take hold in an organization, lack support, and are short lived. Porter and Prenzler (2012a) note, from interviews with police and oversight agency personnel, that one important component of reform efforts that encourages traction is ownership over the reform strategy, particularly local ownership within the agency subject to the change. Interviewees pointed out that, typically, changes to policy or practice are recommended to police by external agencies. Police are then expected to engage in the process of implementation despite not having had any input into what changes might be most appropriate or how goals of reform might best be met. Failure to implement recommendations can result in further external pressure to comply. This lack of ownership may inhibit engagement with the reform process. Walker and Archbold

(2014) also recognize the importance of voluntary police reform, citing the case of the Dallas Police Department as an exemplar (pp. 2 and 4). After a series of shooting incidents by police officers, and ensuing community protest, the police chief proactively issued an Eight-Point Plan for New Policies and Strategic Directives. Walker and Archbold (p. 4) note that "The Dallas Eight-Point Plan represents what is arguably the ideal situation [because]... It was an entirely voluntary effort" and suggest that "In the new police accountability, police departments will respond proactively, become self-monitoring, and develop into 'learning organizations.'" However, although this may be the ideal, Walker and Archbold (p. 4) acknowledge that, currently, most police departments lack the "culture of accountability" necessary to fulfill this role, necessitating external input. Clearly, then, one way to promote engagement and traction of reform, while still preserving the integrity of the system through independent scrutiny, is to involve the police agency in the reform process in partnership, or collaboration, with the external oversight agency.

A framework that addresses "problems" in policing and emphasizes the value of partnerships in doing so is Problem-Oriented Policing. The approach of Problem-Oriented Policing and the Scan, Analyse, Respond, Assess (SARA) problem solving model, discussed in the next sections, provide a framework to highlight a number of activities that police agencies and oversight agencies can engage in as a collaborative process. Each drawing on their strengths, they can identify and analyze problems in the police integrity domain and design and implement solutions that impact positively on the police and communities.

Problem-Oriented Policing Framework

Problem-oriented policing was first conceptualized by Herman Goldstein in 1979 (Goldstein, 2003) and has gained the support of both academics and police practitioners as a means for approaching and tackling law enforcement "problems," particularly certain forms of crime. The popularity of the approach lies in its recognition of the range of policing problems that require tailored solutions, its emphasis on collaborative partnerships with stakeholders, and its reliance on empirical methods of analysis and evaluation to identify problems and test the impact of implemented solutions. The former encourages creativity and cooperation, whereas the latter contributes to organizational learning and improving the policing profession:

> The concept carries a commitment to implementing the new strategy, rigorously evaluating its effectiveness, and subsequently reporting the results in ways that will benefit other police agencies and that will contribute to building a body of knowledge that supports good practice and ultimately, thereby, will also contribute toward the further professionalization of the police. (Goldstein, 2003, p. 14)

Some authors have highlighted the potential of a problem-oriented approach to police oversight through acknowledging that analysis of complaints data can highlight key issues or problems (Walker, 2001). Livingston (2004) asserts that, just as police have begun to move beyond enforcement of the law to embrace a problem-oriented approach, so too should oversight agencies expand their role beyond rule enforcement. Livingston recognizes that this requires collaboration between oversight agencies and police.

SARA Model

Livingston (2004) discusses four principles of a problem-oriented approach to citizen review, focusing on complaints handling: "triage" of complaints, complaints "information gathering and analysis," the "involvement of [subject-officers'] line supervision" in the complaints process, and "monitoring the complaint review process." These four principles demonstrate an application of the SARA problem-solving model (Eck & Spelman, 1987). Arguably the best-known method for undertaking problem solving in policing, SARA represents the four stages of scanning (identifying a problem), analyzing (collecting data to inform the scope or cause of the problem), responding (developing and implementing solutions to the problem), and assessing (evaluating the effectiveness of the response). The process can be cyclical, where the results of the evaluation are fed back into understanding the problem and monitoring the need for further intervention. The process does not necessarily involve all stages, though, or follow this order, and the SARA model is only one model of the problem-solving process; other variations have also been presented (e.g., see Ekblom, 2005; Read & Tilley, 2000). However, as a conceptualization of the basic stages of understanding and responding to a problem, and expanding on the idea of problem-oriented oversight, SARA will be presented here as a guiding framework to understand the contributions (both real and potential) of oversight agencies to police problem solving, or police reform, particularly reflecting opportunities for, or examples of, police–oversight agency collaboration.

Problem-Oriented Approach to Police Reform: Agency Contributions to the SARA Process

The SARA problem-solving model is outlined in Figure 11.1, showing the stages of scanning the environment to identify a problem, analyzing information to understand the problem and inform solutions, responding to the problem by designing and implementing solutions, and finally, evaluating the response to gauge its effectiveness. This section outlines how the functions and activities of oversight agencies demonstrate their position to assist

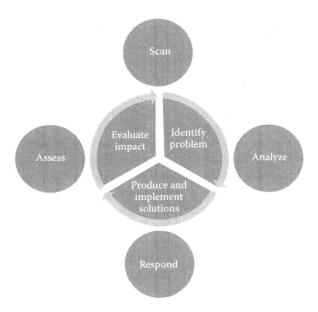

Figure 11.1 Representation of the SARA model (taken from Porter, 2013).

police agencies with reform at each of these stages. This is followed by case study examples that demonstrate the whole SARA process in practice.

Scan

The first stage of the SARA process is to identify a problem. In the present context, the "problem" may be an area of policing practice, or policy, or a pattern of police behavior, for example, that is of concern. Such concerns are frequently highlighted through public complaints regarding experiences with police, with oversight agencies the recipients, or monitors, of these complaints. Although oversight agencies are traditionally tasked with resolving complaints, attention to the underlying issues in individual cases, or more sophisticated analysis of complaint patterns, provides a method for identifying problems that may require reform.

Many authors (including Livingston, 2004, mentioned previously) have highlighted that oversight agencies accumulate information about the policing environment that can be used to build a picture of potential areas of concern. At the lowest, or most basic, level of oversight, agencies may receive appeals from unsatisfied complainants, that is, those who have complained to police but are dissatisfied with the handling or outcome of their complaint, or may audit police systems or practices. For example, in the United Kingdom, the office of the Police Complaints Commissioner for Scotland (PCCS) initiated an audit of the complaints handling process of one police force after a complaint handling review raised concerns (PCCS, 2008). Thus, even individual complaint cases can identify systemic problems that require further action.

At a deeper level, the Corruption and Crime Commission in Western Australia, oversight agency to the Western Australia Police, has conducted in-depth "systems-based evaluations" (Porter & Prenzler, 2012a) to audit police practices in a variety of areas (geographically based and subject/procedures based). This audit process goes beyond dip-sampling cases for purposes of rule enforcement and involves site visits and discussions with personnel to provide a more educative presence.

Agencies with higher powers of oversight may independently receive and investigate complaints or reports of alleged misconduct. Patterns may be identified between a number of cases handled by the agency that suggest systemic issues, or individual matters may be viewed as particularly serious or of significant public interest to warrant further inspection. Although issues may be recognized by staff on a case-by-case basis, the observance of patterns of incidents or existence of systemic problems is increasingly efficient with the keeping of databases that allow statistical examination of cases by a range of features, such as the subject of the complaint, location, the issues involved, and so on. To this end, some oversight agencies are tasked with compiling local or national statistics on complaints. For example, the PCCS, mentioned previously, collects statistical information from Scottish police districts and compiles this into a report on complaint numbers, whereas the Independent Police Complaints Commission (IPCC) for England and Wales collects raw complaints data from the 43 police forces and produces its own statistical trend analysis for public reporting (Porter & Prenzler, 2012b).

In rarer cases, oversight agencies are the sole keepers of complaints databases. In Northern Ireland, for example, the Police Ombudsman receives all complaints against the Police Service of Northern Ireland and produces large amounts of statistical outputs, both publicly on its website and, importantly, in reports to Police Service of Northern Ireland units. Provision of this descriptive data to the police agency allows police managers to interpret the problem areas, or indeed people, under their supervision (Porter & Prenzler, 2012b). Thus, the oversight agency provides the role of scanning and compiling the information but relies upon the police agency to engage with the process and respond to the data.

In Australia, the States of New South Wales and Queensland have systems that allow both the police and oversight agencies real-time access to one centralized complaints database and can therefore utilize this information for "intelligence-gathering" purposes (periodic scans or focused on particular areas of concern; Porter & Prenzler, 2012a). In Canada, the Commission for Public Complaints Against the Royal Canadian Mounted Police (CPC) operates an early invention system on behalf of the police agency—the Multiple Complaint Member Project—whereby it identifies:

> RCMP members who are subject to three or more public complaints, where the allegations are serious in nature (e.g., improper use of force, improper use of firearms) within a 12-month period. Once a member is identified under the current criteria, the CPC shares this information with the RCMP, which is then able to communicate the information to the relevant division and/or detachment. (CPC, 2011, p. 12)

Some oversight agencies also conduct wider environmental scans of issues to proactively seek out emerging trends in policing and to inform possible areas of focus for their own jurisdictions. These can be produced as public literature reviews or agency briefing reports. For example, the Police Integrity Commission (PIC) in Australia published a review of early Intervention Systems (Bertoia, 2008), and the CPC in Canada produced a review of literature on in-custody deaths (CPC, 2009).

The information accessible to oversight agencies can therefore be extensive and an important source for recognizing trends or systemic issues or other matters of significance that may warrant further scrutiny. Thus, oversight agencies are often in a prime position to assist police agencies with proactive problem identification.

Analyze

The previous section included the scrutiny of data for identifying problems at the descriptive level and intelligence gathering. Many oversight agencies are also involved in conducting more sophisticated, targeted forms of analysis, or research, around particular identified problems. This includes analysis of data held on agency databases (described in the previous section), as well as conducting additional forms of data gathering and analysis through specific research initiatives.

There are numerous examples of oversight agencies undertaking targeted data analysis of specific problem areas. For example, in Australia, the Office of Police Integrity (OPI, 2009) in the State of Victoria (former oversight agency to the Victoria Police) conducted a Review of the Use of Force by and Against Victoria Police, incorporating analysis of data from Victoria police's use of force reporting system. The review highlighted necessary improvements in policy, training, monitoring, and reporting practices and urged Victoria police to utilize those data more strategically and "demonstrate a commitment to strategically managing the risk associated with inappropriate use of force" (OPI, 2009, p. 58).

In the United Kingdom, the IPCC for England and Wales undertook analysis of all cases in their jurisdiction of deaths in or following police custody over an 11-year period from 1998/1999 to 2008/2009 and reported on trends in the data that highlighted failings of police duty of care, particularly in the assessment and monitoring of persons in custody. This led to specific recommendations for both police and health care services to improve practices. Similarly, the IPCC has collated and conducted analysis of over 100 investigation reports of road traffic incidents involving the police that have resulted in a fatality or serious injury (Docking, Bucke, Grace, & Dady, 2007). Recommendations of that report have resulted in revised police pursuit guidelines.

Oversight agencies are increasingly engaging in primary research, that is, collecting new data for analysis. In Australia, some states have oversight agencies that are heavily involved in research, with dedicated research teams or units. In New South Wales, for example, the PIC has conducted and published reports on a range of research projects. Recent landmark projects explored and identified potential misconduct risks of individuals (Project Odin; PIC, 2009) and work places (Project Manta; Gorta, 2011) to highlight a framework for proactive prevention efforts. In Queensland, the Crime and Misconduct Commission (CMC; and its predecessor, the Criminal Justice Commission) collected survey data on the Queensland Police Service (QPS) recruits and First Year Constables yearly since 1995 to monitor ethical attitudes toward a range of scenarios. A 2010 CMC report on these data noted decreased ratings of seriousness of and willingness to report certain unethical behaviors in recent years as a potential area of concern for the QPS (CMC, 2010).

In the United Kingdom, the IPCC conducted a project to take stock of their early years of operation around complaints handling. The work incorporated stakeholder discussions and the collection of survey data, which identified dissatisfaction with the complaints handling system as well as underaccess of the system by certain groups. The outcome of the work was a new Statutory Guidance for police complaint handling that the IPCC launched in 2010 (IPCC, 2010). The IPCC noted (see Porter & Prenzler, 2012b) that part of the success of the implementation of the Statutory Guidance was the high level of stakeholder input in its inception, with a number of police agencies/personnel engaging in discussions with the IPCC.

Indeed, in some cases, research and analysis are conducted through collaboration between police agencies and their oversight bodies. This could involve the police agency approaching the oversight agency to utilize their research resources, an oversight agency involving the police in the conduct of a project, or a fully collaborative research endeavor. Police agencies also commonly have research units, often staffed by unsworn (civilian) personnel. Thus, there is capacity for the research areas of both oversight agencies and police to collaborate on joint endeavors. In-depth analysis of identified problems enables the specific nature of problems to be explored and for possible causes to be highlighted. This allows for a more informed response.

Respond

Police oversight agencies were traditionally established to respond to problems of police misconduct, but typically did so on an individual case-by-case basis and in response to a particular complaint of wrongdoing. Responses in these circumstances have included investigations, reviews, targeted audits, and even adopting sophisticated covert methods such as targeted integrity testing. However, beyond a reactive ad hoc response, there are a number of more positive, proactive strategies that oversight agencies are beginning to adopt to address problems uncovered by the means outlined in the sections above.

Oversight agencies frequently have the capability of making recommendations to improve police practices at the broader level, based upon their work in assessing and analyzing problems. Recommendations in these cases are typically directed toward improvements and can concern systems, policies, procedures, training, or any other area of policing. For example, the previously highlighted work of the IPCC in relation to traffic incidents recommended changes to U.K. police pursuit policies, whereas the work of the OPI made recommendations to Victoria police regarding their use of force.

However, although oversight agencies have the power to make recommendations, they rarely have the power to require police to accept and implement them. Police can be held to account publicly to explain their position, but ultimately, the way the police agency operates is up to the head of that agency. Thus, although public shaming can be an effective "stick" to move an agency to change, collaborative efforts in the area of recommendations and implementation are increasingly adopted. Many oversight bodies now involve their police agencies in discussions of the findings of their research activity and the development of recommendations (Porter & Prenzler, 2012a). Indeed, such collaboration can result in recommendations having been discussed, actioned, and implemented before the oversight agency's official report is released. Oversight agencies are often held to account for the number of recommendations they make that are implemented, as an indicator of their performance in terms of providing impact. Although it is recognized that oversight bodies should not be making "easy" recommendations to increase their performance profile, there is perhaps room for flexibility in the measurement of implementation to focus more on the intent of the recommendation rather than the specific practical operation of that intent. It is widely recognized that resources and operational issues known best to police can create barriers to oversight agency-recommended practice. Thus, often, it is necessary for police agencies to propose their own ways of meeting the intent of a recommendation to ensure its feasibility. As discussed earlier, involvement of police at this level can also increase police agency engagement and ownership over solutions.

To further support police agencies implementing their own reforms, many oversight bodies are developing a role in providing education and advice. For example, in the United Kingdom, both the IPCC and the PCCS produce publications of the lessons to be learned from particular cases that they see, to promote the consequences of certain wrongdoing and provide information on best practice to avoid future similar cases. Other agencies are also involved in officer training and providing toolkits for officers to use to aid decision making. For example, in Australia, the OPI had a Corruption Prevention and Education Unit that provided a range of educational and advisory services to the Victoria Police, including training sessions, consultancy, and educational resources. OPI (2012) published an Ethical Health Assessment Tool, a self-assessment tool for law enforcement agencies to measure the strength of integrity systems. The CMC in Queensland also provided guidance and toolkits to Queensland police officers (and other public sector agencies). For example, the CMC produced a number of publications on managing conflicts of interest. These activities help to equip police with the knowledge to tailor their own responses to problems. However, it is important that responses are targeted, informed, and followed up with appropriate evaluation to assess their impact.

Assess

The final stage of the SARA model is the assessment, or evaluation, of any response implemented. Many oversight agencies perform a compliance-oriented function of monitoring, or auditing, whether recommendations have been accepted and implemented adequately by the police. The OPI in Australia, for example, maintained a database of the systemic recommendations it made and the progress of the Victoria Police on accepting and implementing these (Porter & Prenzler, 2012a). The CPC in Canada publishes details on its website of recommendations that remain to be implemented by the Royal Canadian Mounted Police (RCMP) (CPC, 2010). Indeed, as mentioned previously, numbers of recommendations made and accepted are reported publicly by many oversight agencies as part of their own performance framework.

However, although this process of monitoring implementation is important, it does not provide evaluation of whether the response has actually met the intended outcomes or had the desired effect. Effectiveness needs to be measured for a number of reasons, including informing on whether the problem has been "solved" or if an alternative intervention is necessary; informing the allocation of resources; understanding how similar problems in the agency might be tackled; or demonstrating how other agencies could implement similar responses. Despite many oversight bodies publishing extensively on the results of their work, particularly reports on individual investigations or complaint reviews, public reports of formal evaluations are much less prevalent.

In the United Kingdom, the IPCC's work on deaths in custody (IPCC, 2011) reported a marked decrease in deaths over the 11-year period of study, as well as decreases by particular causes of death, and drew inferences on a number of possible influences on this decline. The report highlighted changes in laws and guidelines, improvements in cell design, hospitalization of arrestees, assessments and closer monitoring of detainees, provision of health services to detainees, and a custody visitor scheme. However, this work did not directly assess the impact of the introduction of these interventions specifically. Rather, it provided a retrospective analysis of cases.

To fulfill the evaluation component of the process, the impact of the response must be assessed on the basis of what was intended. In other words, there needs to be clarity at the outset regarding the purpose of the response, what the indicators of success should be, and how those can be measured. Indeed, sometimes, monitoring and evaluation require the collection of specific data and so it may be wise to plan for this at the point of designing the response. For example, perhaps, the gathering of appropriate data or establishing the mechanisms to do so should be included in the initial recommended response plan.

Case Study Examples of Problem-Oriented Police Reform

The previous section presented ways that oversight agency activities can contribute to each of the stages of the SARA model. This section presents more in-depth case studies that illustrate the full SARA process utilized in oversight–police partnership projects, including the evaluation of impact.

Case Study: Portland, United States

The full SARA process can be illustrated with the example of the Portland Force Task Force, a joint initiative between the Portland Police Bureau (PPB) and Portland's Independent Police Review Division. These two organizations (Portland Police and its oversight agency) established the Task Force in 2006, with members from both the PPB and Independent Police Review, as well as from Portland's Citizen Review Committee. The goal of the Task Force was to review the PPB use of force activity, policies, and training, with comparisons to similar jurisdictions, and to highlight potential areas of improvement.

The PPB instigated a new use of force reporting system for its officers in 2004, reporting to be one of only a few similarly sized police departments in the United States to publicly report on this activity (Force Task Force, 2007, p. 4). This enabled the Force Task Force to analyze the use of force data held by the PPB, among other sources of information. They reported their findings publicly (Force Task Force, 2007), making 16 recommendations across the areas of data collection and analysis, policy and training, supervision and management, and intra-Bureau patterns of force. The recommendations were designed to improve the Bureau's management of force and reduce the number of community complaints involving force. The majority of recommendations were specifically directed toward the Police Bureau, and the chief of police agreed to their implementation and invited a follow-up assessment. The 2008 follow-up by the reconvened Task Force assessed the implementation of the recommendations and agreed that at least the intent of all 16 had been met. The Task Force further analyzed the use of force report data of the Police Bureau to evaluate the impact of the changes. The Task Force reported decreases in uses of force and citizen complaints of excessive force, as well as decreases in both officer and citizen injuries (Force Task Force, 2009).

This case illustrates the value of collaboration between the police and external agencies using an approach similar to the SARA model. The Task Force scanned the environment (similar police departments) and analyzed data to highlight specific problems of citizen complaints and agency management of force. The collaborative Task Force provided a number of recommendations, with the actual implementation left to the agencies concerned (those subject to the recommendation). The changes were assessed and evaluated collaboratively by the Task Force to follow not only that the response was adequate but also what impact that response was having on the problems identified at the analysis stage. Thus, the response was evaluated against the intended effects. The reports provided by the Task Force were made public. They highlight that the process was challenging but comment on the "maturity" of the Portland Police to be internally critical and to accept both criticism and reform, showing a commitment to improving its services to the public (Force Task Force, 2009, pp. iii–v).

Case Study: Queensland, Australia

In Australia, the QPS and their oversight body of the time, the CMC, jointly undertook a review of the QPS Taser policy, procedures, training, and monitoring. The joint review was initiated by the Minister for Police, Corrective Services, and Emergency Services in the wake of a Taser-related death in Queensland during statewide rollout of Tasers to QPS officers. The rollout of Tasers was put on hold while the joint review team conducted their work. The review team consisted of officers from both the CMC and QPS who had experience and background in relevant issues such as use of force, operational skills and tactics, and risk management.

The team undertook a review of the available literature on Conducted Energy Weapons, particularly research from the United States and Canada, as well as an audit of QPS Taser data, data collected by the Taser device that record when it is activated, how many times it is deployed, and for what length of time. The literature review and audit highlighted issues and risks associated with Taser use by the QPS. The review team then conducted an assessment of the QPS Taser policy, procedures, and training in light of those findings. The review was published in 2009 (QPS-CMC, 2009) and made 27 recommendations. The report also stated "the paramount importance of ongoing collaboration between the CMC and QPS in monitoring both the implementation of the report's recommendations and emerging research on the effective and safe use of CEWs" (QPS-CMC, 2009, p. 1). The review (QPS-CMC, 2009) was followed by an evaluation by the CMC, published in 2011 (CMC, 2011). The evaluation by the CMC reported that the QPS had

> ...demonstrated a firm commitment to implementing the 27 recommendations from the 2009 QPS-CMC review, investing considerable time and resources to do so. To date, 24 recommendations have been implemented, including all recommendations related to Taser policy and training. Progress continues on the three recommendations related to Taser monitoring and continuous improvement processes that are outstanding. (CMC, 2011, p. xvii)

The CMC reported positive effects of the changes, including decreased Taser uses. This included a decrease in presentations and deployments, as well as "drive stun" uses (where the Taser is held against the body rather than the probes being deployed). The CMC also noted decreases in Taser use in certain circumstances, particularly against handcuffed people, and a decrease in multiple and prolonged uses. The CMC (2011) concluded that there was "no evidence of widespread misuse" and "no indication of mission creep in terms of officers using Tasers in less serious situations" (p. xvii). However, some concerns were raised and suggestions were made for continuous improvement in the area of Taser use, particularly regarding Taser use against members of vulnerable groups and ensuring that QPS standards are consistent with suggested best practice internationally. An additional 21 recommendations were presented in the evaluation report that require further monitoring and evaluation. The CMC continued to review Taser usage reports made between mid-2010 and mid-2012 (CMC, 2012), as well as conducted a more in-depth analysis of incidents of multiple and prolonged Taser use (CMC, 2013).

The Queensland case study illustrates a slightly different implementation of the SARA model from the Portland case study in that the final stage of assessing the implementation and impact of the recommendations was independently undertaken by the oversight body rather than in collaboration with the police agency. The independence of the evaluation by the oversight agency, rather than jointly with the QPS, may add weight to its report in terms of reassuring public confidence in the system. The case study also illustrates the circularity of the SARA model, where the assessment stage can highlight further, or outstanding, concerns that may need additional monitoring or response and further subsequent review and evaluation.

Case Study: U.S. Department of Justice Office of Community-Oriented Policing Services

In the United States, the Department of Justice (DOJ) has many functions targeted toward police reform. Particularly, the Collaborative Reform Initiative for Technical Assistance (CRI-TA), established in 2011, is focused on supporting partnerships to achieve change. The Initiative sits within the DOJ's Office of Community-Oriented Policing Services (COPS Office), an office that promotes police–community partnerships and problem solving, in the spirit of community policing. The COPS Office provides funding to the CRI-TA to support third-party providers to work with police agencies to address a range of criminal justice issues through analysis of policies and practices aimed at organizational transformation (COPS, 2014). The CRI-TA process therefore involves a partnership among the DOJ, an external independent third party (e.g., a consultancy firm), and a police department and follows a method similar to the SARA problem-solving process: identifying an issue, analyzing data to further understand the issue, recommending and implementing a response, and monitoring outcomes. This is in contrast to a formal investigation of a police department by the DOJ Civil Rights Division: an external, imposed investigation, rather than collaboration, ending with mandatory reforms, rather than recommendations.

A number of collaborative reform initiatives have been completed, and recently commenced, particularly on police use of force. These include the Las Vegas Metropolitan Police Department (LVMPD; Stewart, Fachner, Rodriguez King, & Rickman, 2012) and the Spokane Police Department, Washington (Rodriguez King, Saloom, & McClelland, 2014), with new reviews announced in October 2014 for the Baltimore Police Department, Maryland, and Fayetteville Police Department, North Carolina. As the most advanced of these collaborations, the Las Vegas case will be detailed further to illustrate the process.

In 2011, after the results of a media investigation into Las Vegas police shootings was published, and the American Civil Liberties Union of Nevada called for action, the COPS Office approached the LVMPD offering assistance to reduce officer-involved shootings (OISs) through a CRI-TA grant. Over the next 2 years, the COPS Office, LVMPD, and a private consultancy firm, CNA, collaborated to reform the LVMPD in the area of officer use of force. The specific goals were to "Reduce the number of shootings; Reduce the number of persons killed as a result of OISs; Transform LVMPD's organization and culture as it relates to deadly force; Enhance officer safety" (Stewart et al., 2012, p. 7).

The process commenced with a 6-month review of LVMPD's use of deadly force policy and procedures, training and tactics, investigation and documentation, and external review. This included scanning national standards and practices in similar jurisdictions, as well as conducting primary research involving almost 100 interviews with LVMPD officers and community stakeholders, observations of police practices, reviewing documentation, and analyzing police incident data. From this, a total of 75 recommendations (symbolizing 80 reforms) were made across the areas of focus, and an implementation plan, with steps for implementing each recommendation, was included. This was followed by a period of implementation with a review at 6 months and final review at 12 months.

The 6-month review by CNA (Fachner & Carter, 2013) showed that 56 of the reforms had been implemented and a further 15 were in progress, representing 89%. The report also notes a decline in OISs since 2010, stating a number of reforms and events as contributory factors (including the collaborative reform process itself, although the decline since the commencement of the reform process is not as dramatic as the decline since 2010; see Fachner & Carter, 2013, p. 12). The final (12-month) report on the reform progress (Fachner & Carter, 2014) confirms that "the number of OISs by LVMPD continues to be historically low" (p. 6), with 72 of the 80 reforms (90%) now completed, and progress made on a further 5.

The case study illustrates the support of the DOJ in collaborating with police agencies to reach mutually agreed reforms, despite having the power to impose investigation and reform. The Las Vegas case study shows how the DOJ supports an external, independent consultancy firm to undertake much of the process, with full cooperation of the police department and support from the COPS Office. It also demonstrates the process of setting an initial goal (e.g., to reduce OISs) and subsequently measuring success against achieving this goal, as well as the successful uptake of recommended organizational changes. Whereas in the Las Vegas case, the DOJ approached the police department, subsequent cases, such as Spokane, are noted to have involved requests by the police department for DOJ assistance (Rodriguez King et al., 2014).

Challenges of Collaborative Reform

Thus far, this chapter has outlined a model for collaboration between police agencies and oversight agencies, with examples that have led to successful policing reform. However, such a process may not be without its challenges. True collaboration requires a close working relationship, cooperation and shared goals, and, importantly, trust. On the one hand, this may be difficult to achieve between agencies whose primary relationship is based on the idea that trust cannot be placed in police to voluntarily reform; on the other hand, successfully achieving this relationship may erode the independence and accountability (or at least perception of such) that oversight agencies have been established to instill.

Regarding the former, Porter and Prenzler (2012a, p. 220), from their study of police integrity frameworks in Australia, note the possible tension between the traditional functions of oversight agencies as monitors and investigators of police behavior and the more recent functions of providing educational and advisory support services, stating that

> the difference between the coercive, intrusive investigatory role and the col-laborative advisory role was described by one agency as the difference of "using sticks or carrots." Whilst both functions are necessary, these different dynam-ics could create tensions that negatively impact both areas, or each function could complement and inform the other. (Porter & Prenzler, 2012a, p. 220)

The tensions referred to relate to the perception of the oversight agency by the police department and the effect of this on the relationship and degree of cooperation between the two agencies. For example, hostility of police to external oversight has been well documented, including lack of cooperation with external investigations (e.g., Chan, 1999). If such hostility is generalized to all functions of the oversight agency, then this will negatively impact on the degree to which police will take up the supportive services offered by the same agency.

Regarding the latter issue of erosion of independence (or perceived ero-sion), Grabosky and Braithwaite (1986) and Prenzler (2000) discuss agency "capture" as a risk of close working relationships between staff of agencies that should be independent. Indeed, although Livingston (2004) recognizes the importance of collaboration between oversight agencies and police, she argues that it can raise questions as to the independence of the oversight agency:

> [If] participants in the citizen review process work more closely with police to see that the information contained in complaints is effectively used to bet-ter the police organization and enhance police services.... Can the citizens in citizen review processes maintain their independence (and be perceived as independent) in light of this closer collaboration? (p. 669)

However, Livingston (2004) argues that the role of civilian oversight should be broadened now beyond the "first generation" of merely providing independent scrutiny, to a second-generation role of ensuring that the wider problems raised in complaints are adequately addressed by police organizations.

The DOJ Collaborative Reform Initiative, illustrated by the LVMPD case study, enables the involvement of private consultancy firms and other third parties, which may help both to instill trust (through the neutral agenda of the third party) and guard against perceptions of capture of the oversight agency, by providing independence. However, the report of the Collaborative Reform Model in Las Vegas received criticism from the American Civil Liberties Union (2012) for both COPS and the consultancy firm being biased toward police:

> COPS and CNA are embedded within the policing community. COPS provides grants and information to assist police departments in best practices; it is not designed to address complaints of pattern and practices of discrimination. Neither COPS nor CNA has a primary role of "working on behalf of the people at risk of harm." Target constituents are the police, not the citizens. As a result, the 2012 Report suffers from a lack of objectivity and demonstrates a number of fundamental failures. (p. 3)

In Australia, a different approach in the state of Queensland has seen a recent restructuring of internal police review and reform functions with the creation of a new Public Safety Business Agency (PSBA) in 2014 that provides strategic and corporate services for all the emergency services. Thus, many services, such as policy development, reviews, education, and employee drug and alcohol testing, are now independent from the QPS, although staffing includes those formerly working for QPS as well as incorporating the QPS area of education and training (the police training academies; PSBA, 2014). It is too early to assess the effects of this restructure, but the movement of these functions to a new agency could potentially improve reform relationships between the QPS and its oversight agency (now the Crime and Corruption Commission) through its focused remit on improvements and service delivery and its position as a third party. However, currently, the PSBA function seems limited to policy and business services rather than operational policing procedures, although the PSBA (2014) annual report announced that "A significant external review of QPS education and training is being undertaken by the PSBA which will deliver a Master Plan for QPS education and training into the future" (p. 39).

Discussion

The value of a problem-oriented approach to police reform has been described in this chapter through a variety of examples and case studies, with particular use of the SARA problem-solving model. It is clear that oversight agencies are already engaging in a number of activities that could (and do) contribute to problem identification and analysis and designing, implementing, and evaluating responses to improve police practices. There is also evidence that oversight agencies and police departments can work collaboratively in this process, although this is not without its challenges.

For collaborations to be successful, both parties must share the same end goal and cooperate in an open and honest way. Ideally, the partnership would be voluntary rather than imposed. However, Walker and Archbold (2014) cite positive experiences of police chiefs who have undergone a mandatory reform process, for example, as a result of consent decrees in the United States. Indeed, both the Queensland and Las Vegas case studies discussed in the previous sections involved some degree of external pressure or direction to commence the process. As commended in the Portland case study, the important factor is that police agencies enter into the partnership with maturity and the ability to be self-critical and accepting of external criticism. Even if the instigation of the partnership is not purely voluntary, if both agencies are willing to fully engage in the SARA process, therefore allowing collaboration in identifying and designing responses, then commitment to implementing and evaluating reforms should hopefully follow.

Such partnerships, however, need to be adequately resourced, and the DOJ CRI-TA is a leap forward in this regard. The provision of funding (by application) to support collaborative reforms is clearly encouraging police departments in the United States to come forward with requests for assistance. It is important, however, that these partnership projects can demonstrate independence and rigor in their methods, as well as utilize the follow-up review exercise to measure not just whether recommended reforms have been implemented but also the effects of these on a range of outcomes.

Indeed, to fully embrace the Problem Oriented Policing philosophy, responses would need to be innovative; implementation and evaluation would be rigorous, scientific, and experimental (or quasi-experimental; see Tilley, 2010); and efforts would engage a variety of stakeholders. While there is clearly activity emerging in each of these areas, including collaborative efforts, there is a great deal of scope for increasing these activities, particularly in relation to conducting and publicizing evaluations.

Finally, it is important to note that SARA is not offered as a prescriptive model for all oversight work but as a framework for describing a complementary suite of activity that can contribute to reform. While cases of misconduct continue to arise, and citizens continue to make complaints against the police, there is still a place for reactive oversight. Both deterrence and reform are important functions for external oversight agencies in their endeavor to increase public confidence, reduce police misconduct, and improve or enhance police services.

Conclusion

Oversight agencies have much to offer the police reform process, if resourced appropriately. Although issues of mutual trust and independence may present challenges, the case studies presented here show that appropriate partnerships between police and oversight agencies are possible. Further, these partnerships can add value to police reform by enabling problem-oriented work that increases the likelihood of police organizational change and positively impacts on police service members and communities.

References

ACLU. (2012). Collaborative reform process or abdication of responsibility? An American Civil Liberties Union of Nevada Position Statement on the U.S. Department of Justice's Community Oriented Policing Services, *A review of officer-involved shootings in the Las Vegas Metropolitan Police Department* (2012 Report by the CNA consulting company). Retrieved January 15, 2015, from http://aclunv.org/files/ACLUNVStatement-COPSReport.pdf.

Bertoia, T. (2008). *Developing an early intervention system for police misconduct in a law enforcement agency.* Research and Issues Papers, 1. Sydney: Police Integrity Commission.

Chan, J. B. L. (1999). Governing police practice: Limits of the new accountability. *British Journal of Sociology, 50*(2), 251–270.

CMC. (2010). *The ethical perceptions and attitudes of Queensland Police Service recruits and first year constables 1995–2008.* Brisbane: Crime and Misconduct Commission.

CMC. (2011). *Evaluating Taser reforms: A review of Queensland Police Service policy and practice.* Brisbane: Crime and Misconduct Commission.

CMC. (2012). *An update on Taser use in Queensland.* Research and Issues Paper Number 9. Brisbane: Crime and Misconduct Commission.

CMC. (2013). *Multiple and prolonged Taser deployments.* Brisbane: Crime and Misconduct Commission.

COPS. (2014). CRI-TA Frequently Asked Questions. Retrieved January 15, 2015, from http://cops.usdoj.gov/pdf/2014AwardDocs/crita/CRI-TA_2014_FAQs2.pdf.

CPC. (2009). *2008–2009 Departmental performance report.* Surrey, BC: Commission for Public Complaints Against the RCMP.

CPC. (2010). *2009–2010 Departmental performance report.* Surrey, BC: Commission for Public Complaints Against the RCMP.

CPC. (2011). *2010–2011 Departmental performance report.* Surrey, BC: Commission for Public Complaints Against the RCMP.

Docking, M., Bucke, T., Grace, K., & Dady, H. (2007). *Police road traffic incidents: A study of cases involving serious and fatal injuries.* IPCC Research and Statistics Series: Paper 7. London: Independent Police Complaints Commission.

Eck, J. E., & Spelman, W. (1987). *Problem-solving: Problem-oriented policing in Newport news.* Washington, DC: National Institute of Justice. Retrieved from https://www.ncjrs.gov/pdffiles1/Digitization/111964NCJRS.pdf.

Ekblom, P. (2005). The 5Is framework: Sharing good practice in crime prevention. In E. Marks, A. Meyer & R. Linssen (Eds.), *Quality in crime prevention*. Hanover: Landespräventionsrat Niedersachsen.

Fachner, G., & Carter, S. (2013). *Collaborative reform model: Six-month assessment report of the Las Vegas Metropolitan Police Department*. Arlington, VA: CNA Corporation.

Fachner, G., & Carter, S. (2014). *Collaborative reform model: Final assessment report of the Las Vegas Metropolitan Police Department*. Arlington, VA: CNA Corporation.

Force Task Force. (2007). *Use of force by the Portland Police Bureau: Analysis and recommendations*. Portland: Force Task Force to Chief of Police Rosie Sizer.

Force Task Force. (2009). *Use of force by the Portland Police Bureau follow up: Progress report and analysis of recent data*. Portland: Force Task Force to Chief of Police Rosie Sizer.

Goldstein, H. (2003). On further developing problem-oriented policing: The most critical need, the major impediments, and a proposal. *Crime Prevention Studies, 15*, 13–47.

Gorta, A. (2011). *Project Manta Report 2: Managing command misconduct risks*. Sydney: Police Integrity Commission.

Grabosky, P., & Braithwaite, J. (1986). *Of manners gentle: Enforcement strategies of Australian business regulation agencies*. Melbourne: Oxford University Press.

IPCC. (2010). *Statutory guidance to the police service and police authorities on the handling of complaints*. London: The Stationery Office.

IPCC. (2011). *Deaths in or following police custody: An examination of the cases 1998/99–2008/09*. London: Independent Police Complaints Commission.

Livingston, D. (2004). The unfulfilled promise of citizen review. *Ohio State Journal of Criminal Law, 1*(2), 653–669.

OPI. (2009). *Review of the use of force by and against Victoria police*. Melbourne: Office of Police Integrity.

OPI. (2012). *Ethical health assessment tool: A tool for assessing ethical health frameworks in police services*. Melbourne: Office of Police Integrity.

PCCS. (2008). *Review of miscellaneous files by Lothian and Borders police*. Glasgow: Police Complaints Commissioner for Scotland.

PIC. (2009). *Project Odin: Identifying and managing high risk officers in the NSW police force*. Sydney: Police Integrity Commission.

Porter, L., & Prenzler, T. (2012a). *Police integrity management in Australia: Global lessons for combating police misconduct*. Boca Raton, FL: CRC Press, Taylor & Francis.

Porter, L. E., & Prenzler, T. (2012b). Police oversight in the United Kingdom: The balance of independence and collaboration. *International Journal of Law, Crime and Justice, 40*(3), 152–171.

Porter, L. E. (2013). Beyond 'oversight': A problem-oriented approach to police reform. *Police Practice and Research. An International Journal*. Special Issue: Police Oversight, *14*(2), 169–181.

Prenzler, T. (2000). Civilian oversight of police: A test of capture theory. *British Journal of Criminology, 40*(4), 659–674.

Prenzler, T., & Ronken, C. (2001). Models of police oversight: A critique. *Policing and Society, 11*(2), 151–180.

PSBA. (2014). *Annual report 2013–14*. Brisbane: Public Safety Business Agency.

QPS-CMC. (2009). *Review of Taser policy, training, and monitoring and review practices*. Brisbane, Australia: Queensland Police Service and Crime and Misconduct Commission. Retrieved from http://www.cmc.qld.gov.au/data/portal /00000005/content/16225001252029372054.pdf.

Read, T., & Tilley, N. (2000). *Not rocket science: Problem-solving and crime reduction*. Crime Reduction Research Series 6. London: Home Office.

Rodriguez King, D., Saloom, C., & McClelland, B. (2014). *Collaborative reform model: A review of use of force policies, processes, and practices in the Spokane Police Department*. Arlington, VA: CNA Corporation.

Smith, G. (2009). Citizen oversight of independent police services: Bifurcated accountability, regulation creep, and lesson learning. *Regulation & Governance, 3*(4), 421–441.

Stewart, J. K., Fachner, G., Rodriguez King, D. & Rickman, S. (2012). Collaborative Reform Process: A Review of Officer-Involved Shootings in the Las Vegas Metropolitan Police Department. Arlington, VA: CNA Corporation.

Tilley, N. (2010). Whither problem-oriented policing. *Criminology & Public Policy, 9*(1), 183–195.

Walker, S. (2001). *Police accountability: The role of citizen oversight*. Belmont, CA: Wadsworth.

Walker, S., & Archbold, C. A. (2014). *The new world of police accountability* (2nd ed.). Los Angeles: Sage.

Managing Police Conduct

Finding the Ideal Division of Labor between Internal and External Processes

12

TIM PRENZLER

Contents

This final chapter brings together the various themes of the book by setting out the lessons for police complaints and discipline systems from available evidence. The focus is on the design of a model system for dealing with complaints, and also for optimizing police conduct and accountability through enhanced responses to complaints. Three main themes are developed: (1) the importance of independence in investigations and adjudication, (2) the value of alternative dispute resolution, especially an independently managed mediation program, and (3) the importance of the whole system working in support of optimal ethical conduct by police, including the incorporation of a complainant profiling and early intervention system. Despite the emphasis on independent investigations and independent mediation, the model system proposed here leaves large scope for police responsibility for integrity management, including through a scientific approach to recruitment, training, supervision, remediation, and proactive investigations.

Independence

Chapter 1 examined how police complaints and discipline systems, including civilian oversight systems, developed over time in response to corruption scandals, judicial inquiries, and government reviews. The results showed how inquiries and reviews typically identified deficiencies in internal complaints investigations and discipline as key contributing factors to endemic misconduct and lack of public confidence in police. This malaise included inadequate responses to police whistleblowers. These inquiry and review findings then frequently led to in-principle support for independent processes. However, final recommendations tended to pull punches, reverting to a preference for primary police control of complaint responses. The rationale included the need for police to maintain responsibility for integrity and the supposed lack of investigative competency outside policing. In many cases, a reform package that continued to rely on police management of complaints contributed to further misconduct problems. More broadly, continuing reliance on in-house processes meant that persons making complaints (including police themselves) were denied an impartial hearing grounded in an institutional separation of the accused person from the investigating authority. Consequently, an intrinsic "no-win" situation was perpetuated through a straight out denial of natural justice. The view was summed up in an Australian Law Reform Commission (1995) report (pp. 149–150):

> To ask the police to investigate complaints against their own places them in a "hopeless conflict of interest position." Police investigators, whether consciously or otherwise, will tend to be sceptical of complainants and will be "softer" on the police concerned.

Chapter 2 showed how the idea of independence can be mapped across a spectrum: specifically the categories of (1) "insiders" (mainly former police from the same force under scrutiny), (2) "insider outsiders" (former officers from another force), (3) "outsider insiders" (former investigators from allied regulatory agencies), and (4) "outsiders" ("homegrown" investigators from outside groups 1–3, trained in-house). There is likely to be a strong correlation between increased proportions of investigators in the direction of group 4 and increased evidence of impartiality and objectivity in the complaint investigation and resolution process. However, as evidenced by practitioner interviews in the chapter, while outsiders might be considered ideal, there are significant benefits to be had from the inclusion of carefully selected investigators from groups 2 and 3 in terms of knowledge, skills, and commitment.

Chapter 3 reviewed public opinion surveys about preferred police complaints and discipline systems. Public opinion appears to strongly support the independent processing of complaints. Some surveys show extremely high levels of support, above 90%. General support for the principle of independence is, however, tempered by the results for specific questions about how different types of complaints should be handled. Surveys with breakdown questions show support for independence that is centered on serious matters, with varying degrees of support for police management of lower-level complaints. Many of these surveys do not directly canvas the reasons for these views. Available data suggest that distrust or negative attitudes toward police have some influence in turning people away from in-house processes to support external agencies. At the same time, the main reason appears to relate more to the general principle that investigations and adjudication not only need to appear to be independent but should also be genuinely independent through a clear functional separation between the investigator and the subject officer. In Northern Ireland, with the world's most independent oversight agency, public opinion rates have shown extremely high levels of confidence—85% on average across the sectarian divide—in the independence of the Ombudsman from the police, its fairness and impartiality, and contribution to the quality of police work (Police Ombudsman for Northern Ireland [PONI], 2010).

Chapter 4 examined surveys of complainants who had been through a complaints and discipline system. The results showed that the large majority of complainants—typically 70%—were dissatisfied with outcomes and processes in police-dominated systems. Mixed systems produced similarly high levels of dissatisfaction, with the exception of one Philippines study. In some cases, dissatisfaction overall related to dissatisfaction with outcomes; that is, complainants with unsubstantiated complaints tended to be more dissatisfied overall. There was also widespread dissatisfaction with process aspects—such as timeliness, communication, and the commitment and interest of the investigating officer—which could apply regardless of which agency carried out the investigation. At the same time, distrust of police investigating police was a common theme. Complainants frequently referred to officers appearing to take the side of their colleague under investigation. The following is an example of a common response, in this instance taken from a Calgary Police Commission (1999) review of a police dominated complaints procedure (p. 92):

- 68% of complainants reported that the process was biased and cited the perception that investigating officers were biased in favor of fellow officers and that the process was meant to "protect the police."
- Approximately 80% of complainants declared themselves dissatisfied with the outcome of their complaint. Between 33% and 45% of complainants reported that nothing had worked well in the process.

Similarly, in the United Kingdom, a study of complainants' experiences found that "nearly two-thirds of the sample were dissatisfied because they felt it was wrong in principle for the police to investigate complaints against their own number" (Brown, 1987, p. 37).

The complainant surveys showed that, on the whole, the question of *who* handled the complaint was at least as important, or more important, than *how* the complaint was handled. Of particular note was the fact that, under a mixed system, complainants who believed their matter would be investigated by an independent agency felt deeply betrayed when the complaint was referred back to police. For example, in Landau's (1996) study of the system oversighted by the Ontario Police Complaints Commissioner, 75% of complainants interviewed believed the Commissioner was "not at all, or not very involved in their case" (p. 307). A sense of betrayal was evident in comments such as the following (Landau, 1996, p. 304):

- I thought that this organization has their hands tied and they do not have the capability to carry on a separate investigation from the police force. I don't think they could do anything for me.
- It was the greatest shock—as soon as I phoned them, they passed all the information to the police.
- If they really were an independent body, they would do their own investigations from the start.

In the United Kingdom, Maguire and Corbett (1991) obtained similar responses when comparing complainants' experiences of cases "supervised" by the Police Complaints Authority with those managed by police without supervision (pp. 161, 176):

> Respondents whose cases had been supervised were slightly happier than the remainder, but the overall levels of confidence and satisfaction were uncomfortably low... Those who awarded the PCA, as it were, "marks for trying" tended to feel that the Authority's independence and effectiveness were compromised, either by the fact that investigations were carried out by the police, or by close links between the PCA and the police.

Not surprisingly, in surveys that asked which agency complainants would prefer to handle their matter, the large majority expressed a preference for an independent agency. What is also of note in this context is that, as with the public opinion surveys, this view should not be taken as exclusive to police. To quote Landau (1994) again (p. 58):

> Many see the problem outside of the context of the Metropolitan Toronto Police *per se* to one of the nature of organizations in general, "like doctors investigating doctors" or other professional situations in which a "brotherhood" exists.

It was also not surprising that Chapter 4 reported that the only independent agency in the sample—the PONI—generated majority satisfaction among complainants on almost all criteria. Substantive independence appears to have been crucial to its success, but close attention to procedural justice principles also appeared to be crucial. The Ombudsman obtained overall satisfaction levels averaging 57% over 8 years, with peaks of 65% and 63% (PONI, 2007, 2009, 2014a). This was despite minority satisfaction with outcomes—averaging 41%. At the same time, high scores were obtained on most process measures. Crucially, high scores were obtained on fairness (averaging 70%) and impartiality (73%). An average of 69% said they would use the system again. It would appear then that while the problem of evidence in police complaints makes it difficult to generate majority complainant satisfaction on outcomes, the overall experience can still be very positive given independence and quality processes.

Chapter 5 challenged the notion that police—as a key stakeholder group in the complaints and discipline system—are invariably attached to in-house investigations and adjudication. Police have an obvious stake in the complaints and discipline process as the potential subjects of complaints, with varying degrees of experience as complainants themselves and/or as investigating officers and adjudicators. Surveys of police showed highly variable experiences when it came to both police-dominated and mixed systems, with some high levels of dissatisfaction around process and outcomes. Surveys also showed that police are capable of seeing the value of external investigations, at least in terms of public confidence. As with complainants, the chapter highlighted the work of the independent PONI. The Ombudsman obtained overall satisfaction levels among police, averaging 70% over 8 years, with peaks of 74% and 73% (PONI, 2007, 2008, 2014b). Majority satisfaction was obtained on outcomes (averaging 82%), with high scores on most process measures, including an average of 83% for fairness and 91% for impartiality. On average, 70% agreed that the system made police more accountable.

Chapters 6 through 10 reviewed the powers, functions, and achievements of diverse oversight agencies around the world. The sad conclusion from these studies is that most agencies lack sufficient control of the investigation and adjudication of complaints to do the job properly. The result is continuing problems of police misconduct, complainant alienation, and inadequate public confidence in police integrity and accountability. These studies also show a problem with a lack of evidence gathering by these agencies about their impacts. Nonetheless, it is clear that most systems are designed in defiance of democracy and science. They represent a weak compromise. The chapters highlighted the enormous gap between public expectations and real practice in most locations.

The inescapable conclusion from the points made in the previous discussion is that complaints and discipline systems require a large, direct role by oversight agencies in the management of complaints. The evidence is overwhelming that police internal investigations—even where they are conducted professionally—compound the cynicism and distrust already felt by complainants. Oversight agencies that merely audit or review police investigations also aggravate the alienation felt by complainants. At a minimum, therefore, oversight agencies should have control of the investigation and adjudication of more serious complaints and incidents. Obvious examples include alleged assaults involving injuries, deaths, and serious injuries in police custody; traffic crashes; and all allegations of corruption or conflicts of interest (Liberty, 2000). There is also a strong case for all complaints, even the most minor, to be dealt with independently—as is the case in Northern Ireland—given that complaints deemed as "minor" might not be seen that way by complainants (Independent Police Complaints Commission [IPCC], 2009, p. 7). However, where policymakers are unwilling to go that far, one option is for these complaints to be managed by negotiation. Some complainants might be quite happy to have their matter dealt with by a police professional standards office or an officer's supervisor. Others might be adamant that they want nothing to do with police and should be granted the right of an independent hearing. An important qualifier to this point is that numerous complaints will be best dealt with through alternative dispute resolution procedures at the earliest opportunity (see section on alternative dispute resolution). But again, the management of this can be done externally.

This raises an obvious question about how independent systems are to be resourced. In theory, financial costs per complaint should not be significantly different whether managed internally or externally. However, significant efficiencies are likely to be achieved by including police matters within a larger "public sector integrity commission" (Prenzler & Faulkner, 2010). This also has the strong advantage of treating all public servants, police, and politicians according to the same standards and processes of independent scrutiny. It also means that, in most locations, oversight agencies—or "integrity agencies"—will need to have offices in regional locations. This makes complainant and police access much easier, and it means that civilian investigators can easily access police (and other government) premises and quickly take over the scenes of major incidents. Concerns about a possible loss of focus on police-specific issues can be addressed through the creation of a dedicated policing unit within the wider integrity agency.

There is also an obvious question about how more independent systems are to be staffed (Chapter 2). Very few, if any, agencies appear to exclude former police entirely. Some agencies, such as the New South Police Integrity Commission, exclude all former and current New South Wales officers (Police Integrity Commission Act 1996, s. 10). Others are less specific about who can and cannot be employed. Careful judgment clearly needs to be exercised in balancing the needs of real and perceived independence against the advantages of employing carefully selected and supervised former officers. A 2011 review of the Northern Ireland Police Ombudsman is instructive here. The review found in favor of the Ombudsman's independence in processing contemporary complaints. At the same time, it reported that "there is a substantial proportion of investigative staff (around 41%) from a former police background," with the implication that this was above an appropriate threshold for public confidence (Criminal Justice Inspection Northern Ireland, 2011, p. 32). One potentially useful set of guidelines, based on extensive consultation, was provided by Liberty (2000; the UK National Council for Civil Liberties) in relation to the IPCC (p. 40):

> The investigative staff of the IPCC should comprise at least 75% civilians with no more than 25% seconded or ex-police officers.
> The investigations should take place in a team structure reflecting the above proportions.
> The IPCC should have the decision as to who are selected as seconded police officers.
> Investigative teams should always be headed by a civilian team leader.

Liberty (2000) also recommended the creation of disciplinary panels consisting of an assistant chief constable and two nonpolice members (p. 49). Guidelines like these can be very helpful, subject to local conditions and changing circumstances.

The analysis so far suggests that independence on its own will not automatically satisfy the key criterion of stakeholder confidence. External agencies will still need to pay close attention to process criteria of communication, timeliness, and fair treatment. These criteria should be satisfied given the right resources, staffing, and management in what amounts to a win–win outcome for complainants, police, and the public. Again, the example par excellence is the PONI. The Hong Kong Independent Commission Against Corruption is also exemplary, although its jurisdiction is confined to corruption across the public and private sectors. It has been particularly successful in public outreach and obtaining high levels of public confidence in the Commission and in the integrity of public institutions (Graycar & Prenzler, 2013).

Alternative Dispute Resolution

A number of the preceding chapters of this book identified valuable lessons about alternative dispute resolution. The results are particularly compelling when complainant and officer experiences are compared. Mixed results were found for informal resolution and conciliation, with particularly strong results for mediation.

Chapter 4 referred to a number of studies with largely negative implications for informal resolution processes—which normally involve an apology or explanation from a senior officer to a complainant. In Victoria, Australia, "management intervention" was rated unsatisfactory by almost three-quarters of complainants (Office of Police Integrity, 2008). A study of "local resolution" in the United Kingdom found that 41% of complainants were satisfied and 51% were dissatisfied, whereas only 27% of police were satisfied and 54% were dissatisfied (May, Hough, Herrington, & Warburton, 2007). A Cincinnati study found officers fairly divided over informal resolution procedures: 56.5% believed the outcome was fair, whereas 42.1% were satisfied with the process and 47.8% were dissatisfied (Ridgeway et al., 2009).

On a more positive note, in a Northern Ireland study, 52% of complainants stated that their complaint was resolved to their satisfaction through informal resolution (PONI, 2005). In a Queensland study, both complainants and police were very positive about informal resolution carried out by police officers trained by civilian specialists in alternative dispute resolution: 76.2% of complainants and 83.4% of police were satisfied with the process, and 60.1% of complainants and 75.8% of officers were satisfied with the outcome (Criminal Justice Commission, 1994). Satisfaction rates were lower for both groups who experienced a formal investigative process. In addition, the study found that formal investigations took 2.5 times longer to complete than informal resolution (see Ede & Barnes, 2002, p. 123).

As noted in Chapters 3 and 4, complainant dissatisfaction with informal resolution often related to lack of information, nonreceipt of an apology, and police control of the process. Efforts at resolution were often considered tokenistic, providing a convenient "bureaucratic suppression of a dispute" (Young, Hoyle, Cooper, & Hill, 2005, p. 300). In a Northern Ireland survey, 58% of complainants wanted to meet with the officer who was the subject of their complaint (PONI, 2005). For police, dissatisfaction with informal resolution was largely related to perceptions of bias in favor of the complainant, alleged triviality of complaints, delays, and lack of information. A focus group study of New York City police officers who had been investigated found that "the overwhelming majority" expressed a preference for a "face-to-face interaction" with complainants (Sviridoff & McElroy, 1989, p. 36).

There would seem to be a place for a well-managed informal resolution option in a model police complaints system, especially where either party to a complaint is not willing to participate in mediation. At the same time, mediation would appear to be the more desirable default option. In the surveys of complainants and police covered in Chapters 4 and 5, mediation attracted consistently positive responses from both groups. In England and Wales, Young et al. (2005) compared participants' experiences in a form of mediation (conducted by specialist police) with conciliation processes that lacked contact between the complainant and the subject officer. Overall, 61% of complainants and 85% of officers in the restorative group were satisfied, and 33% of complainants and 69% of officers who experienced conciliation were satisfied. In terms of outcomes, 53% of complainants and 86% of police in the restorative group were satisfied, and 33% of complainants and 54% of police in the conciliation group were satisfied with the outcome.

A study in Denver involved completely independent mediators. Schaible, De Angelis, Wolf, and Rosenthal (2012) found that 78.7% of complainants and 80.5% of police who experienced mediation were satisfied with the process, compared with 10.5% of complainants and 12.0% of police in the nonmediation sample. Furthermore, 62.9% of complainants and 72.7% of police were satisfied with the outcome in mediated cases compared with 6.6% of complainants and 48.9% of police in the nonmediated cases.

In Portland, Oregon, 51.6% of complainants and 70.0% of police officers who experienced mediation were completely or partially satisfied with the outcome, 93.3% of complainants and 95.5% of officers felt they had the opportunity to explain themselves, 100.0% of complainants and officers felt the mediator was "fair to both sides," and 96.7% of complainants and 85.7% of police stated they would recommend mediation to others (Independent Police Review Division, 2003).

Given this evidence, we can say confidently that a state-of-the-art complaints and discipline system must have mediation available and should encourage mediation as the likely best option for many complainants. The evidence is variable about who can conduct mediation. Nonetheless, the engagement of mediators external to police is probably ideal. This could involve specialist staff in an oversight agency or government or private sector mediation specialists. A regionalized, public-sector-wide integrity commission would provide a good means of service provision were mediation to be adopted on a large scale that appears appropriate.

Optimizing Ethical Conduct

The first two sections of this chapter advocated independent control of complaints processing and the widespread availability of mediation as key methods for satisfying stakeholder concerns about impartiality and fairness in response to complaints against police. The evidence is strong, arguably overwhelming, in support of these two approaches. But how effective are they in optimizing ethical conduct among police?

Starting with informal resolution and mediation, only one study covered in the book considered possible remedial effects. Young et al. (2005) found that only 2 out of 13 officers who experienced mediation "believed that the complaint would lead them to altering their behaviour" (p. 307). This is disappointing but perhaps not too surprising given there is little evidence that victim–offender mediation reduces crime (Hayes, 2007). A mediation event might take 2 hours and the subjects then return to their normal situation, with its many powerful influences on behavior. However, while other criteria make the case for mediation, the potential for remedial effects should be developed from the lessons learned in the analysis of events covered in mediation.

The evidence is stronger regarding the role of independent oversight agencies in improving police conduct. Unfortunately, numerous agencies show little or no direct positive effect. This is most likely the result of inadequate jurisdiction, powers, and resources. Prenzler's (2009) review of agency performance indicators internationally came to the following conclusion (p. 165):

> The limited evidence suggests that the more interventionist an agency is, and the more it engages in independent investigations or close supervision of police investigators, the more likely it is to score on positive indicators than preceding police dominated systems.

The "positive indicators" included complaint substantiation rates (tending to be somewhat higher under oversight); complaint reduction; confidence ratings from surveys of the public, complainants, police, and experts (e.g., lawyers, academics, journalists); and police acceptance of disciplinary recommendations. The more powerful anticorruption agencies—of the type developed in Australia and Hong Kong—are widely considered to be fairly or very effective in both deterring serious forms of misconduct and in "secondary prevention" by identifying and shutting down more serious misconduct (Graycar & Prenzler, 2013; Prenzler, 2009). However, the most challenging task for oversight agencies is to demonstrate large-scale primary prevention of misconduct across the spectrum—not just unjustifiable deadly force, serious assaults, drug corruption, and extortion but also excessive force, discrimination, oppressive conduct, rudeness, inaction, and other common problems in policing, some of which are manifested in complaints.

Chapter 11 of this book showed that oversight agencies can go beyond deterrence and incapacitation to work with police departments in generating demonstrable improvements in police conduct through changes to procedures, training, and supervision. Again, looking at the example of Northern Ireland, early efforts at cooperation were put on a more formal footing in 2010 with agreement on a "focused PSNI Complaints Reduction Strategy" (PONI, 2013, p. 6). A number of areas of improvement were documented, including in baton use, handcuffing, search procedures, vehicle pursuits, and police responses to child abuse and hate crimes (PONI, 2010). Two of the areas of more demonstrable achievement related to complaints involved measures to reduce duty failure allegations (related to investigations) and incivility allegations (PONI, 2010).

In the bigger picture, it has to be said that the PONI and the Police Service have struggled to address the underlying causes of complaints and to reduce complaints. It appears that increased public confidence drove an initial increase in complaints after the establishment of the office, and this has been followed by a long period of fluctuating complaint numbers (PONI, 2014c, p. 9). However, there are other indicators of success. The issue of the impact of the Northern Ireland Police Ombudsman needs to be placed in the context of the deeply entrenched and extreme sectarian conflict that led to the 1998 Good Friday Agreement and the associated policing reform package (Independent Commission on Policing for Northern Ireland, 1999). The establishment of the Ombudsman's Office was just one element of a complex and interconnected set of changes aimed at creating a less biased, more democratic police service (Ellison, 2007, p. 251). The whole reform process, including police reform, has seen very large reductions in incidents of violence related to sectarian conflict—including killings, injuries, shootings, and bombings (Police Service of Northern Ireland, 2013). There is also good evidence of major improvements in police–community relations. The 1999 report of the Independent Commission on Policing for Northern Ireland (1999) reviewed public opinion surveys and noted a division of approval ratings for police: more than 80% among Protestants and less than 50% among Catholics (p. 13). Improvements have been tracked over time. A 2014 survey found the following positive and consistent views of police (Northern Ireland Policing Board, 2014, pp. 6–8):

- 70% of Catholics and 73% of Protestants considered the performance of the Police Service as a whole as "very/fairly good."
- 68% of Catholics and 77% of Protestants were satisfied police "treat members of the public fairly in Northern Ireland," whereas 10% of both groups were "fairly/very dissatisfied" in regard to fairness.

A repeated concern among critics of civilian control of complaints is that police will abandon responsibility for integrity management and discipline. However, there is a large field of work in integrity management outside complaints processing, and oversight agencies can serve an important accountability in testing the effectiveness of police integrity strategies. Measures will include complaints, as well as stakeholder perceptions and experiences. The strategies that should be managed by police are complex. The presence of oversight agencies does not preclude police from conducting investigations and reviews at their own initiative and meting out discipline where appropriate. Both agencies can engage in covert tactics and integrity testing. In addition, police should be primarily responsible for recruit screening, preservice and in-service training, supervision, and remediation. Complaint profiling and early intervention systems have been shown to be particularly beneficial in reducing complaints, especially repeat complaints against individual officers and units (Macintyre, Prenzler, & Chapman, 2008; Walker, Alpert, & Kenney, 2001).

A small number of police departments are on the record in demonstrating large improvements in measures of ethical conduct, with lessons that have wide application. For example, in New York City, the introduction of a "courtesy, professionalism and respect policy" in two Bronx precincts in the 1990s led to reductions of 54% and 64% in complaints against the trend of increasing citizen complaints during the alleged "zero-tolerance" crackdown on crime (Davis, Mateu-Gelabert, & Miller, 2005). In Tasmania, Australia, police generated an extraordinary 87% reduction in citizen complaints over a decade through a combination of complaint profiling and early intervention and complaint analysis and modified procedures and training (focused on de-escalation; Porter, Prenzler, & Fleming, 2012). The main contribution of the Tasmanian Ombudsman was to verify the strategies and data. In both the Bronx and Tasmanian cases, reductions in complaints were achieved along with reductions in crime. Prenzler, Porter, and Alpert (2013) also reviewed case studies of successful force reduction in policing, using a range of measures including complaints, police and citizen fatalities and injuries, and use-of-force reports.

Two other integrity measures should be briefly mentioned. The legal regulation of policing procedures has also been shown to reduce misconduct. The most outstanding example is the prevention of investigative misconduct, especially coerced confessions, through compulsory recording of police interviews (Dixon, 2006; Graycar & Prenzler, 2013). In addition, recording technology has now evolved to the point where body-worn cameras are showing enormous potential in improving police conduct and reducing complaints, including false complaints. In a pioneering study using experimental and control groups, with 2 years of postintervention data, the body-worn camera initiative of the Rialto Police Department in California was associated with large reductions in police use of force reports and public complaints (Farrar, 2013, 2014).

Conclusion

This chapter has brought together a wide range of evidence from the preceding chapters in this book. The evidence is complex but generally consistent and clear about what needs to be done to optimize the management of complaints against police and ensure best practice in police integrity management more generally. The focus has been on the role of civilian oversight agencies in attempting to redress the many deficiencies identified in police internal processes. It is clear that these agencies are essential to police accountability and the independent management of complaints against police is an essential requirement. A range of performance indicators need to be applied to ensure that agencies are engaged in best practice and achieving their goals. A properly empowered and resourced oversight agency—best structured as a public sector wide integrity agency—should fulfill the aspirations of all stakeholder groups if it is also properly independent and focused on quality procedural justice processes. Investigations and discipline will constitute key roles in determining responsibility for possible breaches of standards and bringing offenders to justice and preventing misconduct through deterrence and incapacitation. At the same time, informal resolution and mediation are essential strategies for a fulfillment of a broader restorative justice mission. The elevation of oversight bodies as authoritative and major players in police accountability still leaves large scope for police responsibility in integrity management. Oversight agencies should not only independently assess police achievements but also work with police, especially through research and policy development, to ensure police practices are as lawful and ethical as they can be.

References

ALRC. (1995). *Under the spotlight: Complaints against the AFP and NCA.* Canberra: Australian Law Reform Commission.

Brown, D. (1987). *The police complaints procedure: A survey of complainants' views.* London: Home Office.

Calgary Police Commission. (1999). *Report. Calgary: Citizen Complaints Review Committee.* Calgary: Author.

Criminal Justice Commission. (1994). *Informal complaint resolution in the Queensland Police Service: An evaluation.* Brisbane: Criminal Justice Commission.

Criminal Justice Inspection Northern Ireland. (2011). *An inspection into the independence of the Office of the Police Ombudsman for Northern Ireland.* Belfast: Criminal Justice Inspection Northern Ireland.

Davis, R., Mateu-Gelabert, P., & Miller, J. (2005). Can effective policing also be respectful? Two examples in the South Bronx. *Police Quarterly, 8,* 229–247.

Dixon, D. (2006). A window into the interviewing process? The audio-visual recording of police interrogation in New South Wales, Australia. *Policing & Society, 16*(4), 323–348.

Ede, A., & Barnes, M. (2002). Alternative strategies for resolving complaints. In T. Prenzler & J. Ransley (Eds.), *Police reform: Building integrity* (pp. 115–130). Sydney: Federation Press.

Ellison, G. (2007). A blueprint for democratic policing anywhere in the world? Police reform, police transition, and conflict resolution in Northern Ireland. *Police Quarterly, 10*(3), 243–69.

Farrar, T. (2013). *The Rialto Police Department's body-worn video camera experiment: Operation 'Candid Camera.'* Presentation at the Jerry Lee Symposium, Washington, DC. Retrieved from ccjs.umd.edu/sites/ccjs.umd.edu/files/Wearable_Cameras _Capitol_Hill_Final_Presentation_Jerry_Lee_Symposium_2013.pdf.

Farrar, T. (2014). *The Rialto Police Department's body-worn camera experiment.* Presentation at The Stanford Center on Democracy, Development, and The Rule of Law (CDDRL). Retrieved from http://www.youtube.com/watch?v=Nlk4tBsENVE.

Graycar, A., & Prenzler, T. (2013). *Understanding and preventing corruption.* Houndmills: Palgrave-Macmillan.

Hayes, H. (2007). Restorative justice and re-offending. In G. Johnstone & D. Van Ness (Eds.), *Handbook of restorative justice* (pp. 426–446). Devon: Willan.

Independent Commission on Policing for Northern Ireland. (1999). *A new beginning: Policing in Northern Ireland.* Belfast: Author.

Independent Police Complaints Commission. (2009). *Annual report 2008/2009.* London: Author.

Independent Police Review Division. (2003). *Independent Police Review Division annual report.* Portland, Oregon: City of Portland, Office of the City Auditor.

Landau, T. (1994). *Public complaints against the police: A view from complainants.* Toronto: University of Toronto.

Landau, T. (1996). When police investigate police: A view from complainants. *Canadian Journal of Criminology, 38*(3), 291–315.

Liberty. (2000). *An Independent Police Complaints Commission.* London: Liberty, The National Council for Civil Liberties.

Macintyre, S., Prenzler, T., & Chapman, J. (2008). Early intervention to reduce complaints: An Australian Victoria Police initiative. *International Journal of Police Science and Management, 10,* 238–250.

Maguire, M., & Corbett, C. (1991). *A study of the police complaints system.* London: HMSO.

May, T., Hough, M., Herrington, V., & Warburton, H. (2007). *Local resolution: The views of police officers and complainants.* London: Independent Police Complaints Commission.

Northern Ireland Policing Board. (2014). *Public perceptions of the police, PCSPs and the Northern Ireland Policing Board.* Belfast: Author.

Office of Police Integrity. (2008). *Improving Victorian policing services through effective complaint handling.* Melbourne: Office of Police Integrity.

Police Service of Northern Ireland (PSNI). (2013). *Police recorded security situation statistics annual report covering the period 1st April 2012–31st March 2013.* Belfast: Author.

PONI. (2005). *An evaluation of police-led informal resolution of police complaints in Northern Ireland: The complainants' perspective.* Belfast: Police Ombudsman for Northern Ireland.

PONI. (2007). *Complainant satisfaction survey 2006/07.* Belfast: Police Ombudsman for Northern Ireland.

PONI. (2008). *Police satisfaction survey 2007/08.* Belfast: Police Ombudsman for Northern Ireland.

PONI. (2009). *Complainant satisfaction survey 2008/09.* Belfast: Police Ombudsman for Northern Ireland.

PONI. (2010). *Developments in police complaints—Ten years on.* Belfast: Police Ombudsman for Northern Ireland.

PONI. (2013). *Annual statistical bulletin 2012/13.* Belfast. Police Ombudsman for Northern Ireland.

PONI. (2014a). *Annual report on complainant satisfaction provided by the Police Ombudsman's Office in Northern Ireland 2013–14*. Belfast: Police Ombudsman for Northern Ireland.

PONI. (2014b). *Annual report on police officer satisfaction provided by the Police Ombudsman's Office in Northern Ireland 2013–14*. Belfast: Police Ombudsman for Northern Ireland.

PONI. (2014c). *Trends in complaints and allegations received by the Police Ombudsman for Northern Ireland, 2013/14*. Belfast. Police Ombudsman for Northern Ireland.

Porter, L. E., Prenzler, T., & Fleming, J. (2012). Complaint reduction in the Tasmania police. *Policing and Society, 22*, 426–447.

Prenzler, T. (2009). *Police corruption: Preventing misconduct and maintaining integrity*. Boca Raton, FL: CRC Press-Taylor & Francis.

Prenzler, T., & Faulkner, N. (2010). Towards a model public sector integrity commission. *Australian Journal of Public Administration, 69*(3), 251–262.

Prenzler, T., Porter, L., & Alpert, G. (2013). Reducing police use of force: Case studies and prospects. *Aggression and Violent Behavior: A Review Journal, 18*, 343–356.

Ridgeway, G., Schell, T. L., Gifford, B., Saunders, J., Turner, S., Riley, K. J., & Dixon, T. L. (2009). *Police-community relations in Cincinnati*. Santa Monica, CA: RAND Corporation.

Schaible, L. M., De Angelis, J., Wolf, B., & Rosenthal, R. (2012). Denver's citizen/police complaint mediation program: Officer and complainant satisfaction. *Criminal Justice Policy Review, 24*, 626–650.

Sviridoff, M., & McElroy, J. (1989). *The processing of complaints against police in New York City: The perceptions and attitudes of line officers*. New York: Vera Institute of Justice.

Walker, S., Alpert, G. P., & Kenney, D. J. (2001). *Early warning systems: Responding to the problem police officer*. Washington, DC: National Institute of Justice.

Young, R., Hoyle, C., Cooper, K., & Hill, R. (2005). Informal resolution of the complaints against the police: A quasi-experimental test of restorative justice. *Criminal Justice, 5*, 279–317.

Index

A Call for Authors

Advances in Police Theory and Practice

AIMS AND SCOPE:

This cutting-edge series is designed to promote publication of books on contemporary advances in police theory and practice. We are especially interested in volumes that focus on the nexus between research and practice, with the end goal of disseminating innovations in policing. We will consider collections of expert contributions as well as individually authored works. Books in this series will be marketed internationally to both academic and professional audiences. This series also seeks to —

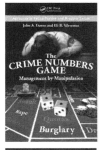

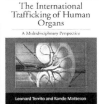

- Bridge the gap in knowledge about advances in theory and practice regarding who the police are, what they do, and how they maintain order, administer laws, and serve their communities
- Improve cooperation between those who are active in the field and those who are involved in academic research so as to facilitate the application of innovative advances in theory and practice

The series especially encourages the contribution of works coauthored by police practitioners and researchers. We are also interested in works comparing policing approaches and methods globally, examining such areas as the policing of transitional states, democratic policing, policing and minorities, preventive policing, investigation, patrolling and response, terrorism, organized crime and drug enforcement. In fact, every aspect of policing, public safety, and security, as well as public order is relevant for the series. Manuscripts should be between 300 and 600 printed pages. If you have a proposal for an original work or for a contributed volume, please be in touch.

Series Editor
Dilip Das, Ph.D., Ph: 802-598-3680
E-mail: dilipkd@aol.com

Dr. Das is a professor of criminal justice and Human Rights Consultant to the United Nations. He is a former chief of police, and founding president of the International Police Executive Symposium, IPES, www.ipes.info. He is also founding editor-in-chief of *Police Practice and Research: An International Journal* (PPR), (Routledge/Taylor & Francis), www.tandf.co.uk/journals. In addition to editing the *World Police Encyclopedia* (Taylor & Francis, 2006), Dr. Das has published numerous books and articles during his many years of involvement in police practice, research, writing, and education.

Proposals for the series may be submitted to the series editor or directly to –

Carolyn Spence
Senior Editor • CRC Press / Taylor & Francis Group
561-317-9574 • 561-997-7249 (fax)
carolyn.spence@taylorandfrancis.com • www.crcpress.com
6000 Broken Sound Parkway NW, Suite 300, Boca Raton, FL 33487